Ten Years of
German Unification

Ten Years of German Unification

One State, Two Peoples

Charlotte Kahn

 PRAEGER

Westport, Connecticut
London

Library of Congress Cataloging-in-Publication Data

Kahn, Charlotte, 1928–
    Ten years of German unification : one state, two peoples /
Charlotte Kahn.
        p.   cm.
    Includes bibliographical references and index.
    ISBN 0–275–96357–8 (alk. paper)
    1. Germany—Social conditions—1990–   2. Germany—History—
Unification, 1990—Psychological aspects.   3. National
characteristics, German.   I. Title.
    HN445.5.K34   2000
    306'.0943—dc21   99–43116

British Library Cataloguing in Publication Data is available.

Library of Congress Catalog Card Number: 99–43116
ISBN: 0–275–96357–8

First published in 2000

Praeger Publishers, 88 Post Road West, Westport, CT 06881
An imprint of Greenwood Publishing Group, Inc.
www.praeger.com

Printed in the United States of America

The paper used in this book complies with the
Permanent Paper Standard issued by the National
Information Standards Organization (Z39.48–1984).

10 9 8 7 6 5 4 3 2 1

Contents

Photographic essay follows page 112.

Preface

This project gave me an unusual opportunity to establish personal connections, check my prejudices against reality, and modify my dogmatic beliefs—the very tasks required of Germans attempting to fashion their future as a unified people within their unified political entity. The steps I took in the preparation of this text have been deeply healing to me. More accurately, not the steps as such, but the many generous individuals and families I was privileged to meet along the way who confirmed my faith in the existence of a measure of goodness and kindness. Some of these acquaintances have become loving and beloved friends.

These good people have helped me with the internal rupture caused first by Nazi discrimination and denigration, then by my forced emigration from Germany (my country of birth), and finally the anxiety I felt adjusting and adapting to new cultures in Great Britain and the United States.

November 1988, fifty years after *Kristallnacht* and fifty years after my departure from Germany, the city of Karlsruhe, my husband's hometown, invited its surviving Jewish former citizens and their spouses or companions to participate in a program of commemoration. I used that as an opportunity to seek answers to a recurring question: What had happened to my German schoolmates and playmates during and after the Nazi era? Of course, I realized that I would not find them in Karlsruhe, or probably even in my hometown,

Duisburg. But I was determined to speak to representatives of my age group.

I decided to conduct interviews and placed notices in the local newspaper asking volunteers to participate in a research project. From the mayor down to the night clerk at the hotel, I received the utmost support in my endeavor: newspaper contacts, interview rooms, telephone, secretarial service, and publicity. To my surprise, before I arrived, sixty-five people had already answered a single notice in the local newspaper, declaring themselves willing to meet with me.

Then, through an unexpected series of events, I found myself interviewing behind the iron curtain one and a half years later. Fortuitously, the existence of an informal East German association of historians had come to my attention and I contacted them. They agreed to help me conduct an investigation similar to the one in Karlsruhe. This time my question was: In what respects do East Germans' experiences and attitudes during and after the Nazi era resemble or differ from those of the West Germans I had interviewed?

Getting to East Germany was not so easy. A visa was required to pass through the Berlin Wall into the German Democratic Republic (GDR). Six weeks before my scheduled departure, I applied for one by submitting a form and surrendering my passport to a special travel agency in New York, which sent on my request to the GDR consulate in Washington, DC. Two, three, four weeks passed. I received promises and reassurances but no visa; worse yet, now I did not even have my passport in hand. Two days before the scheduled flight, the agency assured me I would have my passport back the next day. In fact, just a few hours before my departure, my husband picked up my passport, complete with a visa—dated six weeks earlier, the day following my application! Why? Paranoia? Chicanery? Bureaucratic inefficiency? That's how things are.

The plane I boarded that June day landed at the West Berlin international airport. Accustomed to marching through long airport corridors and waiting on long passport and customs-control lines, I was surprised by the fast pace in Berlin. In fact. I was sped through so quickly that I was still disoriented when my eyes fell on a single long-stemmed wine-red rose rising from someone's hand. Above the flower, the smiling face of Heiner, a young historian, came into focus. Never before had I received such a welcome. My escort had been delegated by his group to shepherd me in his aged *Trabi* (an East German car, smaller than the Volkswagen Beetle) through Checkpoint Charlie (or an equivalent entry point) into East Germany. As it was now seven months since the opening of the Wall, my escort was able to travel east to west and back without difficulty, simply by flashing his identification papers. Still, he cautioned me to wave my American passport only briefly, to avoid suspicion and ensure that the guard would let us pass without inspection. And so it was.

Like the city officials in Karlsruhe, this unofficial group had paved my way. They had placed one notice in each of two very minor Berlin newspapers. One hundred twenty-two people responded! Unfortunately, not all could be interviewed. One historian with the necessary contact at the Academy of Sciences *(Akademie für Wissenschaften)* had procured a room with a telephone for me. Another provided bed and breakfast and many a late-evening snack, accompanied by deep discussions; and yet another family took me along on sightseeing tours and outings. The interviewees satisfied me with "words and *Wurst*" and followed up with clippings, pictures, and references. One family interview was so protracted that the mother left the room for a short while, returning with trays loaded with rolls and sausages for all. Surprised at the generosity, I exclaimed thanks for their many *Wörter und Würste.* I came to experience the warmth and *Menschlichkeit* (humanity) on which the East Germans pride themselves.

Since then, I have returned to Germany several times to listen to elderly Germans, west and east, tell of their life experiences during the Nazi and postwar periods and to East Germans tell of their apprehensions as the barriers between the opposing segments of the country crumbled and then leveled.

In June 1990, in East Berlin, I heard relatively little about the Nazi-era and wartime experiences. My interview partners in the GDR were preoccupied with the impending currency unification with the German Federal Republic (GFR) and the uncertainty about the political future of the country. On October 3, 1990, the unification came to pass, and I became curious about how my interviewees had fared. Therefore, I returned the following year to reinterview several of them.

Other matters required me to be in the Rheinland in December 1991 and, as I had not heard West Germans speak about the impact of unification, I took that opportunity to balance the data by conducting interviews in my former hometown, Duisburg, in January 1992. Again, I was hospitably received and greatly helped.

This year, ten years after the first interviews, I also included middle-aged adults and youths in my group of interviewees. I wanted to find out whether the impact of the unification of the two Germanies was different for the middle and younger generations, who had experienced the course of events at different chronological and developmental ages and who had not had prior experience adjusting to drastic cultural change.

In the course of the 1991–92 interviews and during recent informal conversations with acquaintances and friends in the Rheinland, Baden, and Niedersachsen, it became clear that the greater the distance from the old GFR-GDR border, the less Wessies and Ossies (commonly used terms for West Germans and East Germans) encountered each other and the less intense was the concern about life in the other region. In contrast, those closer to the border mingled more and came face to face with their differences. As a result, their attitudes, reactions, and impressions about the unification were more pronounced. Therefore, I chose Berlin, the liveliest meeting ground of east and west, to find out how the people have fared since the unification.

I tried to observe and listen to my interview partners openmindedly and empathically. In most cases, I succeeded by remaining aware of how greatly Western democratic ideals influenced my personal perspective. At the same time, dormant memories of life in an autocratic society turned out to be easily awakened. On two occasions, the accounts I heard about communism evoked memories of Nazism in me, accompanied by powerful emotions, palpitations, and teary eyes. Fear momentarily threatened to cloud my objectivity, as an interviewee's tale of crossing the border revived old terrors. By the same token, powerful anger overcame me as I heard sad stories from victims of denunciation or of capricious bureaucratic thwarting in the GDR. And I was dumbfounded by tales of Wessie insensitivities that were brought to my attention. Ossies were angry at the shortsighted abrogation of certain admirable East German institutions and outraged by the numerous dishonest business exploitations perpetrated during the beginning period of unification. However, I managed to restrain and contain my personal biases and to adjust my lens to clarity and objectivity.

I was rewarded with full and frank responses. Some interview partners were eager to convey their point of view, several wanted to sort things out for themselves, and a few, who had suffered, needed to unburden themselves. My great satisfaction was to learn that the interview process had been of help to many of the interviewees.

I hope that this record will do justice to their experiences. Though the excerpts from the interviews quoted here constitute oral history and my introductory and concluding comments may make the account psychohistory, this volume is intended to be read neither as a history book nor as a series of clinical analyses. I wish only to record and illuminate the personal aspects of living through political upheaval and adapting to cultural change.

I am deeply indebted and grateful to my husband Gerald Kahn. Jerry, you shared your refined political insights, gave loyal support, advice, and encouragement, and served—not always happily—as my computer-consultant-in-residence. (Without you, I might have had to resort to a quill!) Meinhard Stark, you have been an extraordinary friend, inspiring me with your own works, giving aid on all fronts, and paving my way in Berlin. But for your suggestion that I revisit the topic of unification for the occasion of its tenth anniversary, this book would not have been born. My thanks to Annette Stark for putting up with a houseguest on so many occasions and for so many nights and days. Special thanks to Franziska and Hendrik Stark: to Franziska, for vacating her room and permitting me to luxuriate in the comfort of her *molliges* featherbed, and to Hendrik, for making it possible by letting his sister share his quarters. I am grateful to Family Kircheisen: Sabine, you rescued me from a miserable hotel, chauffeured me, arranged important interviews for me, and included me in family outings. Winfried, thanks for your interesting ideas and for devoting precious hours helping me polish my German. Anne, thanks for the delicious fried potatoes. Heiner Röger—what a *Kavalier* you are—a red rose and "*Helden.* . . ." Thanks for introducing me to "H.H." and for a letter crammed with information and pathos. Katrin Otto, I appreciate your deviating from standard technique to respond to an SOS. Jürgen Köhler, what would I have done without access to a telephone? Thanks. Petra Drauschke, you enriched me with your friendship and your interest in this project. Paul John and Otti de Haan-John, you have been family friends and generous hosts whose expertise I have had to call on too often. Thanks for always having come through with help. Pfarrer Hinnenberg, without your Salvator Kirche parishioners my group of 1992 interviewees would have been small indeed. More importantly, I am touched by the beau-

tiful chapel you created on the site of the former Duisburg syna-
gogue. Ludger and Elisabeth Heid, thank you for your guidance and
for providing a place to work and a place to sleep, and especially for
finding "Ohne Puppe keinen Schritt." Ronald Grele and George
Zimmar, you are the matchmakers. Thanks for helping to make it
happen. Gabriele Hempel, I appreciate your efficiency and the bonus
of parenthetical comments. Alex Page, thanks for your friendship and
for agreeing to be a first reader. Penny McCarthy, your enthusiastic
support encouraged me when I had lost faith, and the generosity with
which you shared your psychoanalytic and editorial expertise did
much to improve this manuscript. Margo Dembo, thanks for hurrying
to help me with translations when the time was short. Jonathan Kahn,
my devoted son, you tirelessly and carefully read each chapter several
times, keeping your sharp eyes on the commas; but I am especially
indebted to you for supplying the idioms and colloquialisms that gave
the interview translations their fluency. Finally I want to acknowledge
my *Gesprächspartner*, my formal and informal interview partners. I
shall continue to think of you often and hope you fare well.

Introduction

Recently, a man related a dream in which he was in a strange town, desperately and unsuccessfully searching for the way back to his hotel. He continued dreaming and found the hotel; but once there, he could not find his room. While associating to the dream, he had a fantasy of leaving the hotel with a small suitcase, which contained his necessities. He then felt uncharacteristically free and relieved.

This person's unconscious mission in life had been to discover a way to get his parents to understand and appropriately respond to his feelings. He wanted them to know what they needed to do to make him more comfortable and in that way to take care of him. In fact, beginning at an early age, he had had to fulfill his own needs by himself, and even those of his parents. Now his responsibilities continue, as his parents have become old and ever more feeble. In discussing the dream, he was able to sort out the realities of today from the residue of ungratified infantile wishes. Once he accepted the pain of his intense frustration and recognized that his parents would never be capable of responding as he would like, he became emotionally free to leave the "hotel" of the past. Relieved of the burden of searching, he is able to focus on the future, to sally forth with the necessary energy and skills in his imaginary suitcase.

This dream and its fantasy sequel could well represent the psychological experience of many a political dissenter. Dissatisfied with his homeland, he may strive unsuccessfully to change it before abandoning it with a sense of betrayal, disappointment, and anger in search of greater freedom, stability, and opportunity for growth. Nevertheless, no matter how unsatisfactory the homeland may have been, leaving the comfort of the familiar is always difficult. Nostalgia for past pleasures, real or anticipated, may retard one's adaptation to the new society. Moreover, the difficulties of adjustment to a strange society are intensified when relocation has been involuntary.[1]

Ten years ago, East Germans and West Germans had to leave the comfort of the familiar for relatively unknown circumstances. When confronting the differences that the forty-year division had wrought between the two Germanies, the West Germans experienced a culture shock. However, greater adjustment was required of the East Germans. It was they who were leaving a familiar politicoeconomic culture and stepping into a strange one. More so than the GFR citizens in the west, former GDR citizens have been involuntarily relocated— not geographically, but culturally and politically.[2] Hence, there is more to report about the East Germans in this book.

In the year 2000, the two Germanies will have been joined under one political umbrella for a decade. While most people appreciate the gains, many of the problems perceived by the citizens who were interviewed during the summer of 1990 remain unresolved in 1998. (For some of the interviewees this was the third conversation. They had granted interviews in 1990, after the fall of the Berlin Wall and again just before the unification. For details, see the Appendix.) In both west and east, some Germans still suffer nostalgia and regret about having given up the old order.

Both West Germans' and East Germans' personal perceptions of the past decade's events will be described in their own words in later chapters. Here, I would like to address the questions: What occurred? Why then?

Soon after the initial euphoria accompanying the fall of the Berlin Wall in 1989, the West Germans awakened to the fact that they had underestimated the decay in the east and overestimated their own economic capacity to cure the ills. To some extent, they also experienced the unification as an involuntary change into which they were misled by politicians and economists who withheld crucial information about the state of the GDR industry and economy. Moreover, many West Germans were accustomed to viewing only their truncated territory as Germany, having written off the districts lost with the defeat that ended the war in 1945. Consequently, West Germans' nostalgia centers around the now-threatened great prosperity of the recent past, and their resentment is focused on increased taxes, even though the tax increases are by no means entirely attributable to the building up of the East German infrastructure.

A significant number of former GDR citizens believe that they were involuntarily propelled into unification with the GFR. Many claim that the goal of the 1989 demonstrations was to reform and transform their existing state. Like the dreamer at his hotel, they held fast to hopes and illusions that the nature and the structure of their political (parent) system contained the potential for gratification, if only its citizens (children) could find the proper means to communicate their desires. However, though the denial of inherent, immutable deficits in the parents—familial and political alike—maintains hope and protects against despair, it also engenders a sense of helplessness and personal failure when changes cannot be wrought. Such clinging to unfulfilled past expectations saps energy and potentially impedes the journey toward realistic goals.

The external conditions of the change brought about by the unification and the frame of mind with which the altered circumstances were encountered vary with the age and development of the citizens involved. Past exposure to differing political systems, the intensity of prior indoctrination, the necessity for finding new ways to earn a livelihood, and the malleability and education of the youth—all determine the adjustment to the unification.

East Germans now realize that subsidized rent, free child care and education, health care and spas, and a guaranteed workplace are luxuries of the past. These so drained the GDR economy that they contributed to the demise of the regime. Yet, many remain deeply convinced that they have inalienable rights to a state-provided job and place to live. Current East German political goals seem to be to receive due respect from the West Germans—not condescension; to attain financial parity with West Germans—not lower wages and less than 100% of the pensions due them; and to enact social legislation to provide a firmer safety net for families, the unemployed, and the sick. Attempting to reach these goals, East Germans have had to travel along paths studded with legal and political road signs that they frequently find difficult to interpret, wrongheaded, and morally and socially obsolete.

Nineteen eighty-nine was the year East Germans confronted their tremendous sociocultural change. Since then they have developed a greater awareness of the limitations of the planned economy, which

mitigated against achieving greater affluence, and the pervasive, in-
trusive secret police establishment, which would always interfere with
personal freedom. Conformists had accepted the GDR society with
its assurance of at least a minimum level of material security at the
cost of free expression and unrestrained personal development. But
ultimately the magnitude of the failure of the socialist experiment,
the selfish betrayal of their leaders, and the web of the secret police
informers the *Staatssicherheit (Stasi)* who had denounced them was
unmasked.

Notwithstanding the name, the German Democratic Republic was
revealed not to have lived up to the standards of democracy, insofar
as "values [and power] were concentrated in relatively few hands."[3]
In addition, the affluence of the Western market economy beckoned,
as did the process of "shaping and sharing" in Western-style democracy.[4]

Not surprisingly, men and women born in the east several years
after the end of World War II remain most attached to the ways of
the *"real existierender Sozialismus"* (the actually extant socialism in
contrast to the ideals of communism) operant in the GDR, and they
remain most hostile to Western ways and values. This is the generation that in school and in mandatory youth groups was inculcated
with the principles of socialism and the socialist perspective on history—including the evils of the capitalist enemy—and who had been
taught about other bodies of thought only from the socialist perspective.

Similarly, West Germans who grew up in the Cold War era cling
more tenaciously to prejudices about East Germans than members of
the younger and older generations. "Wessies" still accuse "Ossies" of
laziness and ineptitude. In response to these accusations, East Germans point with defensive pride to the GDR's superior system of
apprenticeship and extensive opportunities for continuing education;
they rationalize that work sometimes came to a standstill because of
lack of material, a result of insufficient hard currency; and they claim
it was nearly impossible to modernize their factories, because of the
poverty inflicted by the Soviet demand for reparations. Besides, they
believe that paid time off to attend to important family matters is
more important than totally draining workers on the job.

Wessies regard the simpler attire of their counterparts in the east
with contempt. Ossies, in turn, are disdainful of Wessie materialism
and consumerism. They see no beauty in the West German women's

rings and bangles. (It was not intended as a compliment when in East Berlin, in 1990, an acquaintance told me I was easily identified as having come from the West because of my wristwatch. What was so special about my twenty-five-year-old plain, rectangular watch? It was gold!)

Young adults now embarking on their careers have more flexible attitudes. They had the benefit of first attending elementary school or preschool in the GDR and were subsequently exposed to a different curriculum, often presented by West German teachers. Their horizons have been expanded, not only through the introduction of new ideas and facts but, more strikingly, through travel in Western countries and student exchange programs they previously had not even dreamt of. At a young age, they were exposed to two ways of life.

Members of the younger generation seem more able than their parents to integrate the two ideologies, to enjoy their freedom of choice and movement, and to rise to the demands for initiative and competitive efforts. They are less constrained by the cognitive distortions attendant to totalitarianism.[5] In their teens, they were relieved of the totalitarian repression of ambivalence, dissent, and hostility. The strict control of information coupled with propaganda stopped. Thus, the impediments to the process of integrating discordant ideas into existing belief systems were removed, and it became possible to check ideas and beliefs against reality. Distortions could be corrected and rigidity loosened.

The difference between the manner in which the youth and the parent generation tend to organize their understanding of the world can be easily discerned. In contrast to the younger generation, the parents for the most part cling to the rather rigid belief system with which they grew up, although in a few cases they exchanged old beliefs in toto for a new, but equally rigidly construed set of beliefs.[6] One effect of this cognitive rigidity was that as late as five years before the *Wende* (the "turning," the transition) social scientists of that generation continued to make optimistic predictions in support of their ideology, answering such questions as "Will socialism be victorious?" and "When will the USSR overtake the United States?" with statements such as, "according to our accounting, the United States and the USSR will be equal in strength around [the year] 2030."[7]

The grandparent generation had undergone the Nazi indoctrination during their youth and were traumatized by bombings, evacuations entailing separation from family, deportation and population exchange with accompanying loss of property, and homelessness. They had suffered the death of family members on the battlefield, through starvation, or by sickness. With that behind them, they were happy to abandon National Socialism and the Hitler Youth in order to join the Free German Youth (*Freie Deutsche Jugend, FDJ*) and to participate in building a socialist society—or, in the case of the West Germans, to rebuild their houses and commit themselves to a democratic process of government. Having experienced more than one political system and having endured disillusionment at least once before seem to have prepared this generation of East Germans for yet another transition, this time to a Western-style market democracy.[8]

That is not to deny their personal and political sense of abandonment, loss, and betrayal in 1945 and again in the east in 1989 when political leaders were discovered to have abused the people and ruined the country for their own nefarious purposes. However these reactions to the communist leaders often remained unconscious in East Germans until after their anger, mourning, hopelessness, and fear erupted and culminated in the events of the *Wende* (the "turning" of East German policies and politics to a different direction).

Members of the GDR grandparent generation have led enormously complicated lives, and the Wende aroused their fear and shock. Their fear was largely induced by their own negative predictions: devaluation of their savings as a result of the impending currency exchange, vast increases in rent imposed by exploitative capitalists who would take over hitherto state-owned residential buildings, and the insufficiency of GDR retirement pensions in the market society. Their shock was induced by the closing of very many GDR concerns for reasons of redundancy or inefficiency—and also as a result of dishonest dealings by managers and entrepreneurs. This resulted in massive layoffs and, in some sad cases, dismissal without severance pay before the age of sixty—several years before the official retirement age. These layoffs produced anger and resentment and were experienced as a humiliation. An unemployment rate two and three times higher than in the west is demoralizing for old and young alike. Defensively, GDR citizens continue to tout the quality of their products and the modernity of some of their now-idle factories.

As it turned out, the grandparent generation had several advantages over the middle generation. The seniors were pleasantly surprised to discover that their advanced age commanded exceptional benefits. For instance, the regulations governing the unification process provided for a stage of early retirement with pension, and the pension was to be paid in Deutschmarks. At the time of the *Währungsunion* (the introduction of the Deutschmark as the official currency in the still-existing GDR, beginning July 1, 1990) the rate of exchange for savings was set at 1:1, and at 2:1 for amounts beyond a given limit— politically motivated but generous, nonetheless, since the actual value of the Ostmark currency relative to the Deutschmark was less than 4: 1. Pensions were calculated at a 1:1 rate and were to be paid at 85 percent of the amount due, later to be brought up to par according to a schedule, which, however, was not strictly adhered to. East German wages and pensions were calculated to eventually bring them almost into line with those of West German workers, though at this writing 100 percent parity has not been achieved. However, because GDR women had worked in full-time jobs during almost every year of their adult life, the combined pensions of husband and wife exceeded the household income of pensioners in the west. It afforded them travel abroad and a previously unimaginable lifestyle in apartments renovated either by themselves or by the feared capitalist landlords.

During the 1998 interviews, the pensioners seemed calmer than in 1990. They were enjoying themselves and, in some cases, actively pursuing new interests or performing part-time paid services in positions related to their former vocations.

Overall, the youngest fared best, while the middle generation is having the hardest time. Although the seniors are doing well, neither the flexibility in organizing and reorganizing information nor the integrative skills of the young generation were matched by the grandparent generation. However, the elders did have two psychological advantages over the middle generation.

First, they had the benefit of previous experience with ideological, political, and material changes, which possibly "inoculated" them and improved their ability to cope with future stresses.[9] Second, though the seniors had been exposed to totalitarian indoctrination for most of their lives, their perspective had been broadened by exposure to two fundamentally different doctrines—national socialism and communism. This prepared them for a confrontation with yet a third perspective, namely, the democratic principles and process. In discussing this, the interviewees showed some flexibility by permitting themselves spontaneously to perceive some advantages and some disadvantages of both the socialist and the capitalist economic systems.

Nevertheless, these same interviewees had not totally shed the thinking style fostered by totalitarianism, that is, to draw rigid boundaries around belief systems. In their minds they had cordoned off the national socialist ideology, not only because of the horrors perpetrated in its name but also because in the GDR it had been a taboo. Without properly exploring their own experiences or their parents' participation with (or resistance to) the Nazis, they devalued national socialism as "bad" and exchanged this bad belief system in toto for communism/socialism, which they idealized as "good." To protect their idealized belief system from contamination by the devalued one, the interviewees avoided any and all comparisons between the two. For example, when it was pointed out that, despite the vastly different ideological content of the national socialist and communist systems (one based on the purity of the Aryan race, blood and soil; the other, on the rightful dominance of the working class, the producers of goods, the proletariat), a totalitarian process obtained for both (both requiring the submission of the individual to the goals of the group and both enforcing ideological discipline through denunciations, demotions, incarceration, and varying degrees of torture), they closed the discussion. Angrily they pronounced that the Nazis left behind mountains of corpses while the GDR created only mountains of secret service files. The two political belief systems were separated by internal boundaries as impenetrable as the Berlin Wall.

However, when the actual Berlin Wall could be penetrated, East Germans could enjoy the freedom to travel to destinations of their choice and bask in the warmth of the southern sun; read previously unavailable information in Western newspapers; and see, smell, touch, and taste foods that had not bedecked the shelves of socialist markets. They took it all in, expanded their perspective, and over time began to compare and question the distorted worldviews that had been required by the respective totalitarian ideologies. That is to say, of the three belief systems, at least two—communism and democracy—were brought into relation with one another, and their previously impermeable boundaries could now let information pass.

Nonetheless, certain aspects of the emotional "wall in the head" remained, perhaps defensively to protect against a breach in their sense of cultural identity. The discrepancy between the new reality and the familiar, largely unconscious internal images of themselves and the world threatened to be unsettling. Much work of internal synthesizing remains to be done.

Such emotional "walls in the head" continue to interfere also with east-west relationships. Too often Wessies and Ossies meet each other with mutual criticism and suspicion rather than with empathy, and both stumble over their common identification as Germans, in the unified sense.[10]

Among the forty-one interview partners with whom I spoke in 1998, five had distanced themselves from the communist ideology and the political system of the GDR for religious reasons. In accordance with Marx's dictum that religion is the opiate of the masses, religious practice was frowned upon. One religious wife was required by her husband, who was working for the state, to give up her religious affiliation and stop practicing religious rites. She publicly complied, but privately she guarded her belief in God and continued secretly to recite nightly prayers. The religious beliefs to which these five individuals subscribed served as an antidote to the indoctrination imposed at school, in organized youth groups, and at work.

Those practicing their religion sacrificed much. They were discriminated against at work and in the educational system—often not chosen to pursue academic studies or not allotted a place at a university. All five religious individuals who participated in this investigation were delighted with the turn of events in 1989–90. But none of them seemed to realize that the fervor with which they subscribed to their religious dogma is not too different from the communist fervor—with the significant exception that, at this moment, churches are organizing neither crusades nor witch-hunts. In any case, the religious institutions—long undermined by the anticlerical stance of communism—did grasp the opportunity to lend their strength to the opposition movement.

Two nonreligious interview partners also viewed themselves as dissidents. Both of them carried within them a family tradition of difference. One, the son of a communist who was sentenced to death and killed by the Nazis, became disillusioned when he discovered the gulf between the practice of the *real existierender Sozialismus* and the ideals to which he and his father had subscribed. The other, the son of an involuntary immigrant, brought with him the family's perspective of an outsider. After having been denied the pursuit of his chosen career by the state's representatives, he changed his attitude from skepticism to virulent opposition.

These interviewees' experiences show that an organized set of ideas and experiences originating outside a rigid system can serve as a balance and lend a broader perspective on a given dogma and its application.

Germans, east and west, refer to the period between the opening of the Berlin Wall and the unification as the *Wendezeit*, the time of the turning, the transition. The term *Wende* accurately describes the series of events: In the GDR the population was turning away from the then-current regime and its leaders. They gathered in church sanctuaries to organize themselves, took to the streets on peace marches, and demonstrated on the plazas; they attended meetings and heard speeches by politicians, academicians, and writers. Banners were flying, art works graced the Berlin Wall, and everywhere graffiti proclaimed contradictory demands and recommendations. Either the black-yellow-red stripes of the GFR flag or the wreath around the hammer and compass of the GDR flag were affixed to windowpanes. The crowds shouted *Wir sind das Volk!* (We are the people!), which I understood to mean, ours is the power to rule ourselves. No shots had been fired; no government had been toppled; no violent revolution had taken place. East Germans and West Germans simply turned—toward each other.

For some years prior to the *Wende*, the GFR had given behind-the-scenes aid to the GDR, shoring up the ailing economy. Most GDR citizens had long coveted a greater variety and abundance of consumer goods. By Western standards, the East Germans' life was shabby, though compared to other Soviet bloc countries, the GDR was well off. There was no starvation, no homelessness, no epidemic.

The population was not at its nadir or devoid of resources. They garnered the energy to rise up when their mounting expectations for greater personal freedom remained unmet. The people felt imprisoned by travel restrictions and cut off from an important part of the world by the Berlin Wall. Whereas in the past they had ambivalently affirmed the necessity of the Wall to protect their state from infiltration and exploitation as well as from an enervating brain drain, now they demonstrated for a relaxation of restrictions and greater self-determination—a change for the better.

With the 1968 nightmare of Czechoslovakia ever vivid, people hoped for the big Bear to lie down, to pull in his claws. Until 1989, openly expressed differences of opinion, for the most part, had not been tolerated. Group actions were quashed. No significant changes took place. Then the people of the GDR stirred. Mikhail Sergejevitch

Gorbachev announced that Soviet tanks would not move against them. The Soviet Union was spent.

Armed revolution was no longer a necessity, or even a possibility, when the suction into the communist fold and the pressure to resist capitalism subsided and the GDR government, as well as the official political party, lost the Soviet Union's support. The GDR population is basically pacifist; and the government, without the Russian tanks to back it, lacked the requisite force to squash a serious uprising. Though Germans and most others view the German character as disciplined and orderly, social and political chaos remained a possible consequence of the loss of the externally imposed structure and the change in the relative power of the ruled and the rulers. Why, then, did the country not succumb to a chaotic decline?

Under the pressure of the people, the Berlin Wall crumbled. That is to say, the rulers made a concession by liberalizing the travel restrictions. In so doing, they seemed not to have realized that, rather than saving themselves by providing a safety valve for pent-up dissatisfaction and mounting assertion, they were redirecting GDR people's energy from east to west through the now permeable boundary between the two Germanies. The leaders of the GFR feared a flood of immigrants. Accordingly, the GFR stepped into the void with its own considerable economic power, political acumen, and promises of a great blossoming, thereby mobilizing the people toward a new structure. Helmut Kohl metaphorically promised prosperity when he promised "blühende Landschaften" (flourishing, flowering countrysides).

The way had been paved by the recent sub-rosa economic exchanges; a common language and a shared history and culture would provide the vehicles for a move toward a reunification of the German people. Technically, there could not be a reunification of the two states, as the GDR and the GFR had never been one entity. The political event will thus be referred to as unification, but the German people can be said to have reunited.

In the euphoric atmosphere of the opening of the Wall, the extent of the cultural divergence that had developed during decades of separation remained momentarily unrecognized by the general public. The possibility cannot be dismissed that, despite warnings against—even objections to—taking on the liabilities of the east, West German leaders saw a unified Germany as an opportunity to enhance German influence in the European Community of the future. Now the crowds proclaimed, *Wir sind ein Volk!* (We are **one** people). With that, the course of German political and economic history changed.

For the East Germans, immersion in West German culture began with the opening of the Wall. It did not await the official political unification of the two German states. As they penetrated the Wall, East Germans and West Germans greeted each other with embraces and jubilation. An official, government-sponsored welcoming gift of 100 D-Marks (Deutschmarks, the West German currency) awaited the GDR citizens as they arrived in the GFR, seemingly the land of milk and honey. Like Rip van Winkle awakening after twenty years to find himself a stranger in what he knew had been his town, East Germans crossed the border into what used to be part of their own country and confronted strange ways and values.

On November 9, 1989, the Berlin Wall had fallen. Eight months later the D-Mark became the official currency of both Germanies, and West German suppliers filled the shelves of supermarkets in the east. New banks opened their doors. Insurance salesmen and car dealers served—and seduced—the people. Initiation into the market economy was a baptism by immersion. Many very difficult steps toward a calmer, more permanent adjustment were to follow that first euphoric embrace.

During the summer 1991, when I reinterviewed some of the people I had met one year before, I found them to be in the state of "immersion." Immersion is typically the first phase of adjustment to a new culture.[11] It is the time to learn the folkways and values and to acquire a new language. Fortunately, new language acquisition was not necessary in this unification. Usually this phase is followed by taking stock of both the old and the new, often accompanied by some mourning for the familiar aspects of life that are no longer useful and need to be abandoned.

In 1998, seven years later, people seemed to have taken stock, to have evaluated the new and the old, to have accepted some aspects of each culture and rejected others. This level of acculturation has been called the phase of "bicultural identity."[12]

Not all the interviewees were aware of the degree of change in their attitudes and lifestyle as they passed through the phase of bicultural identity. As was to be expected, the youngest in the former GDR had grown seamlessly into the new culture. The seniors were the most aware, recognizing, for example, that they now appreciate the energizing effect of competition and the value of an ability to take initiative on one's own behalf. Before, they had subscribed to competition and initiative only on behalf of the group or the state.

Middle-aged persons had the most difficulty. It may be that some of them did not truly enter into the bicultural phase. They reluctantly admitted that, as a result of unification, material benefits accrued to them, while, in the same breath, they sometimes diminished the value of their gains and bemoaned the social and personal price paid to attain them. It is as if they were being disloyal, even immoral, if they relinquished any socialist values or practices. To some extent, they are living in an uncomfortable state of immersion, reaching forward into a bicultural existence only enough to stay alive. This is the generation that, unlike their parents, had never been exposed to any other than the socialist ideology and had been quite isolated from any but the Communist bloc way of life. Though they have adjusted, they are the least prepared for adaptation. That is to say, they are complying with such requirements as will keep them afloat without integrating such internal, psychological changes as would ultimately enable them to be truly comfortable and perhaps even to effect changes in their environment.

Under those circumstances, establishing a "transcultural identity"[13]—composed of the reworked values of the old fused with the internalized new into a cohesive whole—will be achieved only with great difficulty by most of the adults in their middle years. A transcultural identity is rich. It is expansive: It includes knowledge and perspectives beyond those available to people with more limited life experience. In contrast to the immersion and the bicultural phases of adjustment, transcultural identity is an adaptation characterized by an internal integrity and feeling of comfort.

As a rule, when a person has chosen or is forced to live in a strange culture, the process of acculturation is facilitated by mingling with the "native" inhabitants. Daily contact at work, socializing, sharing meals, helping and being helped, and giving and receiving foster mutual identification. Identification means becoming like or the same as another—taking the other into oneself.

Becoming more like the others in a society is rewarded by acceptance. This is further motivation to adjust and adapt. Of course, it is a recursive process in that the newcomer's ways affect the native. In Germany, as in the United States, the most visible example of this is the variety of foods enjoyed by the locals but introduced by immigrants who, still identifiable as foreigners, have adopted the ways of the land sufficiently to conduct business.

This does not quite reflect the situation of East Germans and West Germans. Most continue to reside in their home areas and to work, socialize, share, and help their neighbors and friends of old. On a daily basis they are not compelled to interact with "strangers"—Ossies with Wessies and Wessies with Ossies—and therefore are deprived of the opportunity to internalize differences. Rubbing shoulders occurs most frequently at work, but exposure to a different ethos at the workplace is not in itself conducive to identification with a different culture. It is often resisted, especially by West Germans, and is experienced as coercive by East Germans. In contrast, friendly, emotional exchanges in the social sphere are more likely to lead to mutual identification. Unfortunately, such social contacts too often have been limited by a lack of propinquity, sometimes avoided out of fear, or rejected when divergent values precluded finding a common ground. For the moment, the nation remains psychologically as two peoples, although Germany is politically one state.

Even identification with a unified Germany is all but absent in both east and west. Many citizens travel throughout the country and enjoy the countryside, but only one interviewee said that he was eager to see the part of "my" country to which he previously had not had access.

Even some young Berliners declare that not Germany, but Berlin is their *Heimat*, which means home with a myriad of emotional overtones that have no satisfactory equivalent in English. The older people say that the GDR was their *Heimat*, implying they are now virtually *heimatlos* (stateless, without a country).

Fortunately, divergent identifications and lack of common ground will be less of a problem for members of the young generation. Though they attend neighborhood schools, they are exposed to the same curriculum and are growing up together in roughly the same culture.

German schoolchildren and university students growing into a united Europe will have the best chance to identify with the united Germany. They will have no significant personal experience of an enemy on the other side of the Berlin Wall. At the most, they may experience the diluted influence of past, divergent political philosophies transmitted by parents, without further reinforcement in school or society at large. Already, members of this young generation have had travel opportunities and exposure to age-mates from all parts of the country as well as from other countries. In the future, they will experience Germany as a whole within borders that define it as one part of the European community. It is to be hoped that open borders will enable them to establish an expanded personality through identification with other cultures while still identifying Germany as their homeland and all Germans as one people. Now, the Wall at the Brandenburg Gate is history. There, Ossie meets Wessie, girl meets boy, and together they launch their future. (One of the young interviewees indeed did meet his companion at the Brandenburg Gate. Together, this Ossie and his Wessie visited the United States, as did another couple in a "mixed" west-east marriage.)

The words of real people explaining their personal experiences during momentous social, political, and economic upheaval constitute the body of this book. Its chapters will address various aspects of the German unification phenomenologically. The topics of main concern to the people I interviewed were the opening of the Wall, the antecedents and sequelae to unification, east-west relations, adjustment and adaptation, conditions and expectations at work, women in the society, youth, and current political attitudes. A chapter will be devoted to each of these topics. However, in presenting their various personal experiences and perspectives, interviewees weave many themes around a given topic. Therefore, this is not a linear, logical, historical analysis. And not every interviewee gave each aspect of the unification equal emphasis. A different combination of voices is heard in each of the following chapters, including mine as I comment and sometimes interpret—sagely, it is hoped, and to the reader's satisfaction.

NOTES

1. Judith Kestenberg and Charlotte Kahn (eds.), *Children Surviving Persecution: An International Study* (Westport, Conn.: Praeger, 1997), p. 297.

2. Ibid., p. 261.

3. Harold Lasswell, *The Political Writings of Harold Lasswell* (Glenco, Ill.: Free Press, 1951), p. 474.

4. Ibid.

5. Charlotte Kahn, Information Control and the Distortion of Cogni-

tion: East Germans Review the Effects of Totalitarianism in Their Lives, *The Journal of Psychohistory*, 19:4 (1992): 409–420.

6. Milton Rokeach, *The Open and the Closed Mind* (New York: Basic Books, 1960).

7. Erich Hanke, *Ins nächste Jahrhundert, was steht uns bevor?* (Leipzig, Jena, Berlin: Urania Verlag, 1984), p. 108.

8. Prior experience with certain crises can provide an "inoculation perspective." Zahava Solomon, *Coping with War-Induced Stress* (New York: Plenum Press, 1995), p. 143.

9. See Solomon, *Coping*, p. 143; Judith Kestenberg and Charlotte Kahn, *Children Surviving Persecution: An International Study of Trauma and Healing* (Westport, Conn.: Praeger, 1998), p. 3.

10. Charlotte Kahn, The Different Ways of Being German, *The Journal of Psychohistory*, 20:4 (1993): 381–398.

11. Nobuko Yoshyawa Meaders, The Transcultural Self. In Paul Elovitz and Charlotte Kahn (eds.), *Immigrant Experiences—Personal Narrative and Psychological Analysis*, pp. 47–59 (Madison, N.J.: Fairleigh Dickinson University Press and London: Associated University Presses, 1997).

12. Ibid.

13. Ibid.

Germany. *Source*: © 1997 Facts On File, Inc. Reprinted by permission of Facts On File, Inc.

Germany: Länder (State) Boundaries and Capitals. *Source*: © 1997 Facts On File, Inc. Reprinted by permission of Facts On File, Inc.

1

Over, Under, Around, and Through!

It was a moment of emancipation and liberation achieved by the people . . . for the people . . . .[1]

In the early afternoon of the fateful 9th of November the Central Committee of the official German Democratic Republic (GDR) political party (*Sozialistiche Einheitspartei Deutschlands* [SED]) prepared a notice that a "resolution detailing a temporary interim arrangement regarding travel and permanent exit from the GDR is confirmed" *(Beschluss zur zeitweiligen Übergangsregelung für Reisen und ständige Ausreise aus der DDR wird bestätigt)*. This notice, edited to deemphasize its temporary aspects, was circulated for approval among members of the Politburo and various ministers and officials. As the plan called for publication no sooner than the following day, the new regulations were distributed with precautions to maintain all due secrecy. The intention was to relieve the pressure of thousands of GDR immigrants at the Czechoslovakian border and also, to some extent, the pressure on the German Federal Republic (GFR), to which GDR citizens had been fleeing via the open borders between Czechoslovakia and the West. An exit permit would still be required, but would be granted in accordance with the travel wishes of the citizen, including "immediate travel."

Günter Schabowski, Politburo member and spokesperson, was absent during the discussions leading to the changes in travel regulations, as he was in and out of the room, speaking to journalists.

However, he did receive the information informally on a ragged piece of paper, which he stuffed into a pile of other pages he was carrying in preparation for a television press conference that evening. Seven minutes before the scheduled end of the press conference at 7 P.M., Schabowski fished out the fateful paper from his pile and, reading the resolution for the first time, inadvertently made the announcement public. This was followed by further questions and inconclusive answers. Five minutes after the end of the conference, the Associated Press announced its interpretation of the resolution as a transitory opening of the borders until new laws were passed. NBC included in its bulletin that the regulations would go into effect on November 10. Hours later, before the officers and soldiers of the border police had been informed, the tumult began.

The inadvertent opening of the Berlin Wall had been preceded not only by the emigration across the Czechoslovak border and the pressure of the throngs shouting: "We want out!" *(Wir wollen raus!)*, but also by demonstrators shouting: "We are staying here," the implication being, staying here to make changes.

The fortieth anniversary of the GDR on October 7, 1989, had been marked by violence. It was not the violence of enraged revolutionaries; this was the violent reaction of a desperate regime gasping for its life.

On that day—and certainly not for the first time—discontented citizens in several GDR cities had attended prayer meetings for peace and gone on to peaceful protest marches and demonstrations. In the evening, an orderly procession moved in the direction of the Gethsemane Church in the Prenzlauer Berg district of Berlin. Outside the church, hundreds of candles were lit to protest the unjust incarcerations; inside, a hunger strike began. Several informal political groups were formed, such as *Aufruf 89* (Appeal 89) and *Neues Forum* (New Forum). The people demanded reform by means of a collaborative process in which citizens from all walks of life would participate.[2]

In response, special police forces were mobilized, traffic was blocked, streets closed. While the demonstrators had called for "no violence!", the militia and the police, weapons in hand, declared themselves ready to defend the socialist regime. Around midnight the order was issued to crush the crowds. In Berlin, as in Leipzig, Dresden, and several other cities, the police attacked with rubber truncheons and water cannons, brutally knocking people down and pulling them by their hair across the cobblestone streets and loading men, women, and children on trucks to take them to prisons.

With mounting dissatisfaction, the crowd of protestors swelled. The following week 300,000 to perhaps as many as half a million people took to the streets in Leipzig. The battles of a true revolution were almost upon the GDR—but, for lack of external support, they were averted. Before the end of his visit to the GDR to celebrate the state's fortieth anniversary, Gorbachev had announced that Soviet troops would not be available for purposes of internal political repression. Thus, the GDR was effectually disarmed. In addition, a Protestant minister and a small group of celebrities (including the Gewandhaus Orchestra of Leipzig conductor, Kurt Masur) persuaded party leaders to issue an appeal against violence, which was broadcast and passed on to the police.

DOROTHEA

Dorothea is a Wessie, a West German, who now works in East Berlin. She is fifty-two years old, born in Palestine one year before the State of Israel was established.

Whenever I drove through the interzone area, I thought: This magnificent country! Why don't the people revolt? Is there no chance that we'll ever join together again?

The opening of the Wall on November 9, 1989, was one of the most momentous events I had ever experienced, and reunification was like a miracle. At the time, most people actually didn't comprehend what had just happened in Germany historically, what was happening here in Berlin, and that reunification was just around the corner. People were streaming in from the East, from the GDR to West Germany.

The TV anchorman was saying: The Wall is coming down, the Wall is coming down. It's going to be opened up. And you saw lots of people standing at the Wall, and at the Brandenburg Gate—behind it, right at the Wall—trying to get through. And I said to my friend: That's impossible, what's happening here. It's madness. There was dead silence in the center of the city; no shouting, no joy, no open windows. Around 7:30, there was still no sound. And tears came to my eyes. Strangely enough, it reminded me of the long division of Jerusalem. I wondered: Don't the Germans understand what's happening here after so many years? Why is it so calm here? No one is shouting. In Israel, people would be dancing the *hora* in the streets, folk dances. It would be a folk celebration. Here, the windows were closed; it was quiet, alarmingly quiet.

And then, one hour later, it started. All hell broke loose here in Berlin. Everybody was yelling, shouting with joy, and it went on and on. And they didn't know what was in store for them.

ERICH

Erich is a thirty-four-year-old Rhinelander who studied at the East German Humboldt Universität and established many friendships in East Germany. He now lives in East Berlin, where he is a partner in an advertising company.

Unfortunately, I happened to be in Düsseldorf on November 9th. As we were driving from the west toward Berlin that night, there was a huge traffic jam on the highway; starting as far away as 20 km (12 mi.) from Helmstedt, the border crossing at that time. And from the east, I'll never forget this, there was I'd say a 70 to 80 km (44 to 50 mi.) backup to the border. It was like a party. And then, we got to the border and it was open. People stood on the highway; they were drinking. The formalities and the guards at the border were friendly. It was a crazy night. Total strangers embraced, and it was very moving. All of Berlin went wild and there were many accidents, because people were driving drunk. Oh, it was really strange.

Strange things happened, because no one in the GDR had any official information or legal framework for dealing with the developments. The border guards didn't know what they were supposed to do.

JOSEPHINE

Josephine, an office worker in an East Berlin firm, is self-educated. She thinks about many things and stays informed on various issues. Though she was born in Cologne on Christmas Day in 1956, her mother brought her to East Germany as an infant. She spent her entire life in the East, her adult years in East Berlin.

At some point, things have to change. I had always believed that, historically, one thing naturally follows another. People cannot possibly allow themselves to be oppressed like this forever, not permitted to travel, to leave, to take a look at what's going on elsewhere in the world.

The GDR's undoing was its dogma. The regime's ideology made it impossible to change the system into something else. German unification would probably have taken place much sooner if there had been no Wall, and that would have been the end of the GDR, too. One way or the other, it would have become Germany again.

At that time, in '89, I thought of participating in the demonstrations, but I was afraid, because you never knew what might happen and I worried about what would become of my child. I was paralyzed with fear that a war might break out, that there would be shooting. When the trains came through Dresden from Prague, that is, when they were passing through East Germany on their way to West Germany, I thought they would never allow them to go through the GDR. People in Dresden tried to jump on board. I couldn't understand why the military allowed it. That's probably what paralyzed me.

WILMA

Wilma is fifty-three years old, married, with an adult son. Both in her childhood and as an adult, she has lived in both parts of Germany. During a serious marital crisis, she returned from the Rheinland to East Berlin to live and work without her husband. Her husband has since rejoined her.

One can still tell which was East Berlin and which was West Berlin, because the streetcar stops at the West border. Whereas the GDR expanded the streetcar network, the public surface transportation in West Berlin is by bus.

When the Wessies come over, one may be really helpful, while another may look out only for his own interests. The Ossies, of course, had gotten a bad impression of them because the Wessies had cheated them. And I wanted to show these people that, well, not every Wessie is like that.

I have heard people from the Ruhr region say: Thank God the East is very far away; we live in our own world here and it's peaceful and quiet. And they were a bit afraid of what might happen when the border with Poland—or even with Russia—opens and more and more East Germans come to Berlin and even farther into the West. People are afraid of violence, which, as expected, has become worse, unfortunately. But the farther west people live, the less they know about what was happening in the East, or what it had been like before. It's still like that today after nearly 10 years.

The Wessies complain and are upset about the *Solidaritätsabgabe* [a surtax imposed to help finance the rebuilding of the decrepit ex-GDR infrastructure and to shore up the ailing economy in the eastern sector of Germany], which at first had a cut-off date, but which continues to be in effect. The taxpayers are hoping not to have to pay for the reconstruction of the former GDR any longer. And so, more than just a few Wessies are saying: The Wall should be rebuilt, but, please, this time build it higher.

HANS

Hans is in his forties. His parents, Erika and Willie, were first interviewed in 1990 and invited him to participate in the 1998 interview. Divorced from his wife, Hans has sporadic contact with his son.

West Berlin was the frontline city and profited from tourists who came to see the Wall. In addition, all its residents were given a Berlin subsidy, that is, a subsidy from Bonn, because they lived, so to speak, on an island in the middle of the Eastern Zone. It was a lot of money and they were all well off. Now, however, everything in Berlin is getting more expensive. The rents are going up because the power is in the hands of only a few individuals, not the People. The landlord wants more and more money, profit, profit, profit. Before, when the GDR still existed, the Western leaders had to allow the population to enjoy a certain level of prosperity. It was a contest between the two systems, between the East and the West.

Now that the entire Eastern Bloc and the GDR have disappeared, the capitalists can pull the strings, politically and economically. They can have their fling and they can be ruthless. Ten years ago, if the GFR had asked of their people that what they're asking today, the people would have said: That can't be; look at the GDR; there's no unemployment there; they don't have rent increases. There was always that example, and that's why they did well over there [in the West] all those years.

After the opening of the Wall, but before the monetary union, the West German currency, the Deutschmark, was not officially valid in the GDR. In contrast to the Ostmark of the GDR, however, the D-mark was considered hard currency and thus preferred. This caused many bitter experiences. Hans describes what happened to him:

Here in East Berlin, if you went into a restaurant, you were a second-class citizen. Wessies were given preferential treatment on principle. The same thing happened to us when we wanted to take a taxi or go to the theater. Ossies were always put somewhere in the back of the restaurant, simply because of their currency. A Wessie would slam down his Deutschmark and the waiters would take his west-money and then pull some east-money out of their own pockets and put that into the cash register. And that was that.

In restaurants, it was customary for Wessies to be seated immediately. All they had to do was walk up to the door. There was a sign there that read: Please wait to be seated. And we would stand there and wait. And, well, if the line was long enough—and they were often very long, these lines—sometimes we stood there for an hour. Meanwhile, someone from the West would come along. You could tell, somehow [that they were Wessies], but I don't know how. And I also don't exactly know how they did it, whether they handed them the D-marks directly or some other way. Suddenly they were inside and we were left standing there. Sometimes it made me furious. It made me sick.

ERIKA

Erika is an energetic sixty-five-year-old woman. She was born into a *Volksdeutche* family in Poland, was deported to East Germany with her family during World War II, married at nineteen, and bore five children (Hans, Monika, and Thorsten among them). She continued her vocational training throughout her life, worked full time, and commanded a very respectable salary.

Sure, the GDR citizen had money but there was nothing to buy. In those days, you didn't ask where it all went, all those consumer goods. Western catalogue firms were supplied by the East. *Quelle* and *Otto-Versand* sold GDR products in their mail-order catalogues; and our entire agricultural production went to the West. After the *Wende*, when our businesses had to close because they were not competitive and our agriculture broke down, the catalogue houses had to look for new sources of merchandise.

In the GDR, you had to stand on line forever to buy television sets. They would always arrive in batches. A store would get fifty sets at a time. Somehow people found out, and they'd put their *Fiffies* ["fifties"—50-Mark bribes (also *Fuffies, Fünfzig-Mark*)] on the counter. Nobody got a set without handing over a tip.

Of course, consumer goods—TV sets, stereo equipment, textiles—were very expensive. But everyday things were cheap. Salamander shoes and fashions from Italy? Obviously, nobody could afford those. There were special stores for things like that, and there was also the *Genex* catalog. That's where GDR citizens could buy East or West German products for west-money. If you had west-money, you could even order cars, but they were Russian cars, a Lada, a Wartburg. You could also buy a Trabi through a catalog; and you didn't have to wait fourteen years. For west-money you could get a car immediately!

Well, where did a GDR citizen get west-money when it was officially forbidden? If you were lucky, you were able to exchange it. For a long time, I wasn't able to exchange any because I didn't have that much east-money.

Only the Intershop had jeans. And you had to have west-money. There was this old man at my job; he was the janitor/doorman and he was allowed to drive to the West, precisely because he was older, over sixty. He asked me once, Don't you need a little west-money for your children? I can exchange it 1 for 3, he said. And of course I jumped at the chance. After that, I always brought home west-money for my children. I mean, I exchanged the money I earned so that the children could have their jeans. Then after the children had worn them out, I sold them to someone else.

That's how the system bred corruption. It had to do with the fact that there were three currencies in the GDR: as we jokingly said, there was the GDR currency, the West German currency, and a third currency which was introduced foolishly at some point by the GDR—Forum Checks. They tried to prevent relatives visiting from abroad from giving you D-Marks by making them exchange their money for Forum Checks, which they could then use to shop at the *Intershops*. GDR citizens could go there too, except that officially, as GDR citizens, you were not supposed to have any west-money. Right?

Things were supposed to be getting better all the time, but I thought: Actually, what's getting better all the time? And there aren't going to be more goods either. They produced, produced, and produced, and still there was never anything to buy.

PAUL

Paul, forty-five years old, grew up in the GDR. Although he admits to the problems that led to the demise of the GDR and has become a businessman, he remains a convinced socialist. He is Petra's husband and Paul's father.

So-called socialism couldn't go on like that. We noticed everywhere that nothing in our daily lives was quite right. Economic development was described in glowing terms but never added up. Every GDR citizen, down to the last employee, knew that the collectives—the state-owned industries—were no longer operating efficiently. But no one really wanted to know. Once they picked up their wages, everything was okay. But then they complained when they couldn't find anything to buy with their money. And so there were protests and demonstrations in the streets. So it's difficult to maintain that only an elite few saw and knew about this.

But you have to focus on what's important to you. Is it important to have a very good car glittering with chrome trim, or is it more important to be able to send your children to college? Or to have free health service? Naturally, attitudes like that were acquired with one's upbringing. Even as a young person you put more value on things like being able to go to a vacation place, or that a mother of three could send the children to camp during their vacations. Now the only people who can send their children to camp are the ones with money. All the others always have problems with the six weeks of summer vacation. On the whole, money plays a much greater role than before.

HILDE

Hilde and her mother were deported from Czechoslovakia to the East German Zone after World War II, when Hilde was twelve. She is now sixty-five, a mother, grandmother, and retired teacher. Hilde describes herself as slow on the uptake:

I had been caught up in the socialist system. However, with the invasion of Afghanistan, I thought, Well, a society that attacks other countries can't be quite right. And so, I began to have doubts. And then I developed breathing problems in Berlin-Buch, that is, in East Berlin. We were being poisoned by the inferior brown coal, by the combustion gases, while they constantly preached to us that the people's welfare was paramount. So, I began to doubt everything. Of course by then it was the 80s already—twenty years after the Wall was built!

In Bautzen, I didn't quite take in the building of the Wall. Bautzen was far away from Berlin. The Berliners were much more conscious of all that.

I was living in Berlin when all the protests and the demonstrations started to happen, but I did not participate. I was afraid of losing my teaching job which, after all, was supporting us. I had to stay at the helm, figuratively speaking, so that our children would grow up to be something.

My son marched in one of the demonstrations. He was locked up for a night in Hohenschönhausen. I warned him: For God's sake, you can't do that; it's dangerous. My whole attitude was fearful.

I was pretty much on the sidelines of the historical events, too. My daughter called in the middle of the night when the Wall collapsed. Sleepy and grumpy, I went to the phone. *Mutti*, my daughter said, do you know where I am? I'm at the Ku'damm [*Kurfürstendamm*, an elegant main street in West Berlin]. For God's sake, I said, Why are you waking me up at this time of night? I'll never get back to sleep! You know I have trouble sleeping, and tomorrow I have to teach. I was very indignant. Well, I reacted quite stupidly, couldn't foresee what was going to happen next.

Yet in 1989, when the stream of people escaping was so big that the country couldn't cope with it anymore, it was pretty clear that it had to be resolved somehow. But at that time it wasn't clear to me that this spelled the imminent collapse of the State.

Every day was historic in 1989–1990. Everything was changing; the border was open and every day there was something new. Changes occurred within days that otherwise would have taken years; one couldn't grasp it all. You begin to realize more and more of the things you misunderstood before, but some of it gets lost, forgotten.

JOHANNA

Johanna is an attractive thirty-six-year-old, who has spent her entire life in West Berlin. She grew up in a lower-middle-class family, has one brother, remained single, and works in a missions program in the Catholic Church.

As a child in West Berlin I really wasn't aware of the Wall very much. There were a few exceptions when the Wall became obvious to me, but it was not a presence in my everyday life. I wasn't aware of it, didn't sense it as a constriction, even though I grew up with it. I also grew up with the idea that the GDR existed as a country, and there was never any question that it was a separate country. Nor did we delve into the background of all this in school.

My mother was pregnant with me when the Wall was built. And this was a profound, terrible experience for my parents. They had relatives in East Berlin and in the GDR. And my mother told me once, she thought the shock she had experienced that day would induce a miscarriage. She was actually afraid that it would have an effect on me. It didn't.

And I remember now that we visited my grandmother. She lived in Marienfelde, right by the Wall. So did my uncle. My uncle's property was bordered by the Wall, and there was a road between my grandmother's property and the Wall. My brother and I were about 7 and 8 years old and we were playing in the trees there. We climbed too far up, so that we were above the top of the Wall. And then we heard voices coming from the guard tower. They were shouting something, but we didn't understand what and didn't pay any attention because we were so absorbed in our games. Then there were shots! Suddenly something whistled past us, and some of the rocks splintered off. The shots had bounced off the rounded top of the wall, or at least grazed it, and some cement splintered off.

We were too young to realize that they might have endangered our lives. They must have had binoculars; they must have seen that it was only children playing. Well, we couldn't figure that out. Later we played there again, simply because we didn't understand what was going on.

There was only one other time when I was even aware of the Wall—and quite a striking experience it was! Going on a trip was always a threatening experience, particularly for us children, not because of the Wall itself, but because of the transit area, the border guards, the weapons. We always had a small car, a Bobby or a Kadett, and you had to wait in line forever at the border, first just to get out of Berlin, and then again to get out of the transit area and back into West Germany. When we set out on these trips, we were always afraid, worried that we would do something wrong. There couldn't be any comic books lying around openly in the car, no newspapers, no photos or film. That would be seen as a provocation and one would risk reprisals at the border checkpoint. It was frightening for a small child to sit in the car and knowing that you couldn't get out; even in the parking lot you weren't allowed to go far away from it, or you'd be in enemy territory, so to speak. We were afraid that something would happen to us. We didn't know what, my parents didn't know either. It was just this uncertainty.

Sometimes we couldn't understand what was happening—coming back from a vacation trip at night, we sleeping children would be dragged out of the car. Then they would take apart the entire car to see whether anybody was concealed in it, whether we were taking somebody out of the GDR; they'd look behind the rear seat, under the car in the gas tank or wherever else. My parents practically taped our mouths shut with adhesive tape. But my experiences at the Wall were limited to these trips.

Today, you know that the drive from Berlin to Helmstedt takes at most three or three and a half hours. Before, when you started out on a trip with the *Pfadfinder* (Boy Scouts) you had to count on at least five or six hours for that stretch, simply because the buses—full of children—were lined up at the border. And if one of the children made a stupid remark, or made a face, or something was off, then the bus was kept standing there in the searing heat at the checkpoint; the children weren't allowed to get out. Sometimes it was all right because there was a nice *Vopo* [*Volkspolizist*, member of the Peoples Police, a policeman] who even told jokes. But sometimes a crease in a child's identity card would cause them to take the child off the bus to be fingerprinted and photographed.

This was the sort of occasion that as a child and young adult made me feel threatened. As a Wessie, I had no connection with the Wall, and yet I, and others, were quite helplessly at the mercy of it, especially since we didn't exactly know the rules, and they, after all, acted arbitrarily.

For the first two or three years [after the *Wende*], I continued to feel that same fear every time we drove by that checkpoint. I always knew: This is where it happened! So I was always aware of that. And a strange feeling would always come over me whenever I saw those kinds of buildings again. Even today, when I drive to Helmstedt and see these old customs clearance facilities—now they've been turned into a memorial to German unity—I think: How long you used to wait here.

HELGA

Helga is a young teacher, a Wessie, who works at a high school (*Gymnasium*) in the eastern part of Berlin. She was a member of a group of teachers interviewed at the school.

To this day, I am amazed that, as a student, I would walk along here with visitors who were staying with me in the western sector of Berlin, and we would climb up to where we had a good view and look across. Yes, we even nodded [to them]. That was a Sunday excursion. One made the best of it. We didn't think about the situation very much. In retrospect, now that the Wall is open and everything has changed, I'm really shocked that I didn't act differently. I was really just vegetating.

Once, I played [on a team] with a girl at my club. She lived in Neukölln in the border zone, right near the Wall. And once she came here just after witnessing an escape attempt by a man from the GDR. They had shot at him, and he didn't make it. Yes, we talked about that. She couldn't do anything about it. That sort of thing came up often. Something happens and it frightens you, but you don't really get involved.

Four or five years later, I went over to East Berlin to buy books because there was good literature available there and it was reasonably priced. It's embarrassing to look back on, but at the time I saw it only one-sidedly. I think that someone with a wider perspective would have gone over there to look at certain interesting things.

On that occasion, I took the subway and I had to change trains at the Friedrichstrasse station. The stations were lighted differently in those days than they are today. Suddenly the contrast with the West became apparent. Some of the subway trains first passed through the East and didn't stop at any stations in the East, they just passed by, moving slowly. It was darker there. Ghost stations.

It was relatively easy to cross the border at Friedrichstrasse. You walked through quite mysterious, dark walkways, past a sort of ticket counter. This all seemed odd to me—it was constructed pretty strangely, a sort of wooden partition. First of all, you couldn't see the other side, like a child that can't look over a certain wall. You could see across only after you passed the customs officers or border officials. The border guards, the inspectors, sat above you and looked down at you, and used a mirror to see what you had brought along. I remember, they used that mirror on me. And then they examined your identity card.

DOROTHEA

Dorothea went to school near Hamburg, but often visited her grandparents in Berlin.

I attended high school in Hamburg, and during vacations I took the train to Berlin to visit my grandparents. The East began once you passed Hamburg. And in those days, the time the train took to go through the Eastern Sector always varied. It could take four hours, but it could also take twelve hours. I remember one time I really wanted to be with my grandparents on New Year's eve, so I left in the morning. We didn't arrive here till 3:00 A.M. the next day! The train went very slowly and stopped at every other station. Then the Vopos would come aboard with their dogs and they searched us down

to our undershirts. I remember that they looked through my note-
books. They took down the little advertising posters that hung in the
train at the crossover to the next compartment and they looked behind
them to see whether there was anything hidden there. You weren't
allowed to go into the dining car until the Vopos had taken your
identity card. I think in the beginning they were confiscated until you
left the East, shortly before you got off the train. You were not allowed
to throw anything out of the window.

We often saw children and young people standing behind these
fences, waiting for someone to throw something to them. Later, when
I was a young woman, we sometimes drove by car to Hamburg
through the East. We would pass through Lauenburg, where people
were lined up outside the stores in long lines that snaked across the
street, across the sidewalks. We couldn't believe that they were really
waiting in line for bread or fruit. Nobody can tell me today that this
isn't true because I saw it with my own eyes.

SOPHIE

Sophie is a sixty-three-year-old West German woman, who never
married. A retired teacher, she lives on a pension. The only child of
professional parents, she grew up near the Berlin Wall. To this day,
she lives in her deceased parents' apartment.

At first, when the Wall was being built, they still helped the people
living there on Bernauer Strasse. Later, all those houses were torn
down. The Wall ran down the middle of the street, and the houses
were in the East—so one could still get some people out by using
bedsheets. There were also groups who built tunnels from here to
there. I even had a colleague at work who helped build the tunnels
and who brought people over two or three times. Then he was arrested
trying to get his girlfriend out and was put into prison. Nowadays,
you can't imagine what that was like. Once he took me to Bernauer
Strasse to climb up the Wall. We were told it was dangerous, that they
might shoot at us from the other side.

Twice, an acquaintance of mine saw people killed at the Wall. These
are images she never can and never will forget. She tells me that, nowadays, when she tries to describe these events to a younger coworker
in the East, the woman doesn't want to hear about it. She can't imagine that such things happened and claims they're not true.

Yes, the truth is, Berlin was closed off, Berlin was tightly sealed.

I always refused to cross the border at any point. I did it once, because I am a member of Amnesty International. When someone from one of these human rights groups got sick and there was an emergency, I went across for 25 Marks—which you had to exchange so that the GDR economy would get foreign money and hard currency. The money was exchanged one to one, D-Mark for Ostmark, a most unfavorable exchange rate for Westerners. This obligatory exchange was not to be underestimated as a source of [hard] currency for the GDR. Nor was the visa regulation agreement that was concluded with the German Federal Republic in the early '70s, because it consisted of a lump-sum compensation from the GFR to the GDR. The fees for the use of the transit highway [from West Berlin through East Germany to West Germany] and the visa fees—which one had to pay individually beforehand—were transferred in lump sums by the West German government to the East German government.

At the border, I was so shocked by the harassment with the mirrors—from above, from below—that I said: I think you people here are inhuman. Of course, I was wearing underwear, but I think this is just too macabre, the way they were examining me from all angles with mirrors. I'm a human being, not a car that you can just inspect any way you like.

As a visitor without any suitcases, I was permitted, like all the others, to stay for twenty-four hours. But I couldn't stand to be there that long. So I picked up the tab for the people sitting at the next table in the restaurant, just to get rid of my east-money.

Most students crossed over regularly, twice a year to go to the Brecht Theater, the History Museum, or the Huguenot cemetery; and to go to the Prenzlauer Berg section where they strolled around. They thought it was awesome to walk on this historic pavement. They tried to ignore the harassment somewhat. Some of them got used to it after a while, but I never managed to do that.

MARTHA

Martha is a teacher from the West, who was interviewed as one of a group in an East Berlin *Gymnasium*.

You had to submit an exact accounting for the books you purchased in the East. One time, I also bought some groceries and I saved the receipts for everything. If you didn't have proof for something you bought, it was confiscated.

It's embarrassing to think that one would go to the other capital with the sole intention of buying books at bargain prices. Actually, the more beautiful buildings are here in the East, and you would expect a student to be interested in things other than just cheap shopping.

WERNER

The building of the Wall came as a complete surprise to almost everybody, as it did to Werner, who went back and forth between West and East on a regular basis. Werner is a professorial type with a physician wife and two teenage daughters.

I didn't think it could happen. But perhaps I underestimated the technology. I looked at a map of Berlin and I said: The traffic system is set up so that you can't divide the city. The underground (*U-Bahn*) and the city line (*S-Bahn*), etc. wouldn't work if you did. I couldn't imagine it.

The day before, I had been visiting my aunt in West Berlin; I came back on the last train late at night on August 12th and didn't notice anything. I was renting a room from an elderly lady at the time. She woke me up the next morning and told me what had happened. It was Sunday, bright sunshine. I got up immediately and since the *S-Bahn* wasn't running, I walked to the Brandenburg Gate. When I arrived—the Wall was built later—there was a wire fence there that you could lift up; it hadn't yet been fastened securely. Not many policemen were standing around either, and so I saw people still slipping through. I was standing right next to the Brandenburg Gate at the left, right next to the wire fence. The border ran down the middle of Friedrich Ebert Strasse. At that time you weren't allowed to use that street. A young man was standing in the middle of the street, and a policeman came over from the West and grabbed his arm to pull him across. A moment later, a policeman from the East arrived and tugged at him, too. He was stronger and pulled the young man over to his side. West Berliners were standing under the trees on the other side, protesting and cursing. Then we were chased away.

This happened near the Soviet Embassy, and the Russians were standing there, watching. Later, tanks showed up. Several people were arrested. Whenever two people were standing around together, a policeman would come running over and simply stand there next to them and barge in on their conversation. And if someone said: Beat it, we want to talk by ourselves, he was arrested. I saw it. That was the direction things were taking.

It happened step by step. They closed the border, but said it was only a temporary measure. A table was set up on the street, and an officer sat there and answered questions. He said: Well, you can see

what's going on here. But you can't go across today; it all has to be
sorted out first. But [you can go] later, next week, or the week after
that, I can't give you a precise date, I can't promise you anything; you
have to understand that. That's the way they reacted. You were given
reassuring, intentionally false information.

After a short time, I realized that it was all lies and that you could
no longer leave. Up to that point, people had often asked me why I
didn't leave since I knew that things were better in West Germany. At
first, I argued with them. I could see that there was hardly anyone
who was actually a convinced supporter of the regime. By convinced
supporter I mean someone who would join the system without getting
anything in return. There were many people who supported the system
just to gain some advantage out of it, and they made fun of it, joked
about it. I felt—I was wrong—that this system would not get far. But
we had to wait decades for it to collapse, because the GDR was a
Soviet satellite state, and I didn't take into account that the Soviet
tanks were the most important political factor.

Most important, I have to say that I used to be a very good short-
distance runner, and since the university is about one kilometer [two-
thirds of a mile] from the Brandenburg Gate I kept thinking that when
the time came I could be on the other side in a couple of minutes.
That was no longer possible.

KURT

Kurt is sixty-two, an East German, a once loyal GDR citizen, for
the most part, satisfied with Socialist policies. He supported the official party line. Now he is retired. He lives with his wife, Käthe;
together, they have three adult sons.

The Wall is there to protect us, that was the official line. The Wall
is there not only to protect us from the outside, but also to protect
us on the inside. The state needed the Wall both internally and externally. The crucial point was that all the intelligentsia who studied at
the university here, the top scientists, they all left! The state was hem-
orrhaging. There's no doubt that it wasn't humane to detain people,
but it was necessary for the state to do that. If it didn't want to go
under, it would have to use means—necessarily and consistently—that
were not humane.

Take the delicate subject of the deaths at the Wall and the guards
who shot people. Of course, you can't call that a good thing, but every
body in the GDR knew it was forbidden to climb over the Wall. If
one didn't understand that, then one surely didn't have any brains.

And it's still like that today: If you own a plot of land and you have a dog running around in your garden, nobody would stop you from putting up a big sign saying: Danger, vicious dog. And if, in spite of the signs, someone climbs over your fence and is bitten by the dog, then people would say: It was his own fault. He had no business there. If I know the Wall is there and there are soldiers posted nearby, then I won't climb over it, no matter how much I'd like to.

WILLIE

Willie, an extraordinarily loyal former GDR police officer, had to take early retirement at the time of the Wende. He is the tall, solid, sixty-seven-year-old husband of Erika, father and grandfather. Born in Hamburg, evacuated during the war to Austria and to Bayern, he found an apprenticeship in the East Zone after World War II. He married Erika and became the father of four sons and one daughter.

The border was sealed tight for a long time, in the '60s. Moreover, it hasn't been proved yet that there was an order to shoot people. They [the border guards] were to prevent border violations, to keep people from breaking through, but there was no order to shoot to kill. The border guards were supposed to shoot only when their own lives were threatened.

The [border guards] were still patrolling singly when an incident occurred where we were working near the canal. But later on, after that, there were always two guards on patrol together. Some construction workers were working there with an excavating machine and one of them went up to this very young fellow, this nineteen-year-old border guard, and asked him for a light for his cigarette. And while the guard was getting out his lighter, the worker shot him and went across. It was so easy to do that here. And from then on, there were always two border guards patrolling together. That must have been 1964 or '65.

When I was a young man in the Army I was stationed in the interior, not at the border. When we did guard duty, we were also given instructions, but never . . . well, it was different there than at the border. There were regulations for the use of firearms, and these regulations spelled out exactly when one was allowed to shoot and when not. That's why the former border guards are in court today and being convicted of having shot people down. And again and again, the cases turn on this shoot-to-kill order. To this day they can't prove that there was ever such an order.

I know from personal experience that there was a special police deployment whenever there were state celebrations, whenever people came from abroad on state visits. And then they would go out of their way to emphasize the instructions on the use of firearms and we were told we were not to shoot while at the border because no shots were to be fired at the West. That was absolutely forbidden.

Actually, a lot of border guards and a lot of policemen were shot by people who wanted to get out! If two or three men were to sneak up to the border in the dark in an escape attempt, I'd defend myself. After all, it was my job to see to it that there was order and security along my section of the border.

ERIKA

Erika, Willie's wife, was separated from her relatives by the Wall and the border politics.

We Ossies really had problems with the Wall. For instance, when my brother died in the West, none of us could go over for the funeral, except one of my children was able to go. You had to show the death certificate as proof, but I still didn't get permission, even though it was my brother, because I was married to Willie, a policeman. That's how it was. So I gave the death certificate to my daughter, but it didn't work for her either. Nobody knows why they wouldn't let her out.

So then they gave my son that little piece of paper. He was allowed to go. He got them to give it to him even though, a few years earlier, he had tried to escape over the Wall and was put in jail. It's all so strange.

But he got there too late. The funeral was already over. From that you can see how good our state really was—how stupid. My son stayed in the West for seven days and had a good time going to Holland with his cousin. Actually he should not have crossed the border because his passport was only valid for the German Federal Republic, but he had a nice time. The relatives all said, Stay here. You'll get an apartment, you'll find work here.

At the time, another of my sons wanted to go to the funeral, too. He was twenty years old in 1988. He went to the registration place on Baumschulenweg and had them write out the thing there. The official wanted to know whether he had already served in the army. You haven't? the official asked. Well, what are you doing here then? So my son had to shove off.

MAX

Max, a large, gray-haired man, is a retired GDR factory worker. He is sixty-eight. He comes from a poor family, his grandparents having been illiterate. He has a daughter by his first marriage. Currently he lives with his second wife, who was present at the interview.

The border guards actually played minor roles here; they didn't have to shoot. There are people who claim that they would have been put in jail if they hadn't. Of course that isn't true. They would probably have been removed from the border, transferred elsewhere, because they weren't suited for border duty. No guard who missed or didn't shoot—which sometimes did happen—was ever punished. Whoever says otherwise is feeding you a line. Soldiers could even refuse to go to the border, but what can you expect from young people like that?

In 1991, I was here at the radio station—it was still GDR Radio then—speaking with the defense lawyer for the border guard who shot the last man to have died at the Wall in February 1989, in Treptow at the border. Chris Geoffroy was the name of the man who was killed. He was twenty years old.

The lawyer for the border guards was a major general. In addition, there was another man from our association, the League of People Persecuted under Stalinism [*Bund der Stalinistisch Verfolgten*], a man who had been in prison for eighteen months because of an escape attempt. The discussion was broadcast live. And this major general claimed what officials still insist on today, that there was no order to shoot.

There was no order to shoot; nobody ever saw it in black and white. But the soldiers say, they were instructed to shoot. That is, every day when they moved out to guard the border, they were given a verbal order to capture people violating the border, or to prevent border violations with all the means at hand, or to "neutralize" those who tried to escape. That was the term. And this former major general told a similar tale. So I said to him: Well, if there was no order to shoot, then shooting wasn't legal; and the soldier who did the shooting should at least have been called in to answer for it and to be disciplined. Yet, quite the contrary, they got special leave and received a reward or even a medal. That's been proven. He didn't quite know what to say to that. And since this order to shoot technically didn't exist, these big generals get off easy.

Frieda, seventy, lives with her scientist husband in a one-family house in East Berlin, where they have raised their two daughters. All family members practice Catholicism. Frieda spent some years as a schoolteacher.

Since I was already over sixty years old on November 8, 1989, I was permitted to visit a woman friend in the West. It was her birthday and at her party I recounted my experiences during the demonstration on November 4th.

Many people spoke that day, among them Markus Wolf, the head of the *Stasi*, the secret police [*Staatssicherheitsdienst*], who had retired a few months before. He is a very intelligent man, the son of the writer Friedrich Wolf. And this Markus Wolf, an ardent Communist, somehow had gotten caught up in this change from ideal communism to what it had turned into at the end: living well and getting whatever one can, and let the devil take the hindmost.

Markus Wolf had relinquished his position a few months before the end of the GDR. Of course, he couldn't say: I don't agree with what's going on anymore; rather, he was already old and supposedly had left his job because of his age. But naturally, this man had been involved in many things that the Stasi had done, for instance, kidnapping people who had secretly fled to West Berlin. These people were then brought back by force, really kidnapped. Wolf was also involved in these things, something he denies today. But, of course, as the head of the Stasi he went through several trials in West Germany. As far as I know, he was given a suspended sentence and probation. Yes, he spoke at the demonstration, and they hissed him because the people knew who he was.

Jens Reich, a professor of molecular biology in Berlin-Buch, also spoke. He had met with nineteen dissidents at Robert Havemann's house. Havemann had been an ardent communist and a professor at Humboldt University. Havemann had rebuked the Communist party for many of their abuses, and because of that fell into disgrace, lost his professorship, and was sentenced to house arrest in his hometown, Grünheide near Berlin. He died one or two years before the *Wende*. After that, his widow, Katja Havemann, joined forces with some students and among these twenty dissidents there were people of all convictions, from Christians to atheists to communists. They said that things here couldn't go on this way any longer; things had to change. And they founded the New Forum, there at Katja Havemann's house.

And this Professor Jens Reich was one of the founders of the New Forum.

The New Forum played an important role at the time of the Wende, and we all hoped that the New Forum would establish itself as a party. We wanted free elections and to know for whom we could vote, because everything that had existed before in the GDR had been infiltrated by the ruling party. And we dissidents said that if we really do gain free elections, then we can't vote for these people. So we hoped that the New Forum would constitute itself as a political party.

In the meantime, other groups had formed in addition to the New Forum. There was the Democratic Awakening [*Demokratischer Aufbruch*] and two or three other groups, but they didn't play as big a role as the New Forum. Later a terrible story emerged—one of the founders of the Democratic Awakening was unmasked as a Stasi agent. The Stasi had their fingers in everything.

But to get back to November 4th. At least fifteen different people spoke, and the last one was Steffi Spyra, an old lady who was a well-known actress here in East Berlin. She said—and her words were often repeated at commemorative events and on commemorative broadcasts—:"We want our grandchildren to grow up without flag-raising ceremonies, without civics classes." And the millions of people on the Alexanderplatz went wild with enthusiasm. It was a unique experience, this event. And five days later the Wall was opened.

Yes, we're still laughing about it today, the fact that it was actually a mistake. But it had to happen. Schabowski had to interpret it that way, so he said; It seems that the borders are open, effective immediately. And the people heard that on the radio, and they rushed out.

HILDE

Hilde was still employed as a teacher at that time

As I was going to work on the bus from Berlin-Buch to Niederschönhausen, I noticed that the people on the bus were happy, cheerful, and exhilarated, and at school the students were very excited. On the other hand, the party leaders and the teachers were all wondering, Mmmmh, what will come of it? The party leadership, the SED, they were pretty glum. I was a minor party member, but only very minor, and had often been kicked around, so I was happy. I thought: Now things will be all right.

Two or three days later, I went to the West for the first time, still afraid that one of the party people might spot me and watch me. But

I was curious and so I crossed over. I picked up some of the welcome money, [*Begrüssungsgeld*], looked around, and went into a bookstore. And I thought, for God's sake, you're already so old, you'll never be able to read all the things you can buy now. But I controlled myself and thought: First you have to sort things out, don't be rash.

KURT

Kurt's mother took him to West Germany when he was fifteen. He spent seven years there, completing his apprenticeship and working, until he decided to return to the East, where he hoped the way of life would conform to the ideals he had learned earlier in the socialist youth group, the FDJ (*Freie deutche Jugend*, a socialist youth group).

You don't have to come up with big theories. Unification would have come much sooner if the GDR had left the borders open at the time, that is, if they hadn't built the Wall. From a present-day perspective, I can't help thinking it's a good thing because it gave the greater majority of people something really positive, right?

Nevertheless, at the time, in my heart, I favored the building of the Wall. It was a major experience for me as a fifteen-year-old boy, leaving the GDR with my mother and seeing thousands of people living in these reception camps in the GFR. And even at that age, I could see that many people left not because of their inner political convictions but for economic reasons. They were saying: I'm leaving the GDR because I can't earn anything in the GDR and I make too little money. Over there, they have bananas, and here in the GDR they don't; and things like that. These people left not because they didn't like the system, but because materially they would be doing much better in the West.

Conditions in the GDR should have been such that people could work, that they could be comfortable, that they could win their Nobel prizes here—could have the space, the freedom to be creative, to develop, to blossom. That is important. Then people would have stayed.

And then came November 9th, the opening of the border. That evening, it became clear to me that there could no longer be a GDR. It was the end of the regime. I didn't realize that it was also the end of Socialism. I still believed that Socialism was something very humane—humane, but badly implemented.

The following day, my older son and I went to West Berlin and our experiences of everything that happened here were pretty vivid. I must say it was very impressive, and I also have to admit that tears came to my eyes. One certainly doesn't have to be ashamed of that.

During those first days especially, masses of people streamed into West Berlin. But what was especially impressive was how the people went back home again. It wasn't as though you passed through the border unhindered. In those first days, you still had your identity card and had to show it. For instance, at the border crossing on Bornholmer Strasse, they couldn't cope with this return parade of people. And the people even shouted: We want to go home! Yes, there are a lot of people who really identified with the GDR—as I did—and who said: That's my home. But from that moment on, it was clear to me that there would be no more GDR. And the political developments in the period that followed have confirmed that.

NOTES

1. Timothy Garton Ash, *Ein Jahrhundert wird abgewählt* [A century is voted out] (Munich: DTV, 1992), p. 347.

2. Hannes Bahrmann and Christoph Links, *Chronik der Wende: die DDR zwischen 7. Oktober und 18. Dezember 1989* [Chronicle of the Wende: The GDR between October 7th and December 18th, 1989] (Berlin: Ch. Links Verlag, 1994).

2

Consensual Rape

The GDR "as it really existed" was different from the description given to well-fed *Wessies*. . . . In turn, the economy "as it really existed" was different from what had been promised to the *Ossies*. . . . Lamentations are rising from the German Vale of Tears.[1]

What actually happened?

They talked about reunification and declared that the Federal Republic of Germany and the German Democratic Republic were two independent states that had never before been united. Consequently *re*unification would have been a technical impossibility; at most there could be unification. It was also argued that there could only be genuine unification if East and West were to adopt a new Basic Law, a new constitution that would represent the values of both parts. This did not happen.

How did unification happen?

In 1989 they were shouting: We are one people. It was a wish that still hasn't quite been fulfilled in 1999. The Germans now have one state, one fatherland (*einzig Vaterland*), but that doesn't make its citizens one people (*Volk*), not by far.

West and East Germans understand a *Volk* to be a community composed of like people sharing a common destiny who speak the same language and have a more or less homogeneous territory, a somewhat homogeneous history and culture. Legends, fairy tales, and folktales;

customs, and traditions comprise the people's cultural assets. What is missing from these definitions is every member's identification with all the other members of the *Volk*—the idea of really belonging together, that each is a part of the whole, and that all are striving toward the same goal, at least in some things—somewhat like a family.

WILMA

Wilma moved back to East Berlin from the West, where she had spent several years as an adult and in childhood. Her work as an administrator in charge of relocation for an architecture firm brings her into close contact with many East Germans.

> I felt that my joy, my feelings, turned it into a *reunification*, especially because many people in the West had relatives in the East whom they seldom saw, with whom their only contact had been through letters, and the letters were censored. But perhaps, on a political level, it was only *unification;* and [economically], since the GDR was bankrupt, it was a *joining*. But from the human point of view, one could say: At last, at last!

ERICH

Erich, the Rheinländer, feels as much at home in East Berlin as in the West. He has had friends in the East for many years, and some time ago he set himself up in business in Berlin.

> It was great. I was terribly happy about reunification. It happened a little too quickly, but it was a historically unique opportunity, and no one knows whether it would have worked later on. It was *consensual rape*.
>
> By definition, it was not rape. That's the point. There was a democratic election, and it was possible to be thoroughly informed about events. But democracy requires openness, a grasp of the situation and reflection. They didn't have that here; they hadn't learned it. Socialism collapsed.
>
> Of course after unification there were human differences and economic-historical differences. Germany always had its poor regions and its wealthy regions, even before the world war. That's why in the midst of all these laments about the failure of our growing together, I think that it's really about trying to glue things together that were never joined together before.

JOHANNA

With her parents, Johanna, a Wessie, occasionally visited her relatives in the East when she was a child. Her other contacts with Ossies occurred in the framework of her mission work and religious education.

In my opinion, it didn't have to happen: first of all not at that time, and second, not in that way. They could have allowed the GDR to grow as an independent country—just as there are several German-speaking countries: Austria, Switzerland, Liechtenstein. They should have given the people the chance to build up their country through their own efforts—of course with assistance, but through their own efforts. We deprived them of that opportunity. When people are permitted to achieve something, even if it takes a great deal of effort, they develop pride and responsibility. We took this away from the Ossies. Actually, we *annexed* them. We told them: You are part of this now, and so you will kindly obey our rules and regulations because our rules and regulations are good. It's a bad idea to do this sort of thing. It would have shown greatness on our part to permit them to coexist as an independent country alongside us, with us. That would have taken considerably longer, but it would have been a more natural process. But what we have now is a completely unnatural process.

PAUL

Paul's ancestors came from Poland or Russia, depending how the borders were drawn at various historical times. His great-grandmother was German and at some point relocated the family to East Prussia.

Based on the premise that these two parts of Germany supposedly belong together, we could also reunite with Austria. We could reunite with Schlesien, with East Prussia. And in the name of reunification, why not maybe a piece of France that once belonged to us? Lucky that the EU [European Union] is coming, because this nationalistic thing is just completely crazy. The point has to be that it's a global exchange.

JOSEPHINE

Josephine is an Ossie who married into a very political family and, though subsequently divorced from her husband, continues to think a lot about political matters. However, she is more of a thinker than a doer.

It was an *annexation*, something similar to "*Heim in's Reich*" [a reference to Hitler's program of bringing Germans living in Poland, Russia, and other surrounding countries back into Germany, *Heim in's Reich* means "Home into the (Third) Reich"]. I'm glad it happened the way it did, without bloodshed, without war, that is, without a civil war. I was really afraid that it might have come to that.

HORST

Horst, who has a Ph.D. in economics, is now a pensioner. As soon as he could, he left the GDR People's Armed Forces and took voluntary retirement. He could no longer bear the conflict between his ideals and the abuses by the party.

My wife was the chief assistant of a well-known Berlin professor. One might say this man was driven to his death after the Wende. It was wrong, the way he was dismissed. Perhaps it [unification] was an *occupation* after all. I've spoken with West German jurists about this subject. And one very high-ranking official from the state chancellery of one of the [West German] states told me: You know, all my professional life I thought about how things should be settled legally if reunification were ever really to come about. I thought of so many different variations; the only one I never thought of was the one that was actually implemented: *Anschluss*, Annexation.

I still think unity is a good thing. The gulf between theory and practice, between assertions and reality, was getting bigger all the time in this country; it had gone beyond a thinking human being's comprehension. The system was totally calcified, rigid and unable to move or change.

For me, the political break came in 1968 with Dubcek. What Dubcek proposed offered a great opportunity for a humane socialism. Actually, this was what had always been in my mind from the time I was young. And I always tried to remain true to these ideals. And so much greater was the shock I felt when they suppressed his [Dubcek's] reform program with tanks.

A very bitter joke was making the rounds at the time—Question: Who are the best foreign traders in the world? Answer: The Czechs, because they exchanged 2,000 words for 2,000 tanks. This referred to the famous human rights manifesto of 2,000 words, which was virtually torn up. Instead they sent 2,000 tanks into the country to suppress it. I was profoundly disillusioned.

At the time, some people refused to join in the anti-Dubcek invasion, there were even some army people among them. But they were demoted on the spot and dismissed in front of the assembled troops. I didn't have that sort of courage. I had to come to terms with myself about that, and I looked for ways in which I could get out of the system. That took quite a while, but I managed to do it by retiring for health reasons.

MAX

Max, the East German factory worker, was unemployed before he retired—a rare occurrence in the GDR. He had refused to join the SED, the official political party, with the result that he was not promoted to the rank due him.

The GDR would have failed eight years earlier from a collapsed economy if the West hadn't invested so much money here. The planned economy didn't work. Here's just a small example: I was working in a factory, and in May of that year I had to apply for items we needed for the coming year. I would tell the planning authorities that I needed two thousand sixty-watt lightbulbs and that I needed fifty replacement switches for the machines. Sometimes, I would suddenly be notified by the machine-building trade authority that the order had been canceled, that the ordered material had been given to the National Defense System [*Landesverteidigungsordnung (LVO)*], because defense preparedness had a higher priority.

But if I got imported Russian lightbulbs because our lightbulbs had been sold to the West in order to get west-money, and if the Russian bulbs didn't last as long, then I would be out of lightbulbs. This was a huge problem, because, although lightbulbs were available in retail stores, factories were not allowed to buy anything in those stores.

In spite of that, we dealt with retail stores whenever we knew their managers. There was some fiddling around: Could you let us have 500 lightbulbs? Yes. But then on the bill, instead of lightbulbs, it would say, for instance, "one refrigerator for the Polish workers who were employed there." This was an open secret in the factory, everybody knew, right up to our head of finance. The plant director once called me up and asked: Do you know that you have no lightbulbs? I said: Of course I know. I had even tried to buy candles, but I couldn't get any.—This is no joke. That's the way it was.

However, the planned economy was not to blame for everything; even the concept of national property was circumvented. The Communist principle is: Whatever is made by the people's hands is the people's property. But in actuality the "society's property [*Volkseigentum*] is not treated as the people's property but as state property. . . . Political power [has] power over the processes of production and distribution."[2] Some laid it out differently: If the industry and the production of the socialist economy belong to the people—and not to one or several entrepreneurs as in a capitalist economy—then everyone could feed at the trough to their hearts' content, couldn't they?

Max

Erich Honecker, our former Secretary-General, once made a speech in which he said, quite seriously, that much more could be extracted from our state-owned industries. Naturally, he meant greater productivity. Many people took him up on it—only in a different sense from the way he meant it. For someone who was close to the source, it really was possible to extract a great deal. Through the business, there were opportunities to buy things one would not otherwise have been able to get. But there was also stealing. There's the story of the man taking sawdust out of a plant in a wheelbarrow. The gatekeeper says to him: What are you stealing there? and the man answers: I can take sawdust home; it's permitted. And he goes home. The next day, he comes along with another full wheelbarrow. Sawdust? the gatekeeper asks. And on the third day, the gatekeeper says to him: You can't possibly use that much sawdust. Tell me, honestly, what are you really stealing? Wheelbarrows! answers the man.

So much had become so run down—private things, too—that it had become a disaster, because there was no material left here, and even the most essential consumer goods were in short supply. If you haven't lived here, you can't imagine what shopping for Sunday dinner on Thursday or Friday was like. You'd go to the butcher and find nothing to choose from, so you wouldn't know what to prepare for Sunday.

Sure. Today there are goods available, and I can go into any supermarket on Monday and ask for a beef roulade and buy it if I have the money. But they promised us too much at the beginning of unification, promises that couldn't be kept. Flourishing landscapes, for instance. They're not flourishing, but if you go through the former GDR with open eyes, then you will see that mighty things have happened here and that many owners have been able to beautify their buildings again. All in all, much has improved since unification.

People on pensions were promised they would be getting 100 percent of their pensions from 1996 on, that is, that West and East pensions would be equal—not that everybody would be getting the same amount, but that it would be calculated on a basis of 1 to 1. And that's still not in effect today, and probably won't be in the near future. Nor were salaries equalized. Until recently a bus driver from the West who drove over to the East was paid a certain amount, and his colleague who drove the same distance in the opposite direction got less. As long as the salaries aren't proportionately equal, it will always stand in the way of good relations.

Another problem is that many businesses were dismantled in the East in order to eliminate competition. But, it wasn't necessary to destroy them. The Federal Republic had made subsidies available for the purpose of putting faltering East German businesses back on their feet. And what did they do? The Western advisers came to make money for themselves, and then they were gone. Those were some of the drawbacks of unification.

ERICH

Erich studied business management at the Humboldt Universität.

Capitalism also means that businesses that are not profitable have to be closed. Accordingly, a necessary consequence of the transformation of the GDR into the Federal Republic was that businesses had to be checked and audited. Capitalism doesn't mean that everything runs smoothly. Rather, it means doing business. And the period from 1989 to 1992–93 was a time for deal makers who wanted to make a lot of money fairly quickly. And very few of these were East Germans. They were primarily West Germans who enriched themselves at the expense of third parties—company bankruptcies and falsified bankruptcies and loan sharks. Cars were sold to people who signed installment contracts, where after half a year, they had to give the car back or had to mortgage their little house [to keep up the payments]. That's capitalism. That's how it works. And now they know—no, not all of them know it yet.

Now, many people are down in the dumps, and they say that everything is so terrible and everything is so mean. But that's hypocritical. They themselves aren't any better. On the contrary, if they had been in that situation, I think they would have done the same thing.

MAX

Max is interested in history and current events. He informs himself.

What makes people even angrier nowadays is that no one has succeeded in getting back the SED's money. The SED sent piles of money
abroad at the time of the Wende or afterward—there's talk that it was
in the billions. The German headquarters for investigating crimes
against the government is right here in Berlin, and the states aren't
providing any experts to look into that. They've found a few millions
in Switzerland. We little people have no idea how all that works.

The Treuhand, an agency established as a trustee for East German
assets, doesn't know either. It was established on February 12, 1990,
with instructions to close down the people-owned (state-owned) enterprises and (real estate) property, "because there is no such thing
as a state monopoly of free trade in a market economy." The Treuhand team dealing with government crimes has had difficulty getting
on the right track, because the comrades "were making full use of
the time [before the summer of 1991] to turn state-owned businesses
into their own businesses. The trackers from the West will never be
able to make up for that headstart. Did the turncoat Socialists arrange
for many hundreds of millions of D-mark to disappear into foreign
accounts, or didn't they?" The search for GDR Party property is drag-
ging on into 1994. " 'In general, it is assumed that, of the billions
in assets of the parties and mass organizations, many millions of D-
marks are still hidden in accounts or in companies, and thus those
who are now actually responsible under the law are deprived of these
funds.' "[3]
Max adds:

In the GDR, there was the KoKo, the Commercial Coordination
Agency. Alexander Schalck-Golodkowski used to be its boss; he's in
Bavaria now.[4]
They sentenced Schalck-Golodkowski only to probation. He was a
very intelligent man who was familiar with capitalism and economics,
and he saw to it that scarce goods—computers, for instance—came
into our country from the West, but not for the people. And he was
convicted because he had imported embargoed goods. Personally I
think that was stupid. One ought to condemn the people in the West
who delivered the merchandise because the embargo existed for the
West and not for the East. But those in the West who delivered the
material are not being prosecuted, at least not so far. Of course things
like that upset people—the fact that the right people are not having
their backsides spanked.

Horst

I had the impression that unification was like a premature birth, and precipitate deliveries can do quite a bit of harm to a child.

They should have taken a little more time with the unification agreement. This unification agreement was a quick, slipshod thing that came into being, of course, under pressure of the currency union, that is, under pressure of the Mark and also under pressure from Bonn to get the thing signed and sealed as quickly as possible.

ECONOMIC CONSIDERATIONS

Even though the Bundesbank and other experts had had worrisome information about the condition of the GDR economy and wanted to inform Kohl, the chancellor made a political decision, calling for the "Immediate creation of a currency union . . . [for] freedom wasn't so important over there any more; it had already been won; now our brothers and sisters were getting more specific: Either the D-mark comes to us, or we'll go over to the D-mark," which wasn't all right with the Wessies at all.[5] At that point unification was inevitable.

OTTO

In the GDR, Otto, who had great difficulties at the workplace and in the SED, took on a leadership role in the GFR official discussions about the unification agreement.

It isn't true that they couldn't have known about it [the dismal conditions in the GDR] over there. I was there when the chancellor was questioned. What did he say? He said: That's not so; after all, I didn't go there, at least not officially, and the people who came over from the GDR didn't tell me about it. So it's no wonder that some old grandmas came to him and said, Mr. Chancellor, everything is so nice here. But the experts over there, the highly paid professors, what did they do? Only one, an economics professor at the university in Paderborn, a small Catholic university, explained in my presence at a conference: It's our fault; we gave bad advice to the government of the Federal Republic.

The Bundesbank didn't want [the unification] either. Bundesbank President Pöhl resigned because of it [when he was overruled]. He knew the sort of disaster it would cause. Everyone else claimed they always did everything right.

ERICH

Erich, the Wessie businessman in East Berlin, explains:

At the time, the [GDR's] industries were ready for the scrap heap, and the experts in the West all said: For God's sake, we're buying a store that's completely bankrupt. Nothing works. But politicians are visionaries, and they said: Those are only details. The West German economy severely overextended itself by taking on a territory one-third its own size, one in need of complete rehabilitation. Naturally that was—and is—a great strain on the Federal Republic's economy.

Otto

People were not aware—that is to say, no one wanted to know how bad conditions really were here. You could pick up any German book published right before the *Wende* and read what a strong solid state the GDR was and what a well-developed economy it had. That simply wasn't true at the time, and one could have known.

And so, rash promises were made, and no management was instituted to cope with these things. They thought you could send over a Western professor or a Western director and he would fix things. They thought that, just because he once rehabilitated a similar plant which was in bankruptcy proceedings, he can do it in the East, too. But conditions were completely different here, and so he stood here helpless in spite of all his former experience and knowledge and had to look on as the enterprise went down the drain.

But the Federal Republic is in good economic shape. We're doing better than people in most other countries—at least conditions aren't worse. And I'm somewhat relieved to know there's at least one country that is not preparing for war or planning to annihilate dissidents.

GILDA AND GERHARD

Gilda and Gerhard are retired GDR journalists.

Gilda

In the evening, we watch the weather map on ARD *(Allgemeiner Rundfunk Deutschland)*. They report on the weather for the West, but not for Germany in general. True, they show Berlin. And Dresden is there too. But actually, they give the weather forecast for the West. To get the weather for Berlin and vicinity, you have to turn on the East German Rundfunk. But ARD is a public broadcasting service, and therefore it should really cover all of Germany. And that's only one of many examples.

Gerhard

The press, after all, is the mouthpiece and is organized by regions. You can see that in Berlin. There are several daily newspapers, which of course try to attract readers in both East and West, and then there's the old standard *Berliner Zeitung* that was published in the East. The men in charge today are all Wessies, but at least they made use of the paper's name. They cultivate a loyal readership because the *Berliner Zeitung* always had the largest circulation in the East. On the other side, in the West, there's the *Morgenpost*. Naturally, the western edition traditionally has a very devoted West Berliner readership. And the same thing goes for the broadcast stations. They have only western artists on their programs. Ordinarily we don't even notice that any more. Sometimes you wonder. Where are the many eastern artists? We do have a few! Well, those they hire to perform on the local programs. No, there isn't a unified Germany yet.

It doesn't matter that the West is the bigger half and the East the smaller one. We want to make a whole out of it. It would have been possible to reformulate the entire system, including the Basic Law (*Grundgesetz*, that is, the Constitution of the Federal Republic of Germany) and include things from the East. That would have been reunification.

Each had its own independent development. But only West Germany's independent developments were recognized. They said to us: You are a dictatorship. And by saying that a dictatorship is not to be equated with a democracy, they brushed aside all the issues that came under consideration.

The GFR Basic Law that supposedly had proved to be so worthwhile for forty years should have been revised. There was a judicial reform in the GDR, a thorough fundamental revision of the criminal code, and something did come of that. But the Federal Republic's Civil Code still contains paragraphs dating back to the turn of the century. Reforms are needed in the Federal Republic, and they should have been implemented by the new Germany. Certainly it wouldn't have been easy, but we have many able scholars who could have done it.

There is still talk about the fact that the German Civil Code ought to be revised. And a few changes, for example in the inheritance laws, have been made. There are codicils as thick as a stack of books, intended to simplify [the law]. On the contrary, it gets more and more complicated. Today's legalities have become completely unintelligible to a mere mortal.

HORST

Horst lives in a well-furnished one-family house in East Berlin. He drives a secondhand Mercedes Benz four-door sedan. After the Wende he and his wife decided to invest in a solid car and not risk having to turn in a less reliable vehicle for another one, every few years.

The unification agreement had two basic errors. The first is the general principle [of] "return before compensation" [*Rückgabe vor Entschädigung*], which applies to almost all the real property that anyone could have acquired by honest means in the GDR—land and houses. That was all declared null and void—forty years of GDR were simply annulled and "return before compensation" became law. Perhaps Americans understand this. It's as if you were suddenly to restore all rights to the American Indians, so that Chief Black Panther comes along and says: Well, this place here is my tribal territory; my ancestors hunted here for 500 years, and now it's mine again, so pay up—What would happen to all the cities and houses that are there?

I bought a house here from the GDR, completely aboveboard with a contract and all the necessary documents and I registered it. I couldn't buy the land because it was not for sale, it was state property [*Volkseigentum*]. The land was signed over to me to use only during my lifetime. There was a deed. After the Wende, I nearly lost the house, because a former owner, a woman from Argentina, showed up and immediately filed an application to get the house back. She came from the same city where Mengele used to live and is the daughter of the former owner, the man who built the house, a man who worked in Auschwitz. He never came back here after 1945. He knew what would have been in store for him because, of course, the Russians were here then. So he immediately escaped to Argentina via the Vatican.

I had to go to court. They wanted to evict me, and I had to fight for five years so that I, an elderly grandfather, wouldn't be thrown out of the house.

The second mistaken decision was to have a court inquiry into political injustice in the GDR. The judiciary can't reappraise political matters; it can deal only with criminal law. They can convict and sentence criminals, but they can't get rid of politics through the courts.

OTTO

Otto knew people in the small towns and hinterland areas of the former GDR.

The same errors in the realm of city planning and regional development that were made in the Federal Republic were simply brought over to the East and fully incorporated there. All the same structures were introduced here because they sent us the same people, and they just did what they were used to doing. It was, so to speak, fallow land. Those pied pipers arrived and said: Your little village is really kaput, but we promise to build something splendid here. Our people believed it all. They believed it because they were hoping that it would bring in big money. So they built sewage plants that were too big, and today these communities are still deep in debt and don't know how they'll pay it off.

ERICH

Erich's mother's family is Hungarian. They still live in Hungary. His father is of Huguenot ancestry from Alsace.

Now, the GDR citizens have to cope with two identity problems. Ten years ago, they suddenly became Germans, no longer GDR citizens, and now in the next 10 or 15 years they'll have to become Europeans.

JOSEPHINE

Josephine is not aware of any identity problems at present. She is middle-aged but has a youthful outlook and is much more flexible than others of her age.

I am not angry that [unification] came the way it did. On the contrary, I see it only in a positive light, because my knowledge base, my perspective, my entire intellectual development has changed. Today I'm much more interested in things, much more open. I have more opportunities to broaden my knowledge. Yes! I no longer live under political or economic pressure. And today, if I want to, I can go anywhere in the world. There are no more barriers. There is no limit for me as a human being.

ERIKA

Erika, born in a tiny village in Poland, now has relatives and friends as far away as the United States. Throughout, she was in correspondence with them, and after the Wende, she visited all of them.

Adapting to the new regime, to the new society wasn't that bad. Actually, everything went by pretty quickly because I became self-employed—something that wasn't possible before. True, it might have been possible during GDR times to run a private business, but I didn't get permission to do that, and they even reproached me for wanting to leave my job at the department store. After the *Wende*, I again went to City Hall with my son Thorsten. We knocked on the office door, and the same woman who had refused my application the last time was still sitting there, and she said: I suppose you want to go into business now. Fine. I will assign you a store and you can go and look at it right away.

JOSEPHINE

Josephine grew up in modest circumstances. Both parents worked, and the children had to pitch in.

Never before had I gone through such financial difficulties. When we first had to deal with west-money, I couldn't grasp the idea of this flood of things I could suddenly buy. I fell into a bottomless pit—I bought insurance policies I didn't need, bought pots that were too expensive—I learned much too slowly how to compare things. Today I'm still paying all that off and trying to adjust.

But the system is developing, and we're changing it more and more. So we have to continue adapting, not just complain all the time. I choose the good out of every society.

KURT

Born in Berlin during World War II, evacuated to East Prussia after the family had been bombed out, returned to Leipzig at the War's end, and then relocated to West Germany with his mother—only to return to Berlin as a young man—Kurt has experience with change.

Oh well, the GDR is gone; it's like having lost a good friend whose funeral I've attended. But then the grave is filled and a little mound is built up over it. You might place a flower on it once a year, but generally you do nothing more. And actually, I didn't want to do any more than that either.

Erich

When it came to the subject of certain basic ethical, moral, or philosophical themes—those things that connect people—there were no major East-West differences in the minds of the people, neither for my friends in the East nor for me now.

[As for the future:] It looks as though Poland probably will join the European Community in 2002, in which case, Germany will no longer be at the far eastern end [of Europe], but in the center again and able to realize its historical function once more. Germany is interesting culturally because it is situated between the East and the West. The Slavic influence in Germany has always been huge, not only because Germany once extended much farther east, but because Berlin was the meeting ground between western and eastern Europe.

It wasn't only Berlin that got its hinterland back with the fall of the Iron Curtain. If I feel like it, I can now go to Posnan or to Almstein without any problems, and anyone from Posnan can go to Berlin just as easily now. Before, people—for instance, someone living in Bromberg—would never have thought of going to Warsaw to shop; they would have gone to Berlin, which is much closer. And the moment the borders are gone and Poland belongs to the EC [European Community], all this will change. With the extension of the European Union, I think an additional process will take place that will make the West-German/East-German question seem relatively minor. I'm looking forward to that because I find it tremendously interesting.

Whenever an illusion is lost, there's all that blaming going on. It's always like that. Today the disillusioned people from the East complain dreadfully about the West because it just isn't what they expected. And the bad-tempered people from the West grumble about the East, saying: For five years now we've been pushing hundreds of billions over there and they're not even grateful.

Nobody ever says it, but they think it. They think it's only the West Germans who pay, but taxes are raised from all [of Germany] and so the East Germans are paying as well. Actually, people are complaining more about misapplied funds, that some of the money is going into the wrong projects, that the money isn't being used in places where it would make sense.

I am willing to pay these taxes because—quite independent of the GDR—I benefit a good deal from the state. After all, the state provides an incredible number of services, and usually I pay nothing for them. You have to take this into consideration—all the services you receive from the state. The biggest highway network in the world is fully paid for by taxes. We have local public transportation. Our underground and city train network to a large extent is publicly subsidized. Berlin has three opera houses, more than twenty theaters, far more than a hundred stages. I know what ticket prices are in America. At the German Opera a center orchestra ticket in row sixteen costs fifty-five Marks. At New York's Metropolitan Opera, it would cost at least one hundred twenty dollars. Our colleges and universities are completely free. In Germany, anyone can go to college. We have kindergartens that are almost free and which to a large extent are subsidized. Street cleaning, the cleaning of the cities, the parks. Hospitals—well, they're getting more expensive all the time, but still, we have basic health care. I pay 300 DM a month whether I'm sick or not. But if necessary, I can go to the hospital, get a cardiac catheter put in, or be fitted for a leg prosthesis.

A healing body aches, and keeping the body healthy can cost the patient, the insurance company, or the state a great deal of money—it is the same with the integration of members of society into the collective German body of state. It takes time. The fracture will heal, but the scars may be noticeable for some time—on into the next generation, the generation after that, even into subsequent generations. It all depends on how one deals with the trauma.

NOTES

1. Michael Jürgs, *Die Treuhändler—Wie Helden und Halunken die DDR verkauften* [The fiduciary trustees: How heroes and scoundrels sold the GDR] (Munich: Droehmersche Verlagsanstalt Th. Knaur Nachf., 1998), p. 9.

2. Heike Solga, Klassenlagen und soziale Ungleichheit in der DDR [(Social) classes and social inequities], *Aus Politik und Zeitgeschichte*, Vol. 46 (1996): 19–20.

3. Jürgs, *Die Treuhändler*, pp. 108–109.

4. Ibid., p. 11. According to Jürgs "67 enterprises in the GDR were under Schalck's jurisdiction; 108 others were well hidden in Western Europe . . . and Schalck was considered a reliable business partner. . . . These firms obtained everything their own state couldn't produce or goods whose export into the GDR was forbidden during the Cold War."

5. Ibid., pp. 64–65.

3

Ossies and Wessies Meet Each Other

It is definitely done with, the mutually pleasant and exonerating relationship that consisted of gifts, mail, and visits, and in which two one-sided developments found their meaningful comple- ment: generous giving and grateful receiving. . . . But now we won't come to visit any more; now we have to work and live together.[1]

It's true they are all Germans and can converse in the same native language; yet many misunderstandings crop up. After forty years they now face each other, overjoyed, until they realize that their differing experiences have turned them into strangers. Ossies and Wessies are surprised at these differences, and often they are critical and mistrust- ful. The "grateful receivers" see the generous givers as arrogant and cold in their personal relations. The "generous givers" think the poor receivers are not sufficiently industrious. The Ossies feel degraded and defend themselves against their inferiority feelings by contrasting their human values with the consumer greed of the Wessies.

ERICH

Erich, a Wessie who has a business in the East, comments:

Ossies say the Wessies are greedy, arrogant, inhumane and interested only in money. These are all stereotypes.

From time to time the Wessies also have inferiority feelings. Some Wessies and some Ossies try hard to meet each other half way. Sometimes these attempts succeed. They introduce themselves to one another and talk about the feelings of community in the GDR, the warmth and the altruism. Wessies and Ossies meet professionally, but less often socially.

WILMA

Wilma is a sensitive woman who has lived in both West and East Germany. For many years she lived with her husband in the Rhineland after he was transferred there by his company. She now lives in the eastern part of Berlin. She says:

> One very important reason why I moved back to the East is that I found people in the former GDR more humane, more sincere and warm. People were there for one another. And that appealed to me very much. Sometimes, I found them pushy when they meddled in my affairs, but it wasn't a case of nosiness. It was concern. Often, even committed former GDR citizens helped me once they had taken a closer look and realized: this isn't a narrow-minded Wessie. She's trying to understand us, to understand why we aren't all jumping up and down with joy about the unification. I had some very good experiences, and I only hope people will realize how important that quality of compassion is.
>
> Yes, and I'm afraid that the western coldness will sooner or later spill over into the East. I hear older people say that this warmth, this sincerity has diminished because now everybody has to fight for himself.

MAX

Max is an Ossie and a retired worker. After he resigned from his job, he did not hear from his pals and coworkers anymore.

> Once we were a community. But that was probably because everybody, or most people, were equally badly off. Let's take a garden plot like this. If you needed a piece of lumber, it was a problem—not a money problem but a procurement problem. And there would be somebody who could get the lumber, but he, in turn, needed an electric wall socket. And that's how it worked, just as in the Stone Age,

when they had no money either. Money wasn't important. Connections were important.

This is not the case today. Today, it's a dog-eat-dog world. A ruthless mentality prevails. We didn't have that in the GDR. People stuck
together because they needed each other.

I went for a visit to the West when my brother turned sixty, and I was
at this party where I met people I didn't know. Afterward, I said to my
relatives, There's one thing I don't understand: In the East when people
get together, they say, "Hey, I have this item; can you get me such-and-
such in exchange, I need it, etc." And here the first question always is:
"What kind of a car do you drive? How fast does it go?"

ERICH

Erich, the young businessman, says:

Yes, the Ossies claim that material things didn't play as big a role
in the GDR, that they were much less concerned with money and were
much warmer and more humane. That's hypocrisy; obviously, if your
money isn't worth anything, you don't have to concern yourself with
it. Everybody had money. But in those days, you couldn't buy anything with it. These days the Ossies are pretty greedy, just like the
Wessies.

In the capitalist system everything revolves around money; not in
socialism. That's why it was easy to have friendly relations with each
other and constantly invite people to your home or put up with them
and ignore the fact that in a friendship there's a kind of equilibrium
of mutual invitations or financial arrangements or gift exchanges. That
was never a problem.

One hand washes the other, of course. One man worked in a factory
and had [access to] tiles for the bathroom—he could filch them, sure,
and another guy could get fan belts for the car motor. So you exchanged things. There was a sort of informal bartering. Yes, it was
really a classical barter economy because money didn't function as a
means of exchange. And when they reminisce—it's called "*Ostalgie*"
("Eastalgia")—they forget that the humaneness that prevailed in the
GDR was partly conditioned by necessity. You might say that this
economy of scarcity and the limited function of money was something
positive insofar as it applied to people and their social relations, but it
was something compulsory because nobody likes to go without things.

Persons with greater material resources and children as they increase their emotional and material resources become more inde-

pendent and self-assured, and can risk being more self-centered. Therefore, the less people need one another, the less they have to worry about protecting the other person and their relationships. It is different, of course, in some family and partner relationships when mutual affection and dependency are stronger. Thus the more permeable boundary between dependent individuals acts to increase the interpersonal warmth—and vice versa.

ERICH

Erich knew people in the GDR while he was still a Wessie student. Some of these contacts petered out, but others continued because some of them were genuine friendships, while others were just mercantile relationships. Erich recalls:

> Before the Wende, whenever you came over from the West, you always brought something with you, goods of some sort. It was a very mercantile relationship, which was the case with this one particular acquaintance for whom I always brought books when I came to visit. He worked in a bookstore and had access to so-called *Bückware* [from *bücken*, to bend down] books in short supply that normally were hard to get. Scarce goods were always put under the counter so that one had to bend down to get them out. That's why they were called *Bückware*. I could get these books from him—very beautiful editions—and in exchange, I brought him books from the West. Officially, of course, you weren't allowed to do that, but a female friend who worked for a South American embassy in East Berlin had diplomat credentials, so she could always bring things over in her car. My friend would say: I need such and such a book, this book, that book; my female friend brought them over. I picked them up at her apartment in Pankow in East Berlin. And then I swapped the books with my friend who worked in the book store.
>
> That was one of those typical relationships where you got along well, but in which there was also a mutual profit. Foodstuffs were also in demand. We frequently brought over coffee, or chocolate. These were available in the GDR too, but the coffee didn't taste good, nor the chocolate. Or, we brought over replacement parts and tape cassettes. And because all that suddenly stopped after the Wende, there was a gradual shift in one's circle of acquaintances. My relationship with this particular acquaintance of mine didn't end because of a quarrel; we simply lost touch with each other.
>
> One's good friends remained. And those friendships went beyond bringing back goods.

Irene, who is retired, grew up in the West and then lived in the GDR. She wasn't dependent on Wessies, so her friendships haven't changed much since the Wende. Irene says:

> Right after the Wende we felt the need to see this person or that person again—and it was mutual. So, a few high school classmates got together, but actually not much happened. We didn't have much more to say to one another than: Do you remember when . . . ? and, How are things now? and a little bit about what was going on. Those with whom we had exchanged letters, those contacts continued; we see each other more often.

It is not unusual for school friends to go their separate ways. Some go to college and follow a career; others marry early, perhaps staying in their small town. At reunions, years later, they find they lack common experiences and have little to say to one another. This may be due to personal differences as well as to the different lifestyles of East and West.

Irene

I have a girlfriend who has always lived in West Berlin. She was always my friend, that is to say, [the border didn't act as] a big moat separating us. Even so, our lives diverged and I realized that she didn't understand me anymore. Some things I just couldn't explain to her because she didn't have the same experiences and values. But it's the same with me: It's only now that I've come to understand some things she told me three years ago. For instance, there was always talk about the Ossies wanting to have everything handed to them, from the cradle to the grave, and she said: It's completely different here when it comes to getting an apprenticeship. You're not guaranteed an apprentice position after you get out of school. I said: I think that's terrible. And she, in turn, couldn't understand that my daughter automatically got a job at the place where she had been a trainee. I said that's how it was. And she said: I don't believe you.

I couldn't understand her either because she had lived in a different world and had experiences and attitudes and ideas that were unfamiliar to me because I had never lived there. So I have to put myself in her shoes. But you can do that only if you are really honest and have an open mind; and only if the other person listens and doesn't have preconceived ideas. Preconceptions are what we excelled at in the GDR! We always knew everything, knew how everything should be. That's how it is, unfortunately.

GILDA AND GERHARD

Gilda and Gerhard were professionally severely restricted by prevailing East German prejudices. Nevertheless, they remain loyal to many socialist ideals while, at the same time, they reach out to the world from which they were formerly closed off.

> Because of recent developments and present conditions in Germany, the wall inside many people's heads is rising higher than it ever was. And that's particularly evident in Berlin. For instance, there are gardens in East Berlin and in West Berlin. People have small garden plots [*Schrebergärten* (allotment gardens)]. And after unification, the East Berliners said: Those people over there aren't so far away; let's invite them over. After all we're one country again, so let's do something together. Maybe a third of those who were invited came. And it was the same the other way around. And in the end, everyone stayed in his own garden because they couldn't find things in common to talk about, and evidently they didn't much want to find them, either.

WERNER

Werner was never enthusiastic about the GDR and, he found out after the Wende, had been spied upon for the Stasi by a woman who pretended to be his girlfriend. Personally and as an academician, he becomes incensed when misinformation, distortions, and prejudices supplant facts. Werner recalls giving a lecture in Belgium:

> Hundreds of people came. During the break there was a discussion. A young woman stood up and asked me to explain why the Ossies are all so lazy. She had been reading the West German press, and they were printing stories like that. We were molded by *Neues Deutschland* and over there, they were molded by the *Bildzeitung* [an illustrated journal]. They knew nothing else.

HILDE

Hilde, the teacher who had spent most of her life in the East, now lives in a senior citizens' residence in the western part of Berlin. She says:

I can only make a general judgment. I dislike most of the average Wessie women. Somehow they're all too closely tied to children, pots and pans, scandal sheets, magazines, gossip, superstitions, stories about royalty, cooking, and baking. Somehow, in some things, they're a little too primitive. A lady with whom I always drive to choir practice, an average Ossie woman, sometimes says unfortunate things, too, like: Everything was better before. She mourns for the Wall. It's a bit stupid to think like that and then to say it out loud, too. People don't like to hear it.

But I've also met somewhat more intelligent people. *Na ja*, there are two or three women with whom I can have a conversation, who don't read those screaming gossip sheets. I hate those picture magazines.

You can't lump all the Wessies together, but most of them have never even stepped on the soil of the former GDR; they don't know the first thing about how we lived there. They even asked me about clothing: Did we have any decent clothes? Did we have a textile industry? I said: You know, you profited from our textile industry, because our textile industry sewed and knitted for you, things you used every day of your lives. Naturally, the label didn't say GDR.

KURT AND KÄTHE

Kurt, the department store manager, and his wife Käthe, the teacher's aide, still live in the East, but occasionally they travel.

We've had many pleasant discussions and conversations here, in the old [original] states of the Federal Republic, and abroad, or when we went to our island, Hiddensee, up near the Baltic Sea. We also got into conversations with West Germans and there was tolerance on both sides. We got to talking to some people who asked us: Do you know how we vote? We vote for the PDS (the left-wing party that succeeded the SED). We looked at each other. Ah, we thought: People from the Ruhr! [Coal and steel workers in the industrial area of the Ruhr have had a communist/socialist political orientation at least since the end of the World War I.] So there's that too. We are willing to be reasonable, but we expect similar tolerance from others.

Instead, we often encountered prejudice. Didn't matter whether we were in Cologne or elsewhere. We'd be sitting there, talking with perfectly nice people, and they'd say: Oh, you're from Berlin. Where, East or West Berlin? At first I always said proudly, East Berlin, but then I noticed that the conversation would break off. And so we got into the habit, whenever the question came up, of saying that we're from

Kreuzberg. And they'd look at us: Kreuzberg? Never heard of it. Then I'd say: Don't you know the song *"Kreuzberger Nächte sind lang"* [Kreuzberg Nights Are Long]. And suddenly we're accepted by total strangers as West Germanic.

ERNST

Ernst, a male nurse, moved to West Berlin only recently. Although he never identified with East German communism or socialism because he is an observant Christian, the decision to move was based on practical reasons.

I think all this business about the East and West Germans is a little ridiculous. They are Germans and that's all there's to it. They just have to sit down together, and maybe even argue it out. But I do think that, unfortunately, many West Germans are very arrogant toward East Germans.

Well, if I've had bananas to eat for thirty years and the other guy hasn't, and he'd even give half his life for a banana, I wouldn't make fun of him. But that's how it's turned out.

Suddenly, the Ossies were generously handed something that was in oversupply anyway. Nobody went hungry because of this. It was no sacrifice, and so the storekeepers found it amusing the first one-and-a-half years. They could always tell who was a Wessie and who was an Ossie. For the Ossies it was a completely new world. A store that had so much merchandise was like a fairy tale, the fabled land of cockaigne. And of course, many of the Wessies noticed their reaction, but weren't so refined, disciplined, and well-brought-up as to keep it to themselves, or suppress it with just a tiny, malicious smile. No, they looked down on the Ossies.

And it hurt us that we were accused of being lazy, because it really wasn't true. We were not lazy. You can't say that about us. That we didn't manufacture beautiful things and that our houses were pretty dilapidated was simply due to the fact that we didn't have the necessary materials.

The Wessies also had the attitude that we never knew how to do anything. And that just isn't true. I'd like to see the West Germans in the same situation we were in, in the GDR; how would they have behaved? They all would have conformed, including the people who now swagger and boast. They would have waved the big red flag, just to scrape by. So, one should approach the matter calmly, tolerantly, and quietly and not constantly put labels on East and West Germans. That's stupid.

Max

Of course, both parts of Germany developed independently of each other. On the one hand, West Germany was very strong economically, but on the other hand it had only one-sided information about the GDR, and that left its mark. Unfortunately, that's now ingrained and you can't get rid of it. It will take generations. If you talk to West Germans today, you still hear all the old fighting words from the Cold War days. They still talk about the "Zone" or the "Sector," or they'll say: First of all, they should learn how to work; or: We earned their money for them, the money they're getting today, their pensions too. After all, they never wanted to do any work, never did any work. These are hard and fast notions that were dinned into them [the West Germans] and which they're still spouting today. It's too bad.

Helga

Before the *Wende*, Helga traveled to the eastern bloc countries. In Prague, she met congenial people with whom she maintained a friendship over several years. They were most generous with her during some financially difficult times in her life. Her dependence on them made her afraid to offend them.

In Frankfurt I got to know my friend's neighbor. She creates exquisite ceramics, and since I'm interested in the arts, she invited me. We got along famously. In the meanwhile, she visited me here, in Berlin and we talked, talked, talked. Finally, the topic of Wessie and Ossie women came up and she said: You know, actually your pension is unjust. I asked her: What do you mean? And she explained: You didn't pay into our [west] pension fund. Your premiums were paid into the GDR insurance in worthless Ostmark, and now our state pays you these high pensions, while I collect only 600 D-Mark.

Oh my God! Should I risk the friendship? Tell her my true opinion? I thought and thought. Seven years ago, I still would have thought: Why have a discussion with her? But I took a deep breath and said: I am of a different opinion. I worked for forty-five years—freelance, to be sure, but I went to my studio every day. If I hadn't worked, I wouldn't have earned anything, but I did and then paid my required premiums plus voluntary sums for a supplementary pension. Still, I didn't amass a fortune. You could afford to buy a car for each of your children; you travel to Canada every year and because your husband was a pilot and you a stewardess, you still can fly free of charge.

She could see my point, but I was appalled to realize that that's how people think when they don't know anything about the East. Imagine someone with a limited horizon, who simply repeats such blather.

FRIEDA

Frieda, a GDR senior citizen, spoke about her "great" gymnastics group. Ossies and Wessies meet in this group; they do their exercises together and use the opportunity to get to know one another better. There are some surprises, but everyone tries to understand and to see things from the other person's point of view. And in this way the wall between Ossie and Wessie is being dismantled bit by bit. They are transcending the political border and getting to know one another as human beings.

> The leader of my gymnastics group is a woman from West Berlin, but she's had contacts in both the East and the West for many years and also worked for the *Volkssolidarität* [formerly an agency sponsored by the GDR, now a club, primarily for seniors]. She has had some negative experiences, but certainly many positive ones, too.
>
> We don't provoke discussions in our group, but when we sit together for a halfhour after the gymnastics class over a cup of coffee, the conversation sometimes turns to political themes. And I've noticed that some of these people—primarily the West Berliners, but also the East German communists—often had no idea how dissidents lived in the GDR and what difficulties we had. They thought everyone was doing as well as they were. Yes, indeed. I told them the story about our children and the official refusal by the authorities to let them attend the university because we weren't a working-class family and because we had ties with the church. They were flabbergasted. They thought, that couldn't be, because in the GDR everybody was supposed to have equal rights.

JOHANNA

Johanna plans educational activities for the Catholic Church and, since the unification, has attempted to reach out to congregations in the East.

> Before the Wall came down, Ossies were not allowed to go to the West. But we Wessies would go over there. Naturally, we would go there relatively frequently and often sent things over. It was hard for us, of course, because, by Western standards, we were a family with a

very modest income. But they didn't understand that because they saw us as the rich Wessies who could get everything. And up to the end, they didn't believe that all of my mother's salary went to pay the rent. We had no financial aid, the way they had over there, where the state subsidized its citizens. But that was never clearly explained to them.

Erich

Once, when I was still a student, before I really got to know the GDR, I got myself into hot water.

I was in the East. We drove by car to the Baltic Sea and back again. That meant filling the gas tank twice, and that cost me a lot of money. In the Federal Republic it was quite customary to say: Let's split the cost of the gas. This was unthinkable in the GDR. Whoever owned the car, paid.

I noticed their reaction as we were driving back, and also when we got back to Berlin, when I said: Each of you can give me ten marks for the gas. Actually there wasn't much I could do with the east-money, but I could have bought some records or books. They looked at me as though I were a tightwad. And so I asked them: Did I say something wrong? It turned out that what I had done was totally taboo in the GDR.

Money just didn't play the same role. You didn't talk about it. It didn't pay for things, either. People would bring two cases of wine along with them when they went somewhere, and then everyone would start guzzling. Nobody would ever have thought of saying: Hey, here's some money to help pay for it. Whoever had something, had something.

A contradiction in logic seems to have arisen here, because although one didn't talk about money, it nevertheless seemed important—important because whoever had money paid and in that way shared his wealth with others. In accordance with socialist principles he is obligated to do that. Yet in this case no one asked whether the owner of the car really had enough money to cover the expense of the trip. No one offered, as is customary in the West, to share in the expenses as well as in the use of the car.

Unconsciously, the exploiter-exploited mentality seemed to play a part in this: The owner of the car was regarded as a rich capitalist who owed something to the "poor workers' children."

Erich realized that the situation was complex:

A certain transactional relationship prevails most of the time anyway, except in a case where someone passionately loves someone else. The ethical/moral message of sharing and of social welfare is a phenomenon that overlaps into religion. It's Christian, it's Jewish, it's Moslem, it's Buddhist. It is a basic ethical value of social behavior everywhere. Therefore, I don't want to nail it down politically.

But there is no altruism. Mother Teresa was very egotistical because she would never have done her work had she not profited a great deal from it—perhaps not materially, but emotionally. So, I think altruism is a theoretical construct. First of all, selflessness is a tautology when considered from an etymological standpoint because selflessness is an impossibility, and I consider it a religious fairy tale.

Many GDR citizens say: Oh, it was so beautiful and so terrific here, but they simply forget the actual circumstances. They're also being hypocritical when they say: We helped one another and we always did so without thinking of money.

Asserting oneself requires a confrontational mentality that can be quite exaggerated and indeed is often exaggerated in a market economy.

Erich

Capitalist society is pushy and ruthless, and I have grave problems with that. I'm not the pushy type. The idea of socialism as a construct has always fascinated me. The fact that it isn't suited for most people is a separate problem.

DOROTHEA

Dorothea was an assistant department store manager. She discovered that certain customs prevailing in the West were just as strange, or perhaps uncomfortable to Ossies as the eastern customs seemed to Wessies.

In a West German department store that employed Wessies and Ossies in fairly equal numbers, it was customary, whenever somebody had a birthday, for each employee to put two Marks in the kitty for a present. Oddly, from the outset, the Ossies didn't join in. Things are different at the institute in the East where I now work. Nobody questions the custom. Money is collected and the coworker receives flowers and congratulations, and everybody pitches in.

In 1992, the rift between Ossies and Wessies in this institute was still very, very wide. Wessies were looked at with great distrust, and the Ossies were much more guarded in their dealings with them. People avoided each other. They didn't get together for coffee. During breaks everyone stayed with his own group, that is, the Ossies had breakfast together whenever their break came at the same time, and the Wessies kept to themselves. It took a long time before any contacts were made.

I know that one of my colleagues feels a great inner aversion toward the West. She says she would never be able to cope in that country. Tears come to her eyes whenever she talks about the West. She thinks it's horrible, quite, quite evil. She would do anything just to have the GDR back. She talks enthusiastically about those days. She's actually a pretty nice colleague who probably managed to become a part of the GDR system back then and who did well in comparison to other people. I don't know why she was well off in those times, which of course makes me suspicious. It isn't that I'm blind, but, still, we work very well together.

By the same token, I have another acquaintance here in the West who won't drive through the East, won't step on eastern soil—that's how strong her aversion toward the East is.

Naturally, these mistrustful feelings don't foster friendships. Rather they cause competition from the get-go. But we Wessies were better at shaking it off than the Ossies.

Our working relationship today is first class. I enjoy being able to say whatever's on my mind. I don't have to be a hypocrite to keep my job. I don't have to say: Everything you did back then was good. I can talk about how many bad things happened in those years. After all, I lived through them too. Nobody blames me for that. I consider my relationships in the East to be better than those in the West.

Unfortunately, in some spheres the opportunities and the desire of Ossies and Wessies to get to know one another were much more limited.

Johanna

Because of its insular location, the church in West Berlin was and is separated from other churches. The members of the congregation are very close. Everyone is related by blood or marriage, and everybody knows everybody else. So you could say these internal church networks here in Berlin still have not opened up. And since the church hasn't really opened up, congregations in the East haven't found their way in. But this local attitude toward outsiders—we are self-sufficient, we don't need other people—is not intended to be derogatory toward others; rather it's that we're self-sufficient, we all know each other, we understand each other. Why would we need anyone else? So, there's a slight arrogance here.

Mind you, there are congregations who sought out partnerships with other congregations in the Berlin vicinity or even in East Berlin and simply said: Let's compare notes. Sure, but my God, I mean, how much contact does one have with people who live elsewhere? I have little contact with people in Hesse or in North Rhine–Westphalia. If you don't happen to know someone there, you don't have any connections with people in those places.

ERNST

Ernst, who is devoutly religious, converted from Protestantism to Catholicism. He is married to a Catholic woman.

There was a strong communal attitude in the Catholic Church in Burg. Of course, that could have had something to do with the fact that it was the only Catholic Church in the area. But that's not our experience in the congregations here in West Berlin. And that's too bad.

ERIKA

Erika was expelled from Poland after World War II and still does not consider Berlin her real home, yet she retained some trust in people. She says:

In our apartment complex, where many Stasi officials used to live, there's a woman who's been delivering the mail for thirty-three years. She has known every family, everything, everybody. And you could confide in her. I don't think she ever repeated things she was told, and she's still like that to this day. Whenever I see her, it's: Hello! Hello! We greet each other and also her husband, a charming person. He's retired now, goes fishing and brings me trout. I think there's a mutual liking there. I can't explain it any other way. I don't think she ever passed along any information.

Before, there used to be a communal feeling in our apartment house; neighbors talked to one another, gave parties. Now, after the *Wende*, everybody keeps to himself here. Everybody thinks only of himself and uses his elbows in this pushy society. There's a lot of envy.

Somebody buys a car, and his neighbor immediately thinks: Hey, I've got to get a bigger one. People compete with each other. Each one wants to be nicer looking and better dressed than his neighbor.

MONIKA

Erika's daughter, Monika, is a secretary. She disagrees:

There isn't that sort of envy among my coworkers. It has more to do with competition for jobs. That's the only thing, but there's no rivalry about material things. We actually get along very well.

THORSTEN

Erika's son Thorsten, who owns a bar, recalls:

Before, there was more of a feeling of togetherness. After work, we'd sit down and eat together. Sometimes we cooked things on the grill, had a beer and talked about all sorts of idiotic things. Now, because of the system [German unification] there are a lot of new friends and you've lost many old friends. Many of the old friends left, even shortly before it happened; others don't drop by anymore, partly because they live far away. My old friends were more open [about personal things], but never really said what they thought [about political things] because they were afraid. I was never afraid to speak my mind.

WILLIE

Thorsten's father Willie is a retired policeman. He responds:

It wasn't as though you had to be afraid that if you said a bad word against the state you'd be put in jail. It wasn't like that. I think that people told me what they thought even when I was in uniform and everybody knew that as a police [*Volkspolizei*] officer. I represented the state. We would have discussions. And I didn't lock up a man because he had a different opinion from mine, and neither did other [policemen]. Nowadays people think, and sometimes come right out and say that we had no freedom; that we weren't allowed to speak openly. That's nonsense. If someone committed hostile acts—after all, there were laws and someone who broke these laws had to serve his sentence just as in other countries.

Willie may be right in saying that not every dissident landed in prison, but there were other ways to mete out punishments. For example, Otto was demoted for acting on his too-literal interpretation of democracy in the German Democratic Republic. And religious Werner was spied upon and not allowed to get his graduate degree.

Willie would like to dispel any possible doubts people might have about him:

> I didn't spy on anyone. Was I spied on? I'd have to look up my file. Probably yes, but. . . .

HORST

Horst, who also used to be in the East German armed services, takes a different stance. He has a hobby. (Horst requested that the tape recorder be turned off while he talked about his hobby, because it is sufficiently unusual and he is prominent enough in the field to be easily identified.) His interests bring him into contact with Wessies. He says:

> My connections with Wessies are primarily built on mutual interests. Their need to talk about things is as great as mine. And we talk primarily about current affairs. Because of our hobby, we can't help getting into such conversations. But it's not a personal relationship. Usually, people who have a hobby like this aren't idiots. Still, prejudices and cutting remarks—oh, well—you can't avoid that.

Luckily he doesn't take it personally.

> But that doesn't affect me, because I know more in this special field than most others. In general though, misunderstandings on both sides have increased rather than decreased. The so-called brothers and sisters in the West and in the East—never in the history of the world has that sort of thing worked out. And if you put stock in that, then you should remember that in the Bible, Cain killed Abel, and that shows you how brothers can act toward each other. In German history there were also two enemy brothers, and each one built himself a castle on adjacent hills on the shores of the Rhine. I never have had any illusions about brotherhood.

Petra is an Ossie with a Ph.D., a university research librarian. She says:

> There are all kinds—Wessies I know well and like and those I don't like at all. Just the same as here, in the GDR. But of course I think that this East-West relationship plays a role, somehow. I was lucky in that I got to know many people from the West right after the Wende, and most of these relationships worked out. That has to do with my work. I work at a center for interdisciplinary feminist research. And of course, many women from similar centers in the West came to see us. And we agreed on almost everything. So we were more concerned with women's issues than with East-West issues.
>
> Once they realized that we could do good work too and that we had excellent professional qualifications, some rivalry gradually emerged. Many Wessie women envied us Ossies, because we had been assured a university education and had completed it already. Most of the Ossie women in this circle had doctorate degrees as well as families. The women from the West thought this was an ideal situation, and none of them could imagine how it could be achieved.

It can be assumed that as a result, the West German women had to reevaluate themselves. Their self-representation could no longer be based on a sense of (false) superiority. In fact, they had to face the greater accomplishments of several colleagues from the East.

Actually, West German mothers with doctoral degrees are not at all uncommon. However, mothers in the West are less likely to pursue full-time careers. Is this attributable to differing opportunities? Societal expectations? Or did those with advanced degrees hold good positions and choose not to go to the East?

Petra continues:

> A student from Hamburg voiced the strongest prejudice I have yet heard. She asked me literally: Yes, but you lived in a dictatorship. Did you ever laugh in those days? Later, I talked with her and we had a good exchange of views. She was grateful when she left. It was good for both of us to have talked about it instead of just saying, Oh, not another one!

Philip, an Ossie, is Petra's and Paul's son. He recently completed high school with the *Abitur*, the final academic high school exam, a

prerequisite for university admittance. Before attending the university, young men in the Federal Republic have to spend several months
in the military or one year in civil service. Philip has chosen civil
service.

I don't want to generalize, to reduce human relationships to the
East-West issue. In my school, there was a fluid transition, so that for
me it's no longer East versus West. I got to know west-people there,
and out of every ten Wessies I would like maybe three, and that's the
same ratio as in the East. I am a human being just like them, just as
good. All right, I grew up in the East, but that doesn't bother me. I
can cope with that. No one's ever treated me condescendingly. And
if I catch anyone doing that, he's not going to do it a second time,
'cause I'm not going to treat him like God just because he's from the
West. I'll treat him like a normal human being, and that's that.

But right after the Wende Philip wasn't that confident:

At first, I was afraid to take the *U-Bahn* [subway] to West Berlin
by myself. I was afraid of those stereotypes lingering in the back of my
mind, like criminals, drugs, youth gangs, especially the stories I had
heard and things I had seen on television. And then, the second or
third time I went over, I was with a friend to buy shoes, and three or
four Turks came walking toward us at a bus stop. They wanted to rip
the earrings out of our ears. We hid in a store. That sort of thing is
due to the many immigrants who came here from southern countries.
And now that we are part of the West, we have to deal with their
mentality, too, not just the West Germans'. So that was another thing
that was new to us. Such masses of foreigners! By the way, they had
quite a different relationship with the East Germans than with the
West Germans.

It is also difficult for his grandparents' generation. The current
atmosphere is vastly different from the one they had most recently
been used to. Gilda and Gerhard, both retired, find that their pensions are sufficient to allow them to travel. Sometimes they stay in a
boardinghouse where they meet other couples.

Naturally, we got to talking with this couple from Aachen. The
husband, especially, was a real German, and he said: You must be glad
to have freedom now. Then we asked him: What do you mean, freedom? Well, now you can travel, he said. We replied: Oh, we could

travel before too, except not to the West. We went to all the eastern bloc countries; we could do that.

We had other discussions that would end with the statement: What this country needs is a little Hitler. This wasn't the first time we had opened up to people and told them about our lives in the GDR and then heard opinions like that. Most of the time, they're interested, sure. But when we hear opinions like that, we know we'll never find common ground. It's a generational problem too. We're convinced that some young people manage better because they approach things differently. But we drag our baggage around while the others carry theirs.

It's not often that you meet people on a high enough cultural level to say: Let's have a talk about things in general, or discuss matters on a wider scale politically. One absolutely should have taken advantage of that sort of thing in Germany, to get rid of the nostalgia about the GDR, as well as the Wessies' pride in what a great democracy the Federal Republic is.

PAUL

Paul, Petra's husband, went into business for himself after unification, but he seems to have retained aspects of the GDR employee mentality. He grumbles:

Rapprochement doesn't mean starting a business here in the East, hiring people, taking your profits back to the old [western] states, and after five years, firing all your workers. On top of that, the Wessies accuse the Ossies of coming over to work and taking their jobs away. Egotism, "looking out for number one," has taken root all too much here, although it's necessary for economic success.

Germans' [Paul means the West Germans, not all Germans] don't know how to deal with other cultures. They always want to teach others something, just as the Wessies want to teach us, the Ossies. You can recognize a Wessie immediately by his bad manners.

Paul says that Germans don't know how to deal with other cultures and that Wessies have no manners. But aren't Ossies "Germans" too? Paul does not identify with Germany. Emotionally he longs to be a warm-hearted GDR citizen and not a bad-mannered, arrogant Wessie German.

Paul

There's this particular lifestyle, you see. When a GDR citizen adopts a certain lifestyle and abandons the old values, it's the same. We've moved apart from each other in the ways we live our lives. I have quite a few acquaintances from work or from the GDR era whom I no longer like because they cringe and fawn and bend and such. I don't know whom they're trying to impress. The people who bow and scrape are all of the same ilk. Yes, we don't care for that at all.

I've also met people at work—from West Berlin and other places, like Tübingen—with whom, by chance, I became close, at first. Then, my wife and I would get together with them socially, and by the end of the evening, we'd feel they weren't the right people for us. It didn't work. It works on the job; we can talk, or help one another, or go someplace now and then to have a drink. But talking on a more personal basis? That would never happen. There'd be nothing to talk about. So we [my wife and I] said to each other: No, that's enough; no more.

SELMA

In 1994 Selma, a teacher from the West, was hired by a school in the East. She reports:

On both sides, there was a feeling of strangeness at first, despite all the contacts and the fact that it had been five years since unification. I never thought I would feel that way. I think that it wasn't until we were working together that our mutual preconceptions became apparent.

One thing I shall never forget: I was still smoking in those days, and whenever I entered the smoking room, all conversation stopped. Over the years, as we worked closely together, this has diminished.

Still, the first thing one colleague said to me was: You're the first teacher at this school with an advanced degree and the title of *Studienrat* [Title of a teacher/professor credentialed to teach at an academic high school]. What he meant was: You have priority; none of us do. Well, I, the secondary school teacher, wasn't aware of that, because in the West, the *Studienrat* title is automatically awarded with the required Western educational background. Here it meant something special.

Although I frequently read about what the forty-year-long separation had actually wrought, I was surprised at the differences in our dealings with each other. Above all, the differences in the way they tackled basic things was new to me, even though I always had had contacts in the East, in spite of the Wall.

Still, I was the enemy of the working class, especially here in Hohenschönhausen, in the section of town where most of the former members of the *Stasi* live, whose children go to this school. In class, I was primarily a Wessie, a sort of alien element. In GDR times, some people were punished if they so much as accepted a package from the West. In certain schools, they were forbidden to accept gifts from the West. These students, who had been raised very ideologically, suddenly had to sit at the same table with a member of the enemy party, with whom they had had no previous contact and with whom they now had to work. Indeed, it was very difficult at first, especially with the older students. But every year it became easier. It's hard; it can't be done all at once.

I think several of my colleagues were afraid that I wanted to take their jobs from them. Along comes a Wessie who wants to be department head. That was going a bit far. There were people who never talked to me, never even said hello. Even today. But I must admit, most of them speak to me now. Most of them now see me for who I am, and not so much for where I came from. And the language teachers especially, the English and French teachers, get along very well with one another.

What shocked me the first year was the concept of "justice of the victor" [*Siegerjustiz*]. They saw me as the representative of a certain occupying power who now arrives and introduces new regulations and tells them what's what and what they have to do. I never saw myself in that role at all. I saw that a majority of the people in the GDR had voted with their feet, demonstrating they no longer wanted [the GDR regime], that they wanted unification.

After the *Wende*, the school system changed, and many Ossies thought we were going to come over from the West and show them how to do everything perfectly. As a result, the GDR teachers were afraid we'd expose some deficiencies, that we would judge them. That's not how it was at all. It was twice as hard for us because, basically we came here as beginners, so to speak, and we had our own problems in certain areas. At first, I wasn't completely aware of that. There was such a crazy attitude of expectation.

I must say, in the beginning I had an incredible fear. Fear of both fulfilling and disappointing their expectations of me—of being able to do everything better and knowing more about everything. At the same time, I was terribly afraid of not living up to such high expectations. It was a tense situation for me.

After half a year, I was desperate. I felt that I couldn't win, that whatever I did or said would always be wrong. If I knew something, then I'd be the Wessie, and if I didn't know it, I'd perturb them. What was I to do?

Although some students and teachers from the West and East see one another every day, and even though some Ossies and Wessies come into frequent contact in their professional lives, it's mostly the older friendships that have lasted. Gilda and Gerhard have noticed how difficult it is to integrate newcomers to the old neighborhood into their circle of friends.

Gilda and Gerhard

In our neighborhood, everyone keeps to himself now. That's how it is. In the past, saying hello was the least one did. Those who moved here recently don't even do that, and everyone closes his door and keeps to himself. The bond, the solidarity that existed before, even in our working lives, is gone. Our daughter has the same impression.

In hindsight, this sense of community grew out of necessity. We had to adjust to one another because we were so confined in the GDR. That's no longer the case. These days, the bond exists only in smaller social circles.

To be fair, it must be said that it has something to do with the generation gap. And it also has to do with Christianity. They dug up the church histories in a few villages and cities in order to create some church holidays, which we didn't have during GDR times. The pursuit of common interests brings people together, and that creates a certain cohesion. Never before have there been so many clubs and private groups where people get together. Before, it was usually arranged through the state or by organizations like *Volkssolidarität* or the *Sied-lerverband* [neighborhood association]. The *Volkssolidarität* primarily took care of older people. Now, it's an independent organization, having been reorganized immediately after the *Wende*. Before, the state provided the means. Now everything costs more.

But there were membership dues then, too, and the lowest membership fee is only 1 DM; that's still not very much. We think it's good that some minimal fees are required so that people contribute if they want to benefit. We think that's as it should be. We admit that many things in the GDR weren't very good, really not good at all. But the feeling of solidarity, of belonging together, was very strong.

For some, this feeling of belonging together has survived the Wende and unification. Gilda and Gerhard talk about their activities.

Recently, we were at a meeting of former journalists. We have some space in the old radio building. Right after the *Wende*, several people—the ones who always organize things—kept us in touch with one another, that is, we collected addresses and telephone numbers and stayed in touch.

Right after we were forced out of broadcasting, we didn't want to have anything to do with the station. And whenever we were around colleagues, there was so much grumbling about how bad things were that we could never get over it.

But then, after a while, we began to organize some events of mutual interest, like meetings that offered information to the elderly about pensions, health, rent laws, and inheritance laws. Of course, these things are of interest not just to older people, because today's rent laws, for example, are completely different from those in GDR times. That's obvious. But many older people won't read the fine print, so we invite experts to talk and answer questions. They can explain the law and tell us where to turn if we have problems. That's very important.

On the one hand, these meetings are intended to bring people together, and on the other hand, to provide information, as well as to organize things like excursions. We pursue common hobbies and contribute the skills we might have acquired through our work. We create opportunities to discover and experience the cultural things that were formerly available to us only through books. There's a lot of interchange and we've built up a circle of acquaintances that way. We go on trips with some of them, visit each other, and share our common interests.

It would be nice if this togetherness would spread.

East and West Germans are still confronting each other, but they are in agreement on the subject of the rightist radicals and their sadistic violent attacks on foreigners.

PHILIP

Philip was still a student who played soccer after the Wende. He says:

Fairly often, we would play against some Turkish teams, like Minerva or Türkium Sports, all of whom came from the West. And we sensed that they felt the East Germans had supplanted them and they, the Turks, were moving down a notch in the hierarchy. The Wessies, in a manner of speaking, are on top, then come the Ossies, then the Turks; it's like being displaced.

There was also the cliché [the *Feindbild*—demonizing the East, painting a picture of an enemy] that the East is full of skinheads who are spreading hatred of foreigners—which, of course, is very relevant right now.

Erich

I myself am not 100 percent German, and thus, in some ways I'm a foreigner, even though I have a German passport. In some respects, the Turks in Germany, especially in Berlin where they constitute a huge proportion of the population, have become the personification of the enemy. That's because, on religious grounds, the Turks have, to a large extent, boycotted Germany's incredibly extensive efforts to integrate them. Their parents came here from Turkey as guest workers in the '50s and '60s. They were simple people, couldn't read or write, but they could shovel coal and functioned accordingly; they thought and acted within minimal but very rigid, dictatorial structures. Then they had children who also came into this country. And the state tried to combine German and Turkish instruction in the schools. But the [Turkish] parents blocked [any interaction with German children]. They said to their children: You're a girl and you'll wear a veil, and you're not going to touch a German boy. And: You're a boy and you better not have anything to do with a German girl.

There are third generation Turks who speak neither proper German nor proper Turkish; they're neither Germans nor Turks, and they are very militant and aggressive.

For instance, more than 70 percent of all crimes against homosexuals are committed by Turks. Yet only 12 percent of the population of Berlin is Turkish. But it would be politically incorrect to say that Turks commit six to seven times more crimes against homosexuals and the homeless, that they beat up bums and other weak people. The Turks are human beings and some of them are swine, just like some other people. But to say this out loud would be considered hostile to foreigners. And that's a major problem.

I'm all for immigrants in Central Europe retaining their culture and identity, but—damn it—I also expect them to play by our rules. Because the very same people mocking the Germans who eat pig knuckles with sauerkraut and drink German beer when they go to Mallorca—after all, they don't have to go to Spain to do that!—are the ones who get all bent out of shape when Germans make fun of the fact that women have to wear their chador. Personally, it doesn't matter to me, but it sets up a certain double standard.

Sophie

When someone from abroad gets the opportunity to live here—legally, for political reasons or for any other reason—he should at least try to adapt himself to certain things. And if he really wants to spend the rest of his life here, then he should also be willing to subject himself to a certain degree of integration; this is unavoidable. I refer to the many Turkish parents I met while I was a teacher here, for whom the children had to translate because the mothers couldn't speak a word of German, didn't even want to learn. And worse, some of the parents would take their girls and boys out of school for a year to attend those Koran schools in Turkey. So they need to decide: Do I want to stay here? If I do, then there must be another way to teach my religion to my child. And I think there must surely be opportunities to study the Koran here.

In spite of that, I must say that the Turkish students were hardworking students, above all the girls who saw that the opportunities for a woman are different here than in Turkey or in the Slavic countries. On the whole, all the foreign students were very industrious. Of course, there were exceptions, too.

Josephine

In Magdeburg there's a housing development occupied mostly by right-wing radicals. They don't let almost any other kinds of people go anywhere near the place, and anyone who looks foreign, even if he isn't, is immediately beaten up. Things like that happen in ordinary German villages, too, where otherwise quite normal Germans in their overalls walk through neighborhoods cursing foreigners. It isn't just rightist radical thugs with their leather jackets, shaved skulls, and baseball bats.

There was a case—and to this day they haven't been able to prove anything—where an entire village—ordinary people, who otherwise bake their apple pies and mind their own business [Josephine used the metaphor, "people who usually pick their cherries" (*Leute, die sonst ihre Kirschen pflücken.*)]—set up a collection and then hired somebody to burn down the building where the foreigners in that village were living.

So, it isn't really the rightist radicals and their political parties that scare me so much as the terrible violence ordinary people are capable of.

If this story is true, does that mean that the "normal" people in the village don't have their aggressions under control, that they delegate an individual to carry out the deed and thereby turn him into their scapegoat? If that were so, the entire village population would have to work through this psychological phenomenon so that each individual and all of them together would take responsibility for these dangerous, aggressive, and hostile feelings and acts. Here a good-bad split becomes apparent: bad foreigners, good Germans; guilty arsonist, innocent citizens. This road does not lead to integration.

Erich

Sometimes I wish the Ossies would go to hell. But feeling that way doesn't make it right. Whenever I have to go far into the East on the *S-Bahn*, I find there are many unpleasant people on the train. Skinheads and thugs. I don't even care about their politics—whether they're right or left—they're stupid; they look stupid; they're aggressive; and I feel uncomfortable. It just happens [that I'm] in the East. But I could be in the West somewhere and they'd have the same types there. When I go to Hamburg, to Wilhelmsburg, things look the same. Or, when I'm in Munich, if I go to Neuperlach, it looks like that there too. Here in Berlin, it just happens that there's a greater concentration of these types. So one can get upset about the Ossies.

Frieda

The media don't help matters, in that they always talk about "the foreigners." Not all Germans are hostile to foreigners. Many just don't want the foreign criminals who are smuggled across the border and commit crimes here. But the media usually lumps them all together; they don't differentiate. If people live here like everyone else, become integrated and do their work, then it doesn't matter at all whether they're German or foreigners. But if you look at the statistics and see that most crimes are committed by a few foreigners who entered the country illegally, you become enraged.

The extreme right has learned to differentiate. They're quite clever. In Sachsen-Anhalt their election propaganda no longer says: Foreigners, get out. Now it's: Foreign criminals get out! And so they've really hit on what the people are thinking. In reality, it isn't like that. This rightist party is against all foreigners; they constantly attack foreigners without knowing whether they've become integrated here and whether they're decent people. They're attacked just because of their skin color. So it's hypocrisy when they say: foreign criminals, get out. They beat up completely innocent people.

And of course, the second issue regarding foreigners is the wage inequity. It's a real issue, and I think the government is to blame. A law should be passed forbidding people to pay foreigners less. That's the reason so many foreign workers are legally employed here. The businesses hire the cheapest labor. And so there are tens of thousands of unemployed [German] construction workers here. But if there were a law requiring firms to pay an agreed-upon standard wage, that would stop immediately. It isn't right for a country's native workers to be unemployed while people from across the border do the work for less money. That's not right. And the government is responsible. And this is one of the points the DVU [*Deutsche Volksunion*, the right-wing party] is attacking, saying to the people: They're taking away your jobs. And with the construction workers, this message falls on fertile soil.

Dorothea

Two weeks ago, my youngest daughter was scheduled to go on a class trip to a lake in eastern Germany. The day before they were supposed to leave, the trip was canceled because youths in the East were attacking children's groups and school classes that were camping there or were staying in youth hostels; they beat them up and then disappeared.

When something like that happens, it has an impact here in the West. It's unbelievable that something like that can happen, that young people would do such a thing. These aren't radical groups fighting foreigners; these youths are attacking the West German school classes and groups going on excursions. Unfortunately, it seems that the youths in the East consider these children from the West as foreigners of sorts. That's another indication that we haven't yet grown together properly—not even our young people.

Germans still have a lot of work to do. What is urgently needed is a series of organized group discussions. Under competent leadership such discussion groups would present an opportunity to explore differences and similarities among West German group members, among East German group members, and between the two groups. They would most likely discover that there are as many differences within each group as there are between the two groups, and as many similarities between East and West Germans as there are among the members of each separate group. Much can be accomplished when human beings begin to see in themselves the qualities they had previously hidden from themselves by imputing them to others. Such splitting of the good—within—and the bad—outside—is what the Berlin Wall was all about and what the "wall in the head" is all about. It's time to dismantle it.

NOTE

1. Hans-Joachim Maaz, *Das gestürzte Volk oder die verunglückte Einheit* [The fallen people or the unsuccessful (crashed) unity] (Berlin: Argon Verlag, 1991), p. 90.

4

Getting By—One Way or Another

With the exception of the tax burden necessitated by the repair of the GDR infrastructure and related expenses, West Germans had little adjusting to do. They are in the majority, and East Germans chose to abandon their socialist system for the market economy. Therefore, it turned out that all the speakers in this chapter are Ossies.

GILDA AND GERHARD

Gilda and Gerhard's views and way of life have changed a good deal since unification. In 1991 Gilda was so woebegone about her dismissal from the broadcast network without severance pay that her anger and sadness, her despair and helplessness resulted in sleep disturbances and depression. Eventually she even suffered a psychosomatically induced angina pectoris.

Gilda

Seven years ago, I was depressed about having lost my job. It was just when the broadcasting network was being liquidated. It was dissolved and then divided into several regional networks. Now there's the Brandenburg Rundfunk, the Mitteldeutscher Rundfunk, and the one in Mecklenburg-Western Pomerania. Those are the three main broadcast networks today. Quite a few eastern journalists have found work and are earning their living there these days. Some of the very young journalists found jobs at privately owned radio and television companies. At least that much came out of it.

Gerhard

One particular generation, that is, my generation (I was born in 1935), is having difficulties finding jobs at broadcast stations or in something like that. New enterprises want dynamic young people, especially those who aren't so encumbered by ideology. We carried a greater ideological burden. As we've said, '91 was the year of this upheaval. And it left very deep scars on my wife and me. It took a long time before we were able to come to grips with the situation.

It was particularly hard for us because we still had the GDR outlook: We planned to work till we were sixty-five and then retire on a pension. But in accordance with a law passed by the Federal government, I was retired at the age of sixty. That meant I would have to retire at the age of sixty after having been unemployed. And so I lost five years that might have been calculated into my pension. Meanwhile, my wife also had to leave the broadcasting company without benefits. She had no social security or pension payments at all, even though she had been employed by the broadcast network for almost forty years. At the time, this put a great strain on us. We had to get through that first, and it took us two to three years.

Gilda and Gerhard were interviewed for the third time in 1998. The first time, in 1990, they had expressed strong misgivings about capitalism even while being aware that the GDR politics imposed serious restrictions upon them in their work. When the truth was in conflict with the party line, material was regularly excised from their reports. They were also somewhat unhappy that, unlike some other reporters, they did not have the opportunity to travel to the West. What was unusual about this couple at that time was the degree of self-awareness. They recognized that in the socialist system they had learned to take initiative only on behalf of the group, never on their own behalf. They expected that not being able to be assertive on their own behalf would be a handicap in a capitalist economy. Gilda and Gerhard also accepted the fact that, after unification, the socialist ideology had no place in Western journalism. Gilda was aware that her angina pectoris was directly related to her feelings. In fact, during the 1991 interview she momentarily permitted her angry feelings to erupt. At that point she appeared more energetic and became again the spunky woman I had met the year before.

Acknowledging their own part in their fate, instead of blaming only the society and the state, actually helped them to take charge of their lives. Gilda and Gerhard are an example of true adaptation. They went beyond merely adjusting to a strange environment. They made modifications within themselves and then acted upon the environment to modify it. They created a better fit between themselves and their surroundings and set in motion a recursive interaction in which their increased ability to take initiative on their own behalf led them to activities that satisfied them. These activities created a change in the environment and strengthened their immediate community, which in turn, gratified Gilda and Gerhard. In 1998 these were their words:

We decided we would make the best of it. We're not doing badly, because we finally did get our pensions, and they're not bad. We're doing things that we couldn't have done in GDR times. We can afford to take many trips, trips into countries we weren't able to visit before. We've been to Cyprus, and Tunisia, to Rome and Spain, and we've traveled in our own country, something we couldn't do before either. Even though we were journalists, we weren't allowed to travel freely. And so we've been exploring West Germany a little bit. We went along the Rhine and to the Black Forest. We have also been to Switzerland and France. So you see, we travel quite a lot. And we take videos wherever we go!

My husband does that. We bought a camcorder in 1991 before we took our first big trip abroad, and we've been using it ever since. You could say that we are now working like pros, because we also have a mixing console, that is, we work with video, with frame, and with music. We mix all that together nicely. Either my husband will write a script or we'll write one together. He also makes the rough cut when we're back home, and then we decide what we'll keep and what we'll take out. Then we pick out the music; sometimes it takes a long time to find the right selection. And then I'll record the script, or we may both do it.

When the video is finished, we invite our friends and show them where we've been. And so far, it's always been well received. And so one grows into this new world—but partially also by getting vicariously involved in the workaday world.

My daughter works as a secretary in television; she's with *Ostdeutsche Rundfunk*, and when she talks about the goings-on among the editorial staff, you know there was more solidarity among coworkers in our day. Today, everyone looks out for himself, and it's an enormous struggle to keep one's job. The reporters and editors have to fight—

they really have to work hard to get their pieces aired. Of course, as a secretary, my daughter is spared this conflict. She never had the experience of being unemployed after the Wende because she was immediately hired by the successor firm. But the collegial relationship changed, the interpersonal relationships, if you can call them that now.

And by talking about all this with her and hearing her talk about the new work environment, we're distracted from our own disappointments and even say to ourselves: Thank God you don't have to deal with this kind of workplace situation. That's what I think, and I've actually gotten a better perspective.

The journalism that's done today isn't my kind of journalism. I must say that, for the most part, we practiced an authentic journalism in the GDR, an honest journalism that went deeper. More humanistic. When we hear pieces today—we listen to radio a lot—we find it superficial, all of it. We often did longer pieces in which we could go into depth a bit, where people could express themselves. It's no longer like that today.

Before, you sometimes produced reports that were not accepted or were cut a lot because they weren't sufficiently socialistic. And it's no different today. We heard from Western journalists—we got to know them because they worked at our facilities—that parts of their pieces that were found unacceptable were cut, too. So that whatever is out of step with the official line, whether in the East or West, is cut. Of course, the official lines were different. That's obvious. We had socialism, and over there it was capitalism.

In capitalism, you have to be pushy, a bit more ruthless in order to be successful. That's the new order, according to stories we hear. But it's like that for our son, too. In GDR times, he had a good vocation as a master carpenter [Holzinnenausbau]. He was thoroughly trained. In GDR days, he was employed by a large company, a state-owned company that was closed after the Wende. So, our son had to redefine himself, that is, he no longer worked on construction sites. He started working as a salesman in a lumber business. He had to apply his expert [carpenter's] judgment, a perspective different from many of the other people's there.

Actually, he wasn't a salesman. He was an expert craftsman hired by this dealer to build the things the dealer sold. He built the pre-finished components and then installed them. Today, doors and windows are his specialty, that is, he installs prefabricated components and does all the preparatory work. But he also constructs things. He has built entire houses here with wainscotting and everything. After all, he had learned how to do all that.

Now he's his own boss. As I said, he was employed, but at a certain point he said to himself, Well if it's going to be like that, if a couple of know-nothings can give me orders and underpay me, then I'm going into business for myself and keep the money that comes in. And that's what he decided to do.

Of course he has to pay taxes, just like every other self-employed workman. That's what we like about the boy. And it's also what we liked after the Wende, if you look at it objectively. Those who could adjust, those who used their heads and said: We have to find a way to cope and make the best of it, adjusted to the changed circumstances. Our son did that brilliantly; he's making good money, and he gets lucrative orders.

Naturally, he's also a good workman. His work is appreciated. Of course, his work was appreciated in GDR times too, that's not what I mean, but here it's quite different, because now you have to make absolutely sure—since these are all private orders for which the customers are paying a lot—that you deliver decent work. If he gets a reputation for delivering good work, he'll be called again and his business will grow.

That's what was missing in the GDR, this competition: This guy can do the job better—and that one can't do it quite so well, so I'll take the first one. Back then, you had to take whichever worker you got; you didn't have a lot of choices. That's a good thing nowadays, and the young people have fully adapted to this. That's obvious.

Our son tells us things and we don't quite know what he's talking about, but we're learning from him and we see the problems facing the young people. We can tell that he has problems with his employees, with doing his accounts, with his tax advisor. That's a new thing, if you're in business for yourself. Another is that the business requires that you're always there. He can only afford to take a short vacation; he doesn't have much time off; he doesn't take Saturdays off; he has to work. For us, these are all new experiences we were faced with after the Wende.

My son's situation exemplifies these differences marvelously. He started his apprenticeship during GDR times. He was lazy, really lazy, even though he's very intelligent. He didn't care how things went at work; a few times, he even called in sick. So he had to put in an extra year as an apprentice to get his proficiency certificate. And after the Wende, when he went into business for himself, my son made a 180 degree Wende [turnabout] of his own. Today, he doesn't keep regular working hours; if something has to be finished, then it has to be finished, even if it takes till 10 o'clock at night. In GDR times, this was unheard of, and he's not the only one. He works for himself, but those who don't, who are employed, have to do the same thing these days, because there are ten people waiting in line to take the job. Competition makes the difference.

We're glad that our children have work, that they're not unemployed, that our grandson has an apprenticeship. The things that have improved for us and that are good for us now are things that also play a role in our family.

In contrast to our children and grandchildren, our brother-in-law, who is of course a member of the older generation, is not doing well at all. He's somewhat limited; he can't do much. His mother was Russian and his father was German, Bavarian in fact. They lived in Moscow for four years. Our brother-in-law was an interpreter, a translator, because Russian was his mother tongue. He earned his living that way.

He's a German citizen, so he worked as a translator for the GDR news agency, and it wasn't bad. But he has a handicap, that is, he has a speech impediment; he's inhibited by it, so he can't work as an interpreter. And unfortunately, his attitude isn't very positive; he's a very negative person, he's depressive, probably because of the speech problem, which he's most likely always had. He graduated from a school for the speech impaired. Somehow, this is a burden for him. So he can't develop freely. After unification, they offered him a few ABM jobs (a program to create jobs). In the beginning, it sounded very interesting, but then it turned out that the employers were only using it as an alibi—employing an ABM worker, that is. He was supposed to work in magazine publishing, but that turned out to be only advertising. Then he was supposed to do research in the cultural sphere, and it turned out that that was only temporary, that in nine months he would have to leave again. And since then, he's just been hanging around. After a certain period of time, he had to report to the employment office, and they classified him as "not placeable."

Since he has a college education, he has a certain market value; so he can't do just any sort of work. He's actually not allowed to accept a menial job because he's too highly qualified. That's the absurd thing about our system. If it were up to him, he would; but then he'd automatically go down a step on the social [security] scale. And then he would have a lower market value, and consequently he'd wind up ever lower in the structure. Unfortunately that's how it is. Because he's over forty he also has to think of his retirement pension. What would be left if he took a job and his unemployment compensation were calculated on his latest qualifying level? If he accepted a lower-level job and then became unemployed again, the qualifying level of his last job would determine his unemployment compensation and his pension. Yes. That's the German law, and it's bad.

It's the age group that was already over forty at the time of the Wende that is most discriminated against. We have a running joke that goes: The capitalists want people who are twenty years old, flexible, easy to employ, and not too highly salaried, with forty years of experience! And no one can do that.

That's why they hold back. Many people ask: Why don't they go to work? They say the East Germans are lazy, things like that. It's not so simple; you have to look deeper; there's a good reason for it. Of course, there are lazy people and there are those who retired years ago on the theory that they'll get their money anyway. But people who became unemployed at the age of fifty can't find work anymore. The men start to drink, they let their frustration out at home, and then they start to deteriorate socially. This is the generation that has to bear the disadvantages of this economic reunification.

ERNST

Ernst was already over fifty at the time of the Wende, but male nurses are always in demand. Moreover, he had always distanced himself from socialism. There isn't even a hint of suspicion that he was ever a party member or that he worked for the Stasi, because he is very church oriented. Ernst believes:

In spite of everything, most people don't need to be unemployed. If I were unemployed now—I'm almost sixty years old—it wouldn't much matter to me; I'd go to the BfA [*Büro für Arbeit* (employment office)]; they know my age; I've been there before, and then I'd get my unemployment money. In any case I'll be getting my pension starting in 2001.

I think everyone can find some sort of a job. You have to look for something else. And if you sweep the streets, work in the park, in the forest, or whatever you do, you don't need to be ashamed of it.

FRIEDA

Frieda's grown-up daughters who also are strict Catholics were able to keep their jobs after unification. Frieda reports:

But it didn't just happen automatically [that people could keep their jobs after the unification]. There was an examination first. All the state agencies were screened by committees from the Federal Republic to determine whether the top positions were occupied by politically qualified people and whether they would be permitted to continue in their jobs. And that was handled in various ways.

Our older daughter is a technical assistant in a meteorological institute that employed about thirty people. After unification, some people from the weather service in Offenburg, that is, from the West, came over and talked with all the employees there. They asked my daughter about her career and, of course, she told them the story about school and how she wasn't chosen to take the pre-university final exam (*Abitur*), how she couldn't go on to the university, and how she was offered a chance for adult education, but only at a technical school, not at a university.

And she was asked what she thought of her colleagues' politics. Who, did she think, might have been a Stasi informant. And she said: Of course, we dissidents have our suspicions, but they might be wrong, and I certainly don't want to harm an innocent person. I don't wish to discuss this. If she did, she would be informing, just like the Stasi collaborators.

The upshot was that gradually they were all transferred. They were asked whether they would like to go to Offenbach or to Potsdam, where there was also a weather service. The director had been in the SED, but she had always protected her institute; now she works in the Senate in West Berlin. My daughter was the only one to be kept on here and she was given official status (permanently appointed as a state employee, akin to civil service).

Frieda's husband was a professor and a member of the Academy of Sciences.

Everyone at the Academy was examined by the Scientific Council. Only scientists from the Federal Republic belonged to the Council. There wasn't anybody from the East on it, and only the eastern institutions were examined.

At the time we thought that was fitting because, generally speaking, there wasn't one institute in the Academy that wasn't led by a Party comrade. They were all comrades. If you weren't a comrade you had no chance of becoming the director of an institute. Still, not all of these comrades could be labeled as loyal to the GDR, and not all were involved with the Stasi. There were some very decent people among them. They all had to hand in reports to the Stasi, but you could phrase a report in different ways. You could keep it loyal to the state, without incriminating anyone. And that's where the Council made its first major blunder because, by and large, all the institute directors were dismissed.

At my husband's institute, where there were almost 300 people including the technical staff, they decided, on their own, before the examination, to take a secret vote on whether they wanted to keep the director of the institute. And between 95 and 100 percent voted yes; they all wanted to keep him. But the Scientific Council paid no attention to this vote. The director was dismissed, as at the other institutes. Many of the institutes were no doubt glad to be rid of their directors if they had been hard-line Reds. But the circumstances weren't the same everywhere, yet were dealt with the same way.

Moreover, the Scientific Council approached these examinations with a preconceived notion, namely: The Ossies had such a great lack of [laboratory] materials and [scientific] literature that they couldn't possibly have been as good as we. And that was the second blunder. The scientists here were really amazing. They obtained materials in the most improbable ways. My sister would send my husband syringes from the West because the ones here were worthless. And chemicals were obtained through relatives or brought over secretly by West German scientists who wanted to help us here. And so the work done here was really a miracle, structured as necessity demanded. And with regard to the [scientific] literature, the important scientific journals were available through the library. Thus our scientists were even able to publish now and then in *Design* [a prestigious professional journal].

Of course, that [the Examining Council] caused tremendous frustration. If your name was on what was called the Blue List, it meant you had passed the examination. Those on the Blue List, not only the scientists, but also the medical/technical staff had to reapply. Everybody. And then all the other scientists were fired, and they had no idea what to do next. In December 1990, after the unification, my husband got his dismissal notice and he went to the employment office and registered as unemployed. Though a scientist with many publications, at almost sixty-four years old, he was not permitted to look for work. Beginning January 1st, he was rehired for a year until his sixty-fifth birthday. That made us very happy, you see, but it was a huge humiliation for all the scientists who had to go through this, no matter how long they had been working, no matter how successful they had been, no matter how many publications they had to their credit. Nothing mattered. They all had to reapply for their jobs.

No one thought this was right. And these are mistakes that can't ever be corrected. It's eaten its way into our hearts. Those are my recollections, the bad memories of that time, of the arrogance of the West German scientists who considered themselves superior to the scientists here. There are good people here and good people there and bad ones [in both places]. But that was not taken into consideration.

It was recognized too late. Years later, some scientific committees published articles that said it had been a mistake to examine only the East German institutes, that the ones in West Germany should have been examined too—at the same time. That would have been the fair thing to do.

Those who remained unemployed could then apply for other jobs. Quite a few applied for work at West German institutes, and many were hired there. But they had to relocate. That was another thing.

There were also so many hypocritical reproaches: Oh, you people in the East are too set in your ways, you aren't flexible enough. We in the West, we move where the work is, and if we find something better somewhere else, the family moves there. You won't do that. You want to stay where you are. But then they found out that it's much worse the other way round. For instance, all those civil servants working for the Federal government have the task of serving the state, wherever it may be. The Bonn civil servants have been demonstrating in the streets for years, refusing to move to Berlin, even though as civil servants they have the duty to follow the government when it moves.

KURT

Kurt completed his apprenticeship in West Germany, worked there for some time, and then returned to the East when he was fifteen. Kurt explains:

Nobody smoothed the way for me, not in the GDR either. For almost ten years, I managed a department store that had sixty employees in Weisswasser in Lausitz, a position that gave me great satisfaction. Plus as manager, I was given a very nice apartment in the GDR-style [high-rise] panel-construction buildings. In 1984, I was offered a position here, in Berlin, by a big firm. It still exists today, *Konsum-Genossenschaft* Berlin. So I took over the management of a supermarket and again got an apartment through the company.

In Berlin, I met the firm's legal advisor who said: For God's sake, do you want to keep on struggling in this supermarket forever? Why not join me in the legal department? Well, I said, I only have an economics degree, not a law degree. Oh, he said, come and see whether you like it. We'll figure the rest out later. So in '85, I began to work in the legal department, and in 1988 I enrolled in a correspondence course at Humboldt University with the goal of obtaining a law degree. And then came unification in 1990.

In the final years of the GDR I worked on the legal staff. Prior to

1990, Socialist law was in effect. After the *Wende*, the GDR, except for Berlin, had a certain transitional period [before Western law took effect.] But in Berlin there were no transitional regulations. The labor laws of the market economy society took effect there after July 1, 1990. So, I had to become familiar with the Civil Code, with Western labor law, if I wanted to continue working in this field. Naturally, for me that meant having to cram many a night in my apartment. And because the firm where I worked was a commercial trading company— which had bit by bit discontinued its commercial activities—12,500 of the employees had to be fired or transferred. So there was a lot to do, and I was actively working on this project.

I dealt with sixty labor court cases on behalf of the firm without being a licensed lawyer. But I handled these proceedings as far as the business' power of attorney permitted. And I must admit that I was proud when some West Berlin lawyer would come over and say: You really did that well.

I would have preferred representing the employees and helping them fight for their rights. But I was hired by the firm.

Kurt's son was as able as his father in managing his life:

Before the *Wende*, our middle son, who's over thirty, was actually the first in our family to have a little more west-money than the others. That's because, two years before the *Wende*, he sailed on the GDR cruise ship *Arcona*, working as the ship's butcher. And this GDR cruise ship used to take workers on tours to Leningrad and all over. Then they would dock in Kiel and pick up passengers to take on cruises for Western firms.

In Kiel, the crew, with official approval, received a portion of their wages in west-money. With that my son opened an account. By the time of the *Wende*, he had more west-money in his account than we had in ours.

Two months after unification, he came home, opened the newspaper and there it was: an ad from a hotel in the Bavarian Forest looking for a journeyman butcher. So he called them and said: Listen, I just read that you need a journeyman butcher. Can I come to meet you and take a look around? He packed his bag, took his knives, and went there. When he arrived, he asked: Can I work for you for a week? They agreed. After a week he came back and said that he would stay there. He's still there. He'd rather be here in Berlin, but he said to himself, I have work there, I make a living there. And so he has adapted.

KÄTHE

In contrast to her husband and son, Käthe, the wife of the department store manager, has never in all her life had the chance to live in a different economic or political system. She has known only socialism. She is much more rigid than her husband and is imbued with anticapitalist stereotypes. She is palpably antagonistic toward employers. (For quite a different attitude, see Josephine in Chapter 5.)

Käthe

Today the employer is on your back! After all, everybody's trying to hang on to his job and doing his best—getting things going, a full 8 1/2 hours a day!—Maybe it's because there are five other people waiting in the wings, or maybe the boss has said: If you can't produce, you're out.

In the GDR, there wasn't this much pressure. There were jobs where sometimes you had to work a full eight hours straight, then, too, but nowadays you have to be there all the time. We had to get used to that, really being there a full eight hours to hold one's own, and leaving your husband or your wife to fend for themselves. Nowadays, I wouldn't want to be a salesperson at Aldi or at Karstadt, for instance, even though I must admit I liked being a saleswoman [before becoming an assistant teacher]. But I wouldn't want a job like that because you come home totally exhausted ["Dann kommst du nach Hause und bist **'ausgepowered'** "].

Is there some truth, then, to the Wessie accusation that Ossies don't know how or don't want to work? Käthe would say, no, it's not like that. Rather the family is more important [to the Ossies] and the worker shouldn't be exploited by the employer.

ERNST

Ernst, the male nurse from the GDR, is a loyal family man but devotes himself to Christ and to the healing of human beings. When he was a young man—through *Aktion Sühnezeichen-Friedensdienste* (a German student organization that wanted to atone for the suffering and the crimes of the Nazi period)—he and some other students went to the former concentration camp Stutthof in Poland. Ernst recounts:

I worked in Poland for four weeks and got to know it a bit—Danzig/Gdansk, Svobod. The most important experience for me was laying a wreath at the cremation ovens in Stutthof. I'll never forget it. That made an enormous impression on me. I think of it every day, and I also remember a Catholic Mass and a Protestant supper I attended in the gas chamber. I knew that what I did was right. This is the path I want to follow. I went home and knew I had to change everything in my life. So, I went to the hospital and worked as a nurse's aide for 250 Mark. Then I enrolled in night school and received a thorough training as a nurse. But as I got a bit older, I wanted to have something more solid in hand, so I continued with my studies and became a floor nurse, because what the other nurses were doing was not enough for me. I absolutely wanted to achieve something. I wanted to prove myself. I did. I was very successful and I was happy. And I had a good time in Burg, in the emergency surgical department of the regional hospital.

When his wife's great aunt died recently, Ernst became the owner of a house in the western section of Berlin. He had it renovated.

I don't want to be judgmental, but those [East-German] workers came over and I had a lot of problems with them. Western firms had hired East German workers and—I'm sorry to say this—they didn't do good work.

Most people in the GDR had worked in state-owned industries. If I worked as a plumber in some plant, it meant working at such-and-such a job and taking home some parts to work on my own project or on someone else's. I'd earn twice or three times as much doing that [as at my regular job]. Say somebody wants to build a house in another neighborhood, then I'd be doing the plumbing work there. Well, on the whole that's how it was.

WERNER

Before the Wende, Werner had moved from one apartment to another in the eastern section of Berlin. His new—that is, the old and run-down—apartment had to be painted. He and the workers he hired bowed to the socialist system. Werner's workers did not leave exploitation and plundering to the greedy capitalist employers.

The working class was the eminent class. They were the people who were most loyal to the system and did the worst work, even though they could [do better]. They saw that the system depended on them, and they took advantage of it, shamelessly. I had proof of that when we moved into this apartment in 1982, during GDR times.

We had to renovate the entire place. We could have gone to a socialist firm and said: We'd like to have the apartment renovated. But we knew they would do a bad job. Instead, we hired a painter who worked privately in addition to his regular company job. He brought other painters along, and one day he said to me, That guy there, he's my boss. So the entire company worked at our place, even the boss. The painter had stolen the supplies for this job from his company, quite openly—everybody did it. At some point this practice had been introduced in the GDR, namely, that one could take material from the socialist companies, free of charge, supposedly for private use, to renovate one's apartment. So people were constantly renovating their own apartments, that is to say, they were lying all the time and were moonlighting all over the place.

And then, things got even better. The boss said to us one day, I won't be here tomorrow. Tomorrow, I'm going to see the mayor. Aha, my wife thought, he wants to complain to the mayor because he didn't get an apartment. But no, it wasn't that. He was a delegate and he was going there to attend a meeting of the town council. That's how the system worked [until it went bankrupt].

Of course we paid the painters quite handsomely. I stayed home the entire time, took vacation time off, and watched them. They had a great time here, got their meals every day, and they earned many times more than what they would have been paid at their company jobs. And then the painters brought along an electrician, and they argued about the quality of his work. You idiot, they said to him, don't you see what sloppy work you did? That's unacceptable. They were capable of good work, but the system spoiled them because nobody cared about the quality of their work, only about their politics and how many jobs they had completed. The apartments had to be registered by May 1st whether they were actually finished or not. It was a kind of contest. Doors wouldn't open because they were stuck, the walls hadn't been painted yet. An inspection committee would come and they would say: Oh well, those are minor defects, but we can overlook them. That's socialism. A system like that can't survive.

During the time of economic expansion, the GFR had invited foreign workers to perform menial tasks. Many of the *Gastarbeiter*, the foreign workers, were Turks. They brought their wives and children to Germany. The Turks multiplied and stayed on.

In the United States, second-generation European immigrants and first-generation Americans generally learn some English, assimilate the prevailing culture, and adopt U.S. citizenship—without necessarily abandoning their native tongue, cultural rituals, or family traditions.

It is not so for the Turks in Germany. Although they are entitled to and receive the same social service and educational benefits allotted to Germans, until very recently, they could not become citizens, even when born in Germany. And, with few exceptions, the Turkish population in Germany makes no effort to adopt Western European ways. Intermarriage is out of the question for them.

The GDR had less need of foreign workers, but for ideological and economic reasons was glad to admit Syrian, Vietnamese, and African students. Love affairs between foreign students and young GDR citizens occurred, and occasionally children were born to the intercultural couple. In one case, the German woman remained in Berlin as a single parent, while the Syrian father of her child returned to his home. The child visits the father annually.

This sort of situation creates conflicts. In the GDR tolerance was official policy, but unofficially, German parents preferred to have their children marry other Germans, or at least West Europeans.

Ernst

My daughter married an African. I did not approve, nor did my wife. But our daughter is very happy with this man and they already have a child, a dear, sweet thing. My daughter is going to be a nurse, too. She's already in training and likes it very much. It was a good thing that she had taken her *Abitur* because many things are easy for her that are difficult for the others. She has no problems at all with Latin words and concepts or with chemistry or physics, subjects she needs to know.

Her husband is also Catholic, from a former French colony. He had to flee his native African country. The other day, he showed me a newspaper article about the crimes being committed against the people there. This is true. But he finds it hard to adjust here.

His views of life are completely different from those of a European, especially when it comes to work. He was a teacher. Before that, he did something else, but he had trouble with his back. And now he works in a restaurant. I don't think it's working out too well. But that's their problem.

He ought to learn more German. He already has a driver's license. But sometimes he's the victim of the German tyranny of law, because wherever he applies for work, he's told that they only hire Germans, or something like that. I don't think that's good, although here in

Berlin the attitude toward "*multi-kulti*" [multicultural] is mixed: some
are for it, some against it. It isn't all that easy to cope with.

While Werner is a German and by no means qualifies as *multi-
kulti*, he is different enough to have experienced much difficulty.
Compliance is not in his nature, so in the GDR he found ways to
circumvent many odious requirements.

I was refused permission to go to the university. Work was mandatory, and they needed workers. And when they noticed that I wasn't
going to school anymore, they sent some people to see me. And they
were going to assign me to become a night watchman—they still had
those out in the country—or to become an agricultural worker or a
surveyor, holding a stadiometer, things like that. And to top it off,
somebody from the army came and wanted to enlist me as a border
guard. At that time, army service hadn't yet become compulsory in
the GDR.

That put me in a pretty difficult situation, but I must say, the people
in my little village—where everybody knows one another and where
we were one of the old, established families—helped me. The barber
said to me, You know, nothing good is going to come of you. You
have to prove yourself. I don't know whether it was coincidence, but
anyway here is what happened: The principal of the elementary
school—I had been his favorite student, his top student—came to see
my mother and said: Please talk to your son and ask him to help us;
we have a big problem. We don't have anyone who can teach Russian,
and your son was our best student in Russian; maybe he could become
a substitute Russian teacher in our school. None of our students will
get into secondary school, and none of them will go on to the university, if they don't get a good grade in Russian. Russian is a major
subject. And so I thought, yes, that's what I'm going to do.

In the end, I didn't get to be a professor, didn't get to be a teacher;
I ended up working in the Museum. There, I was often discriminated
against for political reasons. What helped me was the fact that even in
such a corrupt system, they needed, first and foremost, people who
did good work and worked hard. And even though I wasn't being
paid any more money, I worked longer hours and I did better work
than the others, that is to say, I worked on weekends, at Christmas
time, and Easter too.

I always thought things over carefully and then I would volunteer.

The others tried to avoid being on duty [on holidays]; they wanted to take their children to visit their grandmother or things like that. Of course, I had to discuss this with my wife first, because in the GDR they didn't pay extra for overtime or weekend work. You got a compensatory day off, instead. You couldn't pick the day; it was just assigned, but I'd try to get Friday off, for example. And then I'd go to the library or do something else. But I had the time off. And I worked toward this goal, so that at least I would be able to read books. That was primary.

I put in twenty-six days' worth of overtime in one year. Twenty-six days! Christmas, too. In Germany, it's awful to work on Christmas. Everybody else is celebrating and you're sitting in a museum; you sit at the window; nobody comes in, but they have to have a scientist on duty on the off-chance that someone does. And that's what I did, because I knew that I could avoid certain things that way. Every day I didn't have to go to a [political or union] meeting was a plus for me. I worked that out systematically.

The second thing was Russian. The GDR was a satellite state, linked to the Soviet Union. Up to the very end, the GDR openly declared that its existence depended on the Soviet Union. The Soviet Union established the GDR, Soviet troops assured the continued existence of the GDR, and Soviet wishes and the Soviet example determined everything. Everybody here had to learn Russian, but nobody learned it properly. As I saw it, the Soviet Union was not well loved—notwithstanding the public demonstrations of friendship and jubilation among the people. In a dictatorship it's no problem to get millions of people to go out on the street to cheer and be enthusiastic—the same people who say afterwards: Thank God, they've gone away again; now we can go home. The authorities kept track of all that.

There was a checklist in my department to keep track of who participated [in state holidays, etc.]. Supposedly everything was voluntary. May 1st was a state holiday, but it was customary to go to your department head and to say, Listen, I can't show up tomorrow because my grandmother is terminally ill, or something like that. Then he would say, You don't have to make excuses. After all, it's voluntary. But they made a note of it, and it was much the same with all those things. Pressure was constantly exerted on people.

This pressure inhibited Werner even as a student, and its symptoms have stayed with him.

As a student, I lived in a dormitory, four men in a small room, from my first day there to my last. The other three were all members of the party and one of them later became my department head and party secretary. And the terrible thing was—and this hampered me in my scientific work—I would never write anything down for fear of being accused of conspiracy. I simply can't write things down. I'll be sitting in front of a piece of paper and thinking: No, you can't write that. If you write it this way, no, that won't do either. On the other hand, talking is easy for me.

Later, I gave illegal lectures, and the students never got any written material from me. I never read [lectures] to them, I just talked. I used index cards for quotes or statistics that I couldn't remember, and which I then wrote on the blackboard. Otherwise, nothing.

These were theology students from the Protestant church. Here in the GDR, there were theology departments at the universities, but only Protestant [not Catholic or any other religion]. However, I didn't lecture there because the students were in the FDJ, the communist youth organization, and their lectures were all about Marxism/Leninism. For those not admitted to the *Abitur* because they were sons of ministers, there were church-connected institutions that were affiliated only with the Protestant church and where the state had no jurisdiction. And here in Berlin that was the Paulinum. There were similar institutions in Naumburg and in other cities of the GDR. The students there were all older, had first learned a trade, and then had decided to become theologians after they were more mature and already had families. They lived in a dormitory in the same building where classes were held. If their families didn't live in Berlin, they would always go home for weekends. It was a big sacrifice for them. Their families had to live in virtual poverty because, in the GDR, a Protestant minister earned about 300 Ostmark. That was little more than a scholarship; the minimum pension in the GDR was about 300 Mark. That's how much a future minister with a doctorate degree would earn. In fact, he was fundamentally dependent on charity. As for owning a car, at best he might occasionally see one from afar. Nevertheless, people still studied to become ministers. I taught them, and that's where I gave my lectures. That's how I survived working in the GDR.

I was not paid for my lectures. Of course, I could have received some sort of remuneration, but I didn't want to take money from these poor people. Besides, I had another, quite different, reason. Before I started doing this I took a look at the GDR laws and business regulations. And it said that all outside paid work has to be reported to the company. What would have happened if I had gone to the museum director to report that I had just given a lecture to Protestant theology students? That was out of the question. So I did it without pay. Second, any sort of moonlighting done during working hours had to be reported. So I had to do it after work. And that's where my working on Sundays and my overtime came in handy. I had to give these lectures at an awkward time, Friday afternoon at 1 o'clock. You can imagine what that meant to those young people with families who wanted to get home for the weekend as soon as possible, They had to sit there another two hours right after lunch and listen to me, had to write things down, and ask questions. That was a really great group of people I had there.

Once, a professor from the Catholic Academy in Geneva wanted to give a lecture at the Protestant Academy. There was an unwritten law that if a foreigner or a West German wanted to give a lecture at a conference here, someone from the GDR also had to present a lecture, preferably the principal lecture. And so this Swiss gentleman came to speak about Swiss history. The woman who headed the Academy came running after me at the museum and said: You have to help us out; you're the only one who can help us. If you don't give a lecture, I can't arrange this conference. I didn't have a clue as to what to talk about. So I got hold of some books, read up in them, and then turned all that into a lecture.

Of course, it was agreed that no outsiders would be permitted to come into that house; everybody knew everybody. Once, a student thought the lectures were so good, so interesting, that he brought his girlfriend along. It caused a big uproar. The students were told they weren't to discuss it with anyone. They didn't even tell me about it.

And now, since I figured that after my dismissal [from the museum] here I wouldn't get another job, I waited a year and then applied for an early retirement pension. And I've been getting it since January 1, 1996. As before, I still work on the side but naturally without remuneration. Then I joined the Association of Victims of Stalinist Persecution [*Bund der stalinistisch Verfolgten*]. They told me they were happy that I didn't have a job because it meant I could work for them.

The path was smoothed for Werner's wife:

My wife wasn't even in the FDJ. And in spite of that she worked at the university here. She comes from an old family of doctors, and her father was a good chess player. One day, he told an old man he didn't know well, but with whom he always played chess at his club, that his daughter was studying medicine and that she had problems because she got married in Berlin and wanted to stay there. And the old man asked: What's her name? I'll speak to my son about it. It turned out that the son was Deputy Minister for the University and Professional

School System. Suddenly she had several offers. Now she could take her pick, whereas before, no jobs had been available, none whatsoever. The people in the hospital were all party members, and they all wondered how she got her job there. There had to be some explanation. At the time, neither they nor we knew anything about those chess games.

HILDE

Hilde is a senior citizen. The shadow of World War II has hung over her entire life, and she has never been without insistent feelings of anxiety. As a twelve-year-old child she had to work hard in order to keep from starving to death. Hilde recalls:

> When Germans were expelled from Czechoslovakia in 1945, we were taken part of the way in cattle cars. Then after two or three more days on foot, we arrived in Neudrauschkowitz near Bautzen. A farmer there told us we could stay with him. He gave us a room and food in exchange for working the land. I worked on the farm afternoons after school, as did my mother on Saturdays and Sundays. She also had additional work in the city. So we didn't have to starve. We didn't starve. But today I'm worried about my children.
>
> In 1951, I passed my *Abitur* and I had to find a career quickly because everything was still scarce. They were looking for new teachers. Even though I would have preferred to study something else, I applied because my mother said: My God, you've got to hurry up and earn some money. And so, within two weeks, I was trained at lightning speed in a camp at Kotmarberg near Löbau. That September, I was ready to face a class.

Hilde's children's lives were not so traumatic as hers. Nevertheless, the Wende and unification posed a challenge.

> My son became a telecommunications technician, a job for which you didn't need an *Abitur*, or university training. But he did do an apprenticeship. He installs telephone lines and things like that.
>
> My daughter was hit hard by [the *Wende*]. At sixteen, she had to decide on a profession, and she said: For God's sake, I don't want to work in a city. I want to get out, to work with animals. Then she went into farming and learned how to be a *Zootechniker-Mechanisator*. These nice words mean that she worked with cattle, with cows. As an animal lover she was shocked by what she found. For heaven's sake,

she said, the cows are treated like machines. Whether they're done in, sick, half dead, the main thing is that their udders are still hanging there giving milk. Soon after that, the *Wende* came and her job no longer existed. And because she hadn't learned anything else, she got a job in the city, cleaning, working for cleaning firms.

OTTO

Otto worked in a printing authorization office of the GDR. He had a hard time adjusting to the totalitarian rule and consequently faced major problems.

Everything that could be censored was censored, even labels. Anyone who wanted to print something or to duplicate something had to go to our department, which stamped on a paper-quota authorization. I said: This is ridiculous; treating people like infants and [censoring] labels has nothing whatsoever to do with democracy. Such nonsense. First, get rid of this entire license requirement. Nobody needs that; anybody can print stuff like that, and all the rest simply ought to be freed from controls, because democracy thrives on a multiplicity of opinions. Well, that didn't go over so well. It didn't work, so I was transferred for disciplinary reasons.

But my wife always had work. She's a kindergarten teacher. In the GDR, everything was quite cheap. Groceries were subsidized, rents were subsidized, so were streetcar fares. You didn't have to work to be able to live, it really wasn't necessary. I did whatever I could. My wife arranged for me to go from kindergarten to kindergarten, taking photographs of the children. I photographed them when they first came to kindergarten, when they left kindergarten, when they entered elementary school, on the first day of the school year, at Christmas, and at other celebrations. And the parents bought the photographs from me. That went all right. Even in the socialist system, I had to market myself in order to be successful as a photographer.

5

The Right and the Duty
to Work

Risk-taking instead of a planned economy, mobile middle classes instead of rigid collective combines, achievement orientation instead of bureaucratic lazy bones, expertise instead of party membership, information instead of concealment.[1]

In the Great Society, work shall be an outlet for man's interest and desire. Each individual shall have full opportunity to use his capacities in employment which satisfies personally and contributes generally to the quality of the Nation's life.[2]

WILMA

After unification Wilma, a Wessie, was assigned to help people who had to leave their old run-down apartments in the Eastern section of Berlin.

People would ask me: Why are you working overtime? I wouldn't be that stupid!

I would answer: Just imagine, if I had your attitude you wouldn't be sitting here now consulting with me.

I had applied for a job at an architectural and city-planning firm here in Berlin; they were looking for an office manager, and I had the good luck of being hired. The company was planning to renovate a housing development near Berlin. It was to be the first housing renovation in the state of Brandenburg. They had no experience doing this sort of thing, and what really appealed to me was that I would get to talk with the tenants and assist them in getting the job done.

Every day, the tenants came to see me at the office and made various requests. When they saw that it was all working out without difficulties, without problems, they began to trust me, and some of these people would also bring their private problems to me, because what was happening was too much for many of the old people. They were supposed to get out of their apartments. These apartments had been built sometime in 1915, 1920, and also 1935; they had no decent toilets or baths; the windows were in bad condition. So they had to be completely renovated. And I had to arrange to move these people, to find them other places to live, and that wasn't easy.

Of course, the tenants were compensated accordingly and the move was arranged for them. They really didn't have to lift a finger. But I was repeatedly annoyed by the fact—at any rate I had the impression—gee whiz, you people really could help yourselves a little more. But maybe they were paralyzed by what was happening to them.[3]

Something that still bothers me ten years later is that I have the impression that they ought to have contributed somewhat more to this themselves and not just waited and said: Oh, we've got it coming to us. This attitude was drummed into them over the course of forty years. After all, they had been living carefree lives. Ossies think: The Wessies have lived in a fantastical land of luxury for forty years and now the Wessies ought to give us some of that, and we shouldn't have to do anything to earn it ourselves. That bothers me, I must say. And I tell them so quite openly whenever they complain about the Wessies.

Before I came to Berlin, my friends all warned me. They said: For God's sake, don't move there; Berlin is too full of former GDR people. You won't find a room to rent unless you go to a hotel and pay a lot of money, and you won't find a job either. But I was confident I would find work there.

I've worked at a lot of jobs in my life. Even as a young girl, I had to try to earn some money—at the age of 14 I was already apprenticed as an insurance salesperson. Of course, that wasn't the profession of my dreams because, more than anything, I loved children, and so I studied to become a pediatric nurse. So, basically, I learned two professions. But later, life decreed that I wouldn't practice my second profession either. The last job I had was as a secretary at Radio Free Berlin [*Sender Freies Berlin*]. At the time, there was a well-known director there, and when my husband was transferred to the Rheinland, this director wanted me to stay with Radio Free Berlin.

[In the Rheinland] I tried to go into business for myself in EDV [*Elektronische Datenverarbeitung*], Electronic Data Processing. I sold programs to lawyers, and at that time, I worked intensively in EDV. But first I had to learn the program, and I must say, thank God, I did it.

In spite of all my training and previous work experience, I'm unemployed now, because of my age—and I know and understand how hard it is not to have a job. I'm fifty-two years old. Until you're fifty you've got a chance, but a woman of fifty in Germany no longer has any status. And that is very burdensome.[4]

In Germany, you have to be young, pretty, with [the equivalence of] thirty years of professional experience, preferably no children, totally flexible with regard to work, and willing to work overtime. That's how it is. But employers should take into account that [older employees] have certain qualifications that a younger person couldn't possibly have. But I've noticed that nowadays they'll say: All right, it's better that she not be too qualified, she'll be cheaper. Many women from the former GDR went through retraining, did office work for a year, and then applied for jobs as secretaries. Oh well, [the boss thinks] she'll learn all that soon enough. But what if many things at work suffer as a consequence? That's not something the "masters of creation" take into account.

After the renovation project was finished, I found a job in a property management firm. There, I was faced with "mobbing," that is, reprisals at the workplace. Yes, they make things unpleasant for you at work. They try to push you out of your job.

I had a colleague who was afraid I would take his job away from him because I was just as good as he was. He was nearly the same age, but he wanted to play the boss, didn't want to be a coworker. And that didn't work; we were equally competent. And sad to say, after half a year of this constant fighting, I said I can't go on; can't we solve this problem? But they refused to consider other possibilities. I said: It can't go on like this. Oh, they said, too bad. Then the subject was closed, and I was out in the cold.

PETRA

In her profession Petra deals with matters that concern women in the workplace.

I work in Information and Documentation, and my chief goal is to collect articles and literature that concern women in the East Germany. More and more women from abroad are interested in women's issues, and it is incredibly difficult, because after the Wende so many books were discarded by the libraries. I walked through the city collecting them, picking them up from the sidewalks, all I could find.

Petra recalls having the right to apply for four weeks of sick days—perhaps not all in one chunk, but over a one-year period—so that she could take care of members of her family when they got sick.

> Sick days? I think it was only four weeks a year. I'm not exactly sure whether it was only four weeks; it seems to me as if it was more than that.[5] Things happened in stages in the GDR, and toward the end, I think, there wasn't a cap on how much paid leave you could get. You received sick pay, and after the sick pay, six weeks of wages. Then the amount was reduced and you got somewhat less sick pay. And you could also take sick days to care for your children.
>
> That happened to me with my second child. As soon as he entered nursery school, he got sick, and it got so bad that I worked only thirty-nine days that year, and the rest of the time I was either at home with him because he was sick, or I was sick myself because I was constantly coming down with things I caught from him.
>
> There's always that risk when you hire a woman with two children, especially when she's single—which, luckily, was not the case with me. Nobody takes that into account. No one. It was like that in the GDR, too.
>
> The first thing they all said was: Aha, she's having a child, so she'll take time off, and once she comes back to work, all the children will get sick. I experienced that myself, the looks they gave me, when I came back to work. My colleagues had to substitute for me at my seminars, and that was very hard on them.
>
> I didn't feel well at the time, and as a result, I didn't finish my dissertation and my assistantship ran out. Then the university notified me that, without a doctorate, I couldn't continue to work there, and I should look for another job. And I didn't want to do that because my dissertation was almost finished. All I needed was time to sit down and write it all out. So I decided I wouldn't work at all and I stayed home. Even though that was not permitted in the GDR because of the right-to-work and the obligation-to-work laws, I stayed home anyway because of the children. But that was an unusual thing in the GDR, and I felt pretty peculiar telling someone I wasn't working anymore, that I was at home. So I never said a word about it to anyone.
>
> Oh well, it all adds up, psychologically and physically, how one copes. It was catastrophic. While I was writing my doctoral disserta-

tion, we had to get along without my salary, but at least I had been paid for the sick days.

Getting sick pay was no problem in the GDR. The problem was that every GDR business had to meet a productivity quota, and if it didn't because of a high absentee rate—due to sickness, for example,—the GDR Council of Ministers would reduce or withhold the bonus. But so many firms didn't meet their quotas! That's what accounted for the nation's poor performance.

It's like that today. If someone in a firm is sick for a long time, what happens? First of all he gets sick pay. If he has good coverage, he's paid by his health insurance company; then they decide whether he should go on a disability pension. Every firm looks for ways to replace the sick person with other people. The first six weeks are a loss for the firm; after that, the sick person is paid through another source.

Wilma

When unemployment compensation or public assistance is this substantial, it's easy to say, I'm not going to work anymore; what I'm getting is enough. I have no sympathy for that. The politicians ought to come up with something, because unemployment among young people is absolutely a very serious matter. To a great extent, the politicians themselves are to blame for the way the elections in Sachsen-Anhalt turned out—the success of the DVU [*Deutsche Volksunion*, a right-wing, neo-Nazi party]. They ought to concern themselves more with the young people.[6]

In the past, the ex-GDR citizens had it too easy. Too many things were taken off their shoulders, including the struggle to find work, and they weren't allowed to think much, I'd say. The more I go into the ex-GDR, the more I get the impression that they wanted more and more but were not willing to do much themselves. It's their attitude of entitlement. I've seen an office worker in an agency just sitting in a corner, knitting. Yes, I saw that with my own eyes. And if that's a way to get rid of unemployment, then great! But a lot of people who have to fight for a job nowadays unfortunately haven't yet realized that the state ruined itself that way. No, I'm not in favor of having everything simply fall into your lap.

And that is why I'm so shocked by the fact that the German Socialist Party [the successor party to the SED, the official GDR party] still gets so many votes in the East. It proves to me, in the final analysis, that the people have not understood what a great stroke of luck this event, this unification, was for them.

MAX

As long ago as eight years before unification Max could not find a
job in the GDR. He recalls:

Financially, we were both doing poorly. I hadn't been able to find
work since 1982. I had worked for a company for thirty years and then
I had to stop. Luckily, my wife had a small Lotto store. That netted
us about 800 Mark a month after expenses. There was no such thing
as unemployment compensation in the GDR. After all, unemployment
"didn't exist!" I was fifty-two, had no work, and no pension. That's
how it is.

The first person to be declared unemployed in the GDR was someone in my firm; by then I was no longer there. I hadn't been dis-
charged. It was like this: I wasn't in the Party, because when I had
been locked up by the Russians in Sachsenhausen [a Nazi concentration camp] at the age of fifteen right after the war, I swore I'd never
again join a political organization. So I wasn't in the Party. But to get
ahead in the firm even a little, one had to belong. I had been hired as
a deputy foreman, and they told me I had to join the working-class
party: You have young people reporting to you and you have to educate them in the spirit of Socialism. I didn't join and I gave them my
reasons.

That happened earlier, in the '70s. They sent me to see the Party
secretary.—Every large company had a full-time SED Party secretary
on its staff.—And on behalf of the Party, he tried to enlist me, to
convince me. I told him: If the GDR newspapers would print the story
that the Russians continued to run the Nazi concentration camps, then
I would consider joining. But as long as they concealed the fact that
so many people died at the hands of the Russians, I wouldn't join the
Party. And I shouldn't have said this.

First he accused me of being a liar. So, the next day, I took along
my Certificate of Discharge from the camp [to show him]. And I'm
convinced, even now, that the good Party secretary really hadn't
known that these camps existed after 1945. He was shocked, and they
never tried to recruit me again. They never talked to me about joining
the Party again. But I couldn't get ahead [in the firm], either. On the
contrary, apprentices I had trained passed me on the way up, so to
speak, and later they became my supervisors because they had joined
the Party.

It got to the point where, on August 1, 1982, after almost thirty
years of working there, I signed a so-called contract of termination
[*Aufhebungsvertrag*]. There were two kinds of dismissal. They still

exist today, I think. In the first, the employee could give notice; he had to give two weeks' notice. The company could also fire someone, but only when it reduced the number of its employees. And even then it couldn't really fire anyone, only transfer them, try to find them another job. It was hard for the company to kick someone out.

Second, there was the termination contract. That didn't require a period of notice; it could happen from one day to the next, and it said "by mutual agreement for health reasons." And after I thought about it, I wrote out this termination contract here at home. That was on Sunday. Early Monday morning, I went in and handed it to them. An hour later, I was dismissed—now they could say: "Finally he's gone."

Today, you use that modern term *mobbing*; that word didn't exist back then. You have to think of it like throwing in the towel. They made things so unpleasant for me that I left. So it goes.

In 1972, the company doctor who had been treating me had forbidden me to work three shifts for health reasons. I had worked three shifts for more than twenty years, always changing shifts [*Wechselschichten*]. But in 1982 my pension application was rejected on the grounds that I could have continued to work three shifts, which was in direct contradiction to my company doctor's orders.

After that, I tried to find a job at another company, but I never got one. I knew what the situation was, how things were in the GDR. In the GDR, there were so-called insurance identity cards, little booklets that were both your pension document and a record of your sick days. Every year, they entered the jobs you held into these booklets. Everything was recorded there—it was actually more thorough than today. Sure, you could apply for work at another company with this insurance identity card, and then they'd give you a questionnaire and say: Come back tomorrow. Meanwhile, they phoned your old company. And that's how things went for me until 1990.

My son-in-law had his troubles, too. He had antagonized someone at Interflug [the GDR airline, counterpart to Lufthansa] and did the same thing I did. He decided on his own to stop working for Interflug. That happened shortly before the *Wende*, and from then until after the *Wende*, he was with the State Art Dealers [*Staatlicher Kunsthandel*], which was still in existence; the GDR didn't disappear until October 1990.

After unification, Interflug no longer existed and he applied to Lufthansa in Frankfurt am Main. They hired him and he lived there for more than a year, while his wife and two children stayed here. And then he managed to return here because Lufthansa came to the Schönefeld airport in Berlin. He's still with them today.

ERICH

Erich, the Wessie, owns an advertising firm in the eastern part of Berlin. His partners are from the former GDR.

Ten years ago, unemployment in West Germany was 8.4 percent, and actually it's still 8.4 percent there; yet it's 14 percent for the country as a whole, because all the unemployed [ca. 20%] are here in the East. I don't want to generalize, but a great many people who used to live in the GDR never learned to take responsibility, because they lived in a system that had as its primary motto: "You needn't worry about anything; we'll do it for you. The state will take care of everything." And compared to America, the Federal Republic of Germany certainly does a great deal, but it's not much compared to the GDR. And because of all the propaganda after the Wende, people expected that nothing would change except that the stores would be full and they could travel anywhere they wanted and would earn just as much money. But very few people saw the infrastructure problems, the economic problems the GDR would have to face. And the big politicians in West Germany didn't want to hear anything about it, either.

In the West they're saying: All the Ossies ever do is complain and make demands. They're lazy and keep their eyes glued to the clock. These are all prejudices. One of my friends was an actress, not the big time; she did children's theater and acted in provincial theaters. Financially, she is much worse off now than in the GDR because the provincial cultural institutions no longer exist and she has to work much harder now to get acting jobs. She could have left, but she wanted to stay in the GDR, because she thought she'd have to work too hard in the West. She saw that quite realistically. She said, I have my two-room apartment here, I'm doing great. Besides, she's lazy. She admits it. She says: I'm a lazy person. Well, lazy is a bit of an irony, because she reads a lot and is well educated, but she doesn't feel like standing in line everywhere and kissing everybody's ass—excuse my language—just to get a job.

"Things are working well here," she said at the time; "I have no ambitions to leave." After the Wende she said: "I think it's wonderful, but now things are getting harder for me." And that's true. Now she has to perform at parties, or at company celebrations, and has done some promotional tours for a laundry detergent—things like that, which she wouldn't have done and didn't have to do before.

WILLIE AND ERIKA

Willie and Erika's son-in-law is a scaffold builder:

Sometimes, he has enough work and earns good money. Then he'll be home for two weeks, without work, and money is in short supply. It's already been eight years since the Wende, and construction activity is gradually slowing down. Many construction companies have gone bankrupt even though they're far from finished with the work. They've still got many years' work to do on the Potsdamer Platz, those people and their construction cranes

Johanna

Johanna's brother is a Wessie.

My brother studied Economics and Communications at the university here in Berlin. He's trying to find a job in advertising—but things are very, very bad, almost hopeless. He's working. But these are just temporary jobs. Now and then he takes practical training courses or works for advertising agencies. He'll be on the road for half a year doing certain advertising projects in various places. So his studies are being drawn out but he doesn't make any progress, professionally. And that is very hard for a Wessie.

Erich

The Ossies complain that they get lower wages than the Wessies. The way a Wessie sees it, there are two areas of the country: the southern areas, that is, Habsburg, and the northern ones, dominated by Prussia, by the Hohenzollern. There are wage differentials between north and south, too. So, in Büsum near the North Sea coast, you'll earn considerably less than in Munich [in the south]. But nobody's making a big fuss about it. Let's assume there's a ball-bearing plant in Chemnitz [in the East] and one in Essen [in the West]. Back then as well as today, productivity was often lower in the former GDR or in Sachsen than in Nord Rhein-Westfalen. And since the employers' organizations set wages in line with productivity, they would pay correspondingly less in those regions. For one thing, this definitely has something to do with their inferior machines; I don't know whether they also work more slowly.

Willie

Willie, the Ossie, began his GDR career on the railway police force.

Eight years after reunification, a worker here still earns less than over there, even though he does the same work. And they're supposed to earn even less in the future. That's what it says in the newspaper.

The *Deutsche Reichsbahn* (German National Railway) doesn't exist any more; now it's the *Deutsche Bundesbahn* (German Federal Railway). Let's take one railroad worker, a brakeman who works here in Berlin, or in Hamburg or Cologne. If the Berlin brakeman earns less than the one in Hamburg; that isn't right. I don't know whether the man in Hamburg earns more than the Bavarian, but that wouldn't be right either.

His wife Erika

You have to take other things into consideration. Perhaps the rents and fares aren't as expensive in Bavaria as they are in Hamburg. One ought to add all that up and figure it out. You can't always state it just like that.

Willie

This business ought to stop, and the unions should be told, that's enough. From now on, raise only wages in the East. That's what the unions should do, now that the government can't stop the unions from acting. But they [union leaders] always see themselves only as the representatives of their local membership, and those members [also in the West] want the union to see to it that they get higher wages and shorter hours.

In Germany, there's also a united labor union, a parent union of which all the different trade unions are members. First you choose your trade union and then you choose the top leadership, that is the DGB [*Deutscher Gewerkschaftsbund* (German Federation of Labor Unions)]. It's all very neat and orderly. But since 1990, the DGB has always acted on two separate levels, for the East Germans, let's say for the East German masons or plumbers, and then for the West German masons or plumbers.

When Ossies and Wessies work together in the same company, the wage differences are not that significant. However, their attitudes toward work can be markedly different.

Erich

It's not often that Wessies and Ossies work together in one company. But in Berlin it sometimes happens, and wage differences aren't a huge problem. I once had a trainee from the East in my firm, and he was pretty slow and somewhat whiny, but that type exists in the West too. I can't pin that on the East, but previously, all my trainees had been from the West, and they were all fine. Then along came this woman, and she was always asking: May I do this, and I'd like to come to work earlier, and, and, and. But she would put down her pencil and stop work at 6 o'clock on the dot. She did so many little things like that, and then we'd say: She's an Ossie. But that's not typical; I want to emphasize that. It's only one example.

Dorothea

I was a manager of a department store. After 1994, we became very disappointed in many of the newly hired Ossies. We had to fire them, because they simply couldn't understand work productivity. Many of them still did not understand competition—working well enough to keep your job, performing better, working harder, doing overtime as a matter of course.

Erich

Ex-GDR citizens, naturally, have a problem with the fact that the Turks who live in the Federal Republic have a higher social status than they do. This has changed somewhat recently, but after the Wende, there were many Turks who lived here, earned good money, became rich. Often, they owned restaurants, vegetable stores, or retail shops. They work like crazy, they're incredibly hardworking. The last thing you can say about the Turks is that they are lazy. They also had good incomes. And some East Germans are a rung below the Turks on the German social ladder. And of course that's a problem that can lead to outspoken hatred.

JOSEPHINE

Josephine is an Ossie:

We're upset because so many foreigners are working here, but the foreigners' approach to work is different from ours. They just do it.

ERIKA AND MONIKA

Erika, now retired, and her adult daughter Monika, who is a secretary:

Erika

Not everything in the GDR was bad, by no means. Today, as a mother of five children, I wouldn't be able to get my certification, or get a job—no one would hire me with five children. What Western manager would hire me? No one.

Monika

You wouldn't want to work now, either. These are different times. Nowadays, once they have one or two children, women don't want to work any more.

My girlfriend is working again. She was unemployed for two years. She had an office job at Shell. Now she works in an office again. She wasn't doing well financially those two years. She had little income, two children, and no husband. But she managed. Even so, she had to exert herself; again and again she had to go to the government agencies to pick up her money.

JOSEPHINE

Josephine is ambitious and a hard worker. As the oldest of her siblings, she was responsible for many of the domestic chores.

Many people simply come to terms with being unemployed. Some think it's better to pick up their government welfare allowance instead of working. I'm familiar with this attitude: Well, if I don't find a job, I'll go to the welfare agency. We had two or three people who were sent in to work by the welfare agencies. One 29-year-old woman had never worked in all her life; she was a Wessie, mind you, who had lived her whole life on welfare agency handouts, and another one, too, who hadn't worked for many years.

We have terrible unemployment here in East Berlin, and it's even worse farther east. But this, this lethargy at the employment offices, that's not for me. No. If they worked harder, not so many of them would be unemployed. I've been unemployed three times already, in 1992 and for a short time in '93, and three times I found another job. And not through the employment office or through anything else, but through my own initiative, because I added to my education, learned something during those times when I was unemployed—and not only then, but also in between. I can't just stay at the same level, I have to add to my knowledge so that I'll get another job.

A lot of people, I'm sure, aren't to blame for becoming unemployed, but if they really wanted to, they could find jobs today. Absolutely. But you have to change your current educational level, so you can get back into the job field. Firms are constantly growing, so you have to grow too. And people just aren't doing that.

When I was unemployed, I wasn't doing well either, because the unemployment money doesn't amount to much. But my friends didn't take my situation seriously They said: You'll find something again. You're never unemployed for long.

I keep my eyes and ears open in my neighborhood. I see too many people who resign themselves to being unemployed and don't work for years. I know them personally and it makes me mad. So they get vocational retraining, begin a new career, and then they [stop working] again, and once again get a full payout from the [un]employment office. That just can't go on. It can't go on. It's like a bottomless pit. What the state gives you was earned by the taxpayers in the first place. It's only through taxes that the state has any money. But these people don't think of that. Those are my taxes too, and it makes me angry.

Most of my acquaintances and friends say: I'm working to make money and I don't care what happens after that. Yes, earning money, of course, that's the main reason to work. And I don't differentiate between East and West in that; it's the same in both places. And I think it's the same in other countries too. But not for me. I work because I enjoy it; I like to work. I wouldn't know what to do with myself here at home. It wouldn't satisfy me, not at all.

Of course, I've set a minimum [wage] for which I'll work. I won't work for nothing because then I might as well stay at home. During these years after the *Wende*, I've given this a lot of thought. I've reached the point now where I can say that I'm working because I want to. And when I've found a company—like the one I'm with now—I'll be there for them, [committed to them] as long as I work there.

I mean, the success of the company depends on how well I do my work. If I work badly, the firm will suffer, because an employer is nothing without his employees.

But most workers don't identify that closely with their companies. They show up, do their job and go home again. Yes, that's how it is. Our people haven't emerged from their GDR way of life yet. I myself haven't quite done that either, but I'm getting there; I have a goal.

You have to be prepared; you have to learn things:

I do a bit of free-lancing on the side. I don't earn a whole lot, but I want to see what it's like being on my own. From time to time, I go to a meeting or somewhere to check something out. For instance, I'm interested in the construction process; how things work at a construction site, what the logistics are. I have a friend who works in that field and I ask him endless questions, and it makes him happy to explain things to me.

And does the average employee read the *Wirtschaftswoche* [Economic Weekly]? I don't know anyone among my acquaintances who does. When they find out that I read it, they always ask me: What do you hope to get out of that, what's the idea? Well, quite simply, I know what's going on, not everything, but I know a bit about how the stock market is doing, what some of the big firms are planning, which of them intend to reduce their workforce, And I already know that Bölsunger, a huge construction firm in Berlin, wants to reduce its workforce on a major scale. Actually, people do know about it, because it's already been made public. But they wake up to it only after it's already happened.

I have a woman friend who holds a very good position in her firm; she's an important person there, and by now she's been working there for twenty years. The firm came through the *Wende* very well and is now privately owned, but economically they're doing poorly. The bankruptcy vultures are hovering close by. She knows that she'll be terminated at some point, and she's known for some time.

I've advised her not to wait till the last minute. She says, she can't leave now. She has this vague hope that the company won't go bankrupt and that she'll get severance pay for having worked there twenty years. But if the company does go under, which seems more and more likely, then she won't get a penny, won't have added to her education, and will be pounding the pavement at the age of forty-three, trying to find a new job.

It's strange—I can't communicate my experience to others, or what I think is right—not even to my daughter, even though she has profited from what I've done.

I've also noticed that it's always more difficult to find a job while you're unemployed and out of the loop than if you're looking while you still have a job. I've been thinking about what it means for me to look for work, to actually go back to work. Well, it means, someone wants to buy me and I want to sell myself. I am the product and he is the buyer. Then I realized—from background knowledge and from reading—that this is purely an advertising/customer relationship. And that means I have to market myself as well as possible.

But it also means that I don't have to grovel before the person who offers me a job, who says O.K. you can work for me, just because I'm afraid I might lose that job again. I'm in a probationary period right now, and I don't knuckle under, not at all. I work there as though I'd been there for ten years already. It takes me four weeks to get used to a job, to learn to do the work, to get to know the field and the products. Yes, then I'm all set and things are off and running.

And I'm a "mensch" about it, too. I don't start at 8:00 in the morning and then drop my pencil at 4:00 P.M., not caring what happens then. Not at all. I work to the end of the day. If my work isn't finished at 4:00 P.M., then I stay until 5:00 P.M. or 6:00 P.M., whether he tells me I'll be paid for the overtime or not. And if he doesn't pay me [for the overtime], okay; but I'll keep track of the time, that's for sure.

Then at some point I'll say: Look, I've got something to do today. Maybe I have to go to the dentist or someplace. Why should I take vacation time for that? I worked overtime on these and those dates because it was essential for the business, and today it's not like that, it's slow, so I'd like to have the time off today to go to my appointment. And that fascinates the employer.

HANS

Hans, a young Ossie, is Erika and Willie's son. His sister Monika is a secretary, and his brother, Thorsten, has been the proprietor of a bar ever since unification.

Hans is no friend of the entrepreneur. Nevertheless, as an employee, he seems to feel somewhat inferior to his brother, the entrepreneur. He recalls what it was like for him in GDR times:

> I was always employed, and I don't think that's bad, even now. In the GDR, I drove a taxi. The entire taxi system in East Berlin was a big VEB [*volkseigener Betrieb*] industry, a people's, state-owned, industry. All the vehicles were parked in a big yard. You went there and you were assigned a taxi by your foreman. You got the motor vehicle documents from your supervisor. [He would say:] Here, you take this taxi out for eight hours. Then, you drove around and you had to bring the taxi back to the yard; you parked it there, and then you spent some time with the other drivers. You also spent an hour eating in a big dining hall there, and you chewed the fat and exchanged stories, and then you went home.

Today Hans is employed by a private taxicab owner.

> Today, things go like this: everyone basically keeps the taxi at his house. Most of the time, two men share one car. One drives during

the day, the other at night. The car doesn't belong to me; it belongs to someone else, my boss, who's also my friend. I drive the taxi for him. He drives too, and there's also a third guy. There are three of us, the boss and two employees. In effect we're three friends. Ownership relationships are different. The car doesn't belong to me or to my coworker, but to our boss, and we drive for him. Everybody's on his own.

It's not the way it is in a big company. The boss isn't doing much better than I am. He's got to keep his head above water too; he isn't getting rich in the process. For me it's enough; I'm content if everything stays the same.

Monika

As an employee, if I disagree with something or have a different opinion about how to do the work or about other things, then I have to speak up. Not like a bull in a china shop, of course. After all, the boss is a human being and I'm a human being too, so I have to be a little diplomatic.

If I can help improve the work routine by offering my ideas and thoughts, if I adjust my hours sometimes when we're very busy—well, my God, the firm can only be as good as I am. And in a slack period, during so-called vacation time or during some other time, well, I can make use of that then. It's teamwork.

Also, I'm firmly convinced that the whole wage system today—unions, wages—makes the large firms thoroughly inflexible. And consequently, they can't react [to the market], and so they have to set high prices. I'm glad I'm not entrenched in one of those wage systems. There are only two employees here. When we need additional workers, we hire students through student employment bureaus. The students like doing the work. They can always use some extra money, and they're on the books and pay their taxes. These are workers who are expert in the field and it presents no problem. A company has to have a stable economic foundation and grow slowly. If the company expands too quickly and doesn't build up reserves, it will fail.

HORST

The subject of unemployment preoccupies almost all German citizens. Horst is a former officer in the National Peoples Armed Services of the GDR:

Is the problem only the capitalist who wants to pocket everything, or also the machines, which make human beings superfluous? In the latter case, we might as well be back to the English Luddites. No, of course it isn't like that. I don't think so. I think that the distribution is unfair; it doesn't work anymore. For instance, if Mercedes makes profits in double-digit billions per year, but doesn't pay a single mark into the German state coffers, to the German finance minister, because they can spread it out and so very cleverly gyp the national treasury through their export business, investing, and whatever—something isn't right in this country. Hamburg has I don't know how many millionaires, and of those, only two or three pay taxes; the others even get a tax refund because they are supposedly in the red. There's a construct, a financial, legal construct, called unrealized revenue [*entgangener Gewinn*]. You can deduct unrealized revenue as a loss. Actually, that's an invitation to cheat the state. And if I've got a good tax advisor and a good lawyer, I can pocket billions and pay nothing. That can't turn out well. No state can do that.

This state is finished. All the states I've lived in up to now always thought they were unique on this earth, eternal, invincible, and they thought they would exist for 1,000 years. I'm sixty-seven years old now and have already survived two out of three of these "thousand-year" states, without any ado. And the third is wobbly, wobbly like a wounded buffalo. And I ask myself: How long can it go on? When this buffalo falls, who will get squashed?

PAUL

Paul is about forty-five years old. After he passed his *Abitur* in the GDR, he joined the People's Police. While working there, he continued his studies and earned his Ph.D. in economics. After the Wende he went into business for himself.

I joined the police, studied at a university on the side, and worked on the force the entire time. I took this path because of the work/study combination in economics and data processing. In those days, [data processing] was already in the early stages of development, and the police—even in the GDR—knew how to do such things at a time when other agencies and businesses didn't. In addition, I was paid more while going to school and had a sure prospect of finding work after graduating. Another reason for [signing up with a branch of the armed services] was that my father had been in the army, and naturally his friends influenced me.

Now, I'm the managing partner in a corporation. We sell orthopedic appliances. Sales to the patients go through health insurance providers. The health insurance concerns pay, and I only have to organize things.

It's the easy part of life, organizing things. I'm glad to contribute something in the field of public health. It's rewarding to deal with something real. Better than just money, money, money.

There were large cooperatives in the GDR. Farmers worked in LPGs [*Landwirtschaftliche Produktionsgesellschaft*], Agricultural Production Cooperatives. If they hadn't jeopardized the [socialist] land reform by passing these property restitution laws [laws regulating the return of, or compensation for, state-confiscated property], then more collective farms with new technology and good land would have survived, and a few in the West, in the "old" federal states—mostly small family farms—would have had to close down. The GDR worked considerably better in this field. They acknowledged that. That's why we have these court proceedings now, but it isn't finished yet.

It's very hard. If I were in a microelectronics business where they produce chips in West Berlin or in Oranienburg or in Henningsdorf, Brandenburg, I'd be pressured by technology. The only difference is that the company here, in Henningsdorf, is more modern because it was built later. The remaining [East German] businesses are considerably more competitive in world markets than those in the old federal states. The Western companies are waiting to turn them into a branch. They only need to buy them up and then produce the products here. Well, these matters are done on an intra-German basis; it's seldom that outsiders come along.

KURT

Kurt, though retired, represents the view of the department store manager.

This demise of businesses is a logical development. Since the socialist system had to be integrated into the market economy, no other outcome was possible. The [Eastern] industries just couldn't stand their ground in comparison with the market economy industries.

We knew that we had considerably lower productivity per man hour than any industry in the market economy. And in the official party documents you can still read, over and over again, that work productivity must rise to exceed that of the GDR. But it never happened, because the state didn't have the resources to modernize its industries. They should have modernized them, but that would have meant [layoffs and] having to recognize the existence of unemployment in socialism. The state just didn't want to do that.

They said, Things that aren't allowed to happen, can't happen. The unemployed, for the most part, were somehow occupied, kept busy, but that didn't result in productivity. So, even though they had a lot of people working on something, output was reduced.

SOPHIE

Sophie is a Wessie who has lived in a democratic society all her life. She used to be a chemist and then a teacher. Now she is retired and, except for tutoring one elementary pupil, has hardly any contact with young people anymore.

Seen from a purely economic viewpoint, it took five people over there to do what one person did here. And the young people over there can't cope with competition or Western economic technology. They can't work it out. Maybe the next generation will, the kids who are fourteen or fifteen years old today, who know how to use computers just like our people here. But the nineteen- and twenty-year-olds still have problems because they grew up with parents who always had work and free medical care. That's all gone now. And they can't grasp that. For them, a free market economy is something like black magic, not something worth striving for.

Petra

One could accuse the Ossies of not knowing how to work, but it might be that Wessies are clinging to prejudices from the days before the *Wende*, like: If everything was so bleak in the GDR and they couldn't produce quality products, then they can't be good workers.

But on direct contact it becomes clear that most Ossies had continuous training up to a certain level, and that, on the whole, that level was higher [than in the West].

Petra continues:

I once heard a woman from the West say that she always had the feeling—and found it was true—that people from the East had a better education, better basic knowledge, and a more solid apprenticeship than people in the West—political propaganda aside. She would have been happy if her son had gotten his education "over there" because she would have known that, except for the political orientation, he would have had a good education, even though she had heard—and wasn't sure whether it was true—that the West didn't always recognize what had been learned in the East.

Knowledge and ability qualify a worker, but don't guarantee him a job. It has been more difficult since unification to make one's way, even in the professions. Conditions have changed, and not all physicians who practiced in the GDR adjusted to the new system. For medical students, too, the future looks dim.

Paul

These days, there's no guarantee that a physician would even find a position. In the GDR, a doctor who completed his education knew that afterwards he would be assigned to this or that hospital, or he could apply for a post. There were hardly any unemployed doctors. They trained just as many doctors as were needed, and maybe a few extra. Some also went abroad, always paid for by the state. But today! We have, let's say, 4,000 unemployed doctors, not including the medical students. They'll go to hospitals as residents to get their training, but they have no rights at all—[in matters such as] the amount of their salary, whether they leave after the two-year limit, or whether they get a position. They haven't a chance to become specialists.[7]

And the number of doctors who can go into private practice in Germany is restricted by the health insurance plan. In any one city there can be only so many physicians, so many surgeons, so many orthopedists, and so on. Doctors could be told to move elsewhere, to be flexible. But their education and the potential is much too valuable, I think. Should I assume that doctors—4,000 in Berlin alone—are not at all flexible? That's a bit much.[8]

There were also "unification winners" in the employment market. As a consequence of the newly introduced curriculum in East Berlin schools, a few teaching positions became available. Selma, Marion, and Gabrielle, teachers trained in West Berlin, found jobs in their fields.

Selma

After I had children, I stopped working for a time. I just didn't want to go back to school. But then, when my children got bigger, I felt like it again, and I thought: Now that you've got the chance, why not apply? And it worked out right away. So you could say that I was a western "unification profiteer" because I got a job in the east, a job as a teacher. The west, you know, had been closed to teachers for a long time.

Marion

And I lost my job! Actually, I was unemployed because of a glut of teachers—which was partly due to the fact that the Wall was open and the entire corps of teachers had to be distributed somehow.

I am relatively young. I just took my state exam in 1996, and you could call me a young teacher. So I was glad when I got a job with the church as a religion teacher. That's a special situation. I'm employed by the church, not the state. And right now, the church is hiring only for East Berlin, if any religion teachers are hired at all. The old western districts aren't getting any new teachers. I still live in the west, but I work in the east.

Selma

Officially, teachers are hired by the state school office because they're civil servants. I considered carefully whether to apply for a job in the East. I had applied to all twenty-three districts [of Berlin]. My chance came when Russian stopped being taught as the second foreign language and they switched to French instead. My colleague and I, who had had the same education in Berlin, were hired as French teachers here in 1993 and 1994. Right after that, there was a hiring freeze.

Gabrielle

I had expected to be unemployed after my teacher training. Surprisingly, there was suddenly an opening. And I even had a choice. I could choose between Köpenick, Hohenschönhausen, and Potsdam.

Selma

And I could chose between Pankow, Weissensee, and Hohenschönhausen, but that was only because there weren't enough trained teachers in the East to meet the sudden demand for French teachers. So we sort of slipped in.

NOTES

1. Manfred von Ardenne, from a speech in the Dresdner Kulturpalast as quoted in Michael Jürgs, *Die Treuhändler* (Munich: Knaur, 1997), p. 16.

2. Lyndon B. Johnson, Manpower Report of the President, March 5, 1965, in *Public Papers of the Presidents of the United States: Lyndon B. Johnson*, book 1, 1965, p. 262.

3. "Individual initiative is the social capital of a functioning democracy. Except that public spirit . . . is having a particularly hard time in our coun-

try." Adalbert Evers, Das politische Defizit der Wohlfahrtsgesellschaft [The political deficit of the welfare society], *Universitas*, 50 (1995): 590, 734.

4. Christiane Ochs and Brigitte Stolz-Willig, Wie im Westen, so auch auf Erden? Zur Situation der Frauen in den neuen Bundesländern [As (it is) in the West (of Germany), so (shall it be) on earth? (a contribution) to the situation of the woman in the new states in the GFR]. In Dirk Nolte, Ralf Sitte, and Alexandra Wagner (eds.), *Wirtschaftliche und soziale Einheit Deutschlands* [Economic and social German unity] (Cologne: Bund Verlag, 1995), pp. 329–351. "New jobs [are being] preferentially filled with male workers . . . [and] girls have more problems than boys in finding a place to receive training, and after their training they are rarely kept on" (p. 333).

5. 2. Rechtsvorschriften auf dem Gebiet der Förderung und Unterstützung von Ehe und Familie [Laws to promote and support marriage and family], 2.7. Verordnung zur Sozialpflichtversicherung der Arbeiter und Angestellten I—SVO [Mandated insurance for laborers and employees], V. #24–28 and #31; #40; VIII #44, #46; IX #46–53, in *Familiengesetzbuch* [Book of Family Law] (Berlin: Staatsverlag der DDR, 1989). Besides maternity leave with pay, sick pay is available for working mothers at 90 percent of their salary up to six weeks; after that, 75 percent if she has two children, with incremental increases for each additional child, up to 90 percent after the fifth child. Single parents caring for sick children are paid on essentially the same basis for a duration of four weeks yearly if they have one child, with incremental increases to thirteen weeks with five or more children (pp. 96–101).

6. According to Richard Schröder, Schluss mit dem Mitleid, *Der Spiegel*, No. 19 (May 4, 1998): 26–27, "More workers than unemployed people voted for the DVU. . . . Also, most of the violent young people who hound foreigners or beat them up (*Zecken klatschen* [literally, swat the ticks]) usually do it after work hours.—[T]hey have jobs, and in spite of that they have this monstrous rage in their bellies."

7. Weniger Weiße Kittel [Fewer white coats], in *Berufswahl-Magazin* (February 1998), Verlag Transmedia. Currently there are 10,000 unemployed physicians and only one-fourth or one-fifth of the physicians can expect to be employed. However, alternatives present themselves in the form of research, marketing, environmental medicine, and clinic administration and in the *Bundeswehr*. Opportunities also exist in other European countries; for instance, Norway complains of a dearth of physicians, and for some time Great Britain has offered jobs to German doctors (p. 28).

8. David Schoenbaum and Elizabeth Pond, *The German Question and Other German Questions* (New York: St. Martin's Press, 1996). The German courts have ruled that a recipient of unemployment benefits may "turn down a job in the neighboring district because of the cultural stress the alien environment might subject him to" (p. 230).

Picture of man attempting to climb over the Berlin Wall

At the Wall

The world, still innocent—radiant.
And then, from the bright sky,
barely visible, sneaks in
the calamity forged by man.

A storm brews, the earth trembles,
it no longer wants to bear
its bursting, breaking, screaming—
its nature's disturbed rhythm.

Look with watchful eyes
upon the world. Ask questions.
To avert the calamities
created by man's own hand.

Muller-Holtz
12.5.90

The border between East and West Germany is open; still, a pedestrian has to pass the checkpoint.

GDR railroad stock, 1989

Ornate building in East Berlin showing signs of decay, 1989

Rally at East Berlin's Alexanderplatz. The sign recommends:
United States of Europe (USE)
540 million people—540 million citizens
no more nation-states
no more border problems
no more military alliances

Billboard (stored in East German garage): Free elections and a new constitution.

Communist-inspired sculpture in an East Berlin park

West German residences in Essen-Steele, 1990

West Germans shop and socialize in Essen-Steele.

6

Women at Home and at Work

We all profit from an equal-rights partnership.[1]

WILMA

Wilma, a Wessie, has changed her way of life substantially after a marital crisis.

In getting to know the women in the East, I developed a great respect for them. I admire them for the way they coped with their time at work. I believe that these women were more emancipated and more self-assured than women in the West. The women in the West—and at that time I was still one of them—hid behind their husbands. The husband brought home the money, so he also ruled the house. In the East, the woman had the same right to work outside the home as the man. They coped with their work on a daily basis and ran their households as well. The disadvantage for the children was that at six o'clock in the morning, no matter what the weather, they would be taken to day care.

Of course I'm proud. Now I can say, I did it. I've changed a great deal. In the past, my family was the alpha and omega of my existence, and my husband was the head of the family; I was merely an appendage allowed to perform some social duties. Unfortunately, it's very much like that at the workplace: A woman with the same job as a man is given the title "secretary," while the man is called "specialist." I've completely broken out of this situation and have built up something on my own; I said to myself: You're the office manager now. Suddenly, not only my husband's, but my name was in the newspapers too. And naturally, he had to come to terms with that, that his wife was developing a self-confidence she did not have before our marital crisis.

Yes. I worked for some time as the office manager in a psychological institute and read a lot, absorbed much of the literature, and discovered that other people have similar problems in their lives. I became interested in discovering how they overcame them. Unfortunately, it's true that people often give up too quickly.

DOROTHEA

Dorothea is a Wessie mother of three:

The women in the West had to become emancipated. Over there [in the East], women received job training from the outset. They worked in industrial firms, doing even men's jobs. Of course, that was possible only because children and grandparents were protected by social welfare, that is to say, institutions were set up—kindergartens, old-age homes—and made available to the people. We didn't have this here in the West. I mean, for a long time, you had to pay a lot of money to send your children to kindergarten. Then there was a time when you didn't have to pay at all, and now once again you have to pay a lot for it. I think the social welfare policy for children, young people, and old people was much more positive in the GDR than in the West. That's what I hear, it's not based on my own experience.[2] I think people here said: Women should take care of the children. Quite simply, women belong in the kitchen. And the women certainly went along with that. There were very few women who entered male professions, whereas in the GDR, many of them did just that. Hardly any women here are master craftspeople, women masons, for instance, but over there, some women did that.[3]

IRENE

Irene, the former teacher and journalist who has been living in the East since she completed her *Abitur*, attended a class reunion in the West after the Wall came down.

The women from the East [who attended the class reunion] all had professions and degrees. Those from the West, with only one exception, were all housewives and complained about their husbands. They had had no personal intellectual growth. To a certain extent, I found that to be characteristic because not many western women were working. And whether this was good or bad remains an open question. But the women from the East were all self-confident and when they talked about themselves, the others were simply amazed. At first, the Wessies all came driving up in their cars, and later they sat around and told their stories: After their *Abitur* they worked for about a year or they went to college. When their first child arrived, they stopped. Later, after we Ossies left [the reunion], we thought, Oh Lord, we weren't so badly off after all.

Even the wife of the president of a very well-known West German bank seemed to think so. She spoke with an employee of a small [East German] savings bank who had barely managed to survive the GDR years. The Wessie woman said, oddly and without empathy, how happy the Ossie woman must be because here in the East, women could all develop themselves so well, all doors were open to them, while she, the banker's wife, was very unhappy with her life.

HELGA

Helga, although divorced from her alcoholic husband, is still supportive of him when he is in dire need. Her daughter, in turn, was unexpectedly loving and helpful when Helga had a cancer operation, but overall, she is quite independent. Helga lives alone but maintains a passionate relationship with a man she met in her youth, lost track of, and found again when they were both older.

My Frankfurt friend is educated, but she hasn't fulfilled her potential. She stayed home to raise her children, takes self-improvement courses, does quilting and ceramics; and she helps other women when they have troubles with their men. The other day, my friend commented: When I look at you, I see that you are totally independent, free to arrange your life as you wish. When I have problems, I can't solve them because they hinge on finances. I could not live on my small pension. True, my husband's pension is huge, but we'd have to sell our house. So I told her: You've been married such a long time, you're not thinking of a divorce, are you? It's a little late for that. But these [West] women are, in fact, in a miserable situation of dependency, because they stopped working and, so to speak, sacrificed themselves to the family. That's so different here.

Dorothea

The development of women in the western part of Germany did progress, although very slowly. Here in the West, when a child was sick, mothers had the right—and later fathers did, too—to stay at home for three to five days every year [in contrast to four weeks in the GDR]. She continued to get paid if she presented a doctor's certificate. Of course, for the employer this means a loss of workdays. And if a woman had three children, that added up to fifteen days a year, whether she used them or not. This was one of the reasons why employers didn't like to hire women with children. So there was discrimination against these women.

I never used up the days I had coming to me. First of all, thank God, I always had such a good relationship with my employers that I never needed anything like that. He let me take work home with me; or if that wasn't possible, I saw to it that a friend would stay with the children.

Legally, an employer could not fire a woman for that reason [equal rights law]. But it wasn't difficult to "*mob*" the women—it's called that nowadays—until they left on their own. Women with children had a very, very hard time; it's still hard for them today. And it wasn't like that in the GDR. There, women and children were protected. That was an important difference. And I also think that women who speak enthusiastically about the GDR nowadays are referring precisely to the social support given to children and their parents.

ERICH

Erich, the businessman, grew up with a stay-at-home mother. Her musical career did not necessitate daily absences from the household.

In the GDR, having children had a different economic function than here. Future workers were needed. And the idea that all women in the GDR were permitted to work? That's nonsense. It wasn't that they were permitted; they *had* to work because it was important to the economy. The GDR had a very low level of mechanization; everything was done by hand, and consequently there was no unemployment. If you were to turn off all the machines in this country, you'd have zero percent unemployment too.

And that's why, toward the end, almost every woman over there was working, and here [in West Germany] some women were still sitting at home. And now they receive lower pensions and they're envious of the others. This is bad. Even though the pensions over there aren't big.

There's a lot of dissent among the women's groups right now, I think. They have differing views of what it means to be emancipated. In the East, I think, being emancipated meant having practical career training and working productively.[4] Here, it was more in cultural areas. It was easier for women to pursue artistic careers; they had more freedom. They could also go into non-demanding vocations. There were no discussions like that over there.[5] And I think that these are significant differences.

JOSEPHINE

Josephine, who grew up in the GDR, was required to perform many household and child-care chores, because both her parents were employed full time and her mother's schedule was variable.

In principle, men and women in the GDR had equal rights. If a woman wanted, she could work, but she didn't have to. But in the family? No, actually there were no equal rights in our family. My father is the head of the family and my mother obeys. For instance, my parents didn't let me be confirmed; but really it was my father who did not permit it; my mother had no say. My mother worked too; she earned less than my father, but I don't think that was the reason. I think it was just my mother's upbringing.

My mother is the youngest of six children. Her siblings were all boys; my mother was the only girl. And according to the stories I've heard, my grandma obeyed [her husband] the same way in her household. Whatever grandpa said was done. Grandpa ruled.

Especially in the east of Germany, the prevalent view is that Germany has become a state that is hostile to its children. Government support for mothers is lacking.

ERIKA

Erika raised five children in the GDR and now observes her grandchildren growing up.

Things are pretty hard for someone with three children looking for an apartment. In the GDR, families with lots of children received preferential treatment and were given places to live. Children could go to vacation camps—three weeks for twelve Marks, but they were only allowed five Marks pocket money, so that no child would have more than any other, to avoid bragging and showing off. And nowadays, at vacation time, you have to pay 300 to 400 Marks a week. In addition, there was day care for children from the age of six weeks on, and

kindergartens after that. Toward the end of the GDR, there was even
a law to protect mothers, allowing them to stay home for three years—
not at full pay, but with some money and a guarantee that their jobs
would be held for them. But in any case, the three years were calculated into their retirement pensions. The entire problem of dealing
with children was handled much better in the GDR.

WERNER

Werner is very religious. Although only nine years old at the end
of World War II, he was aware that his parents were against Hitler,
and weekly classes in religion were secretly conducted in their living
room. In the GDR, he instructed Protestant seminarians who were
preparing for the ministry, and he made every effort to shield his
daughters from communist indoctrination and to expose them to religion.

We didn't use the state kindergartens, even though there was one
in the very house we lived in at the time. Instead, every morning, my
children and I took a bus for eight stops to a church-run kindergarten
because I didn't want them to be raised with communist ideas. And I
had to adjust my work hours because I had to go back to pick them
up. I went to all this trouble just to avoid the state kindergarten.

WILMA

Wilma raised her son in the West. At the time, not enough child
care facilities were available.

I think it's very sad that they haven't done anything to create more
kindergartens. I had problems in the West when I wanted to place my
son in kindergarten. He doesn't have any children yet, but if he did,
unfortunately he would have exactly the same problems, if not worse,
finding an opening in a kindergarten today.

On the whole, the unified German state doesn't protect women
sufficiently and does too little for families when the women stay home
or are dependent. They work from morning till night, do the household work, and raise the children. I think there ought to be a pension
for housewives, not just child benefits. The allowance for children goes
straight into the family budget, but a woman should receive specific
remuneration for her work. Women and girls could be required to put
money into a fund which would then be paid out when they become
mothers. That's the way health care insurance works today.

Yes, I now think thoughts that hadn't come to mind for many years.

It's too bad that nothing has been done for women in this regard. And I have to reproach women for not rebelling; they let people walk all over them. Women would have more influence if more of them went into politics. But then, of course, there's always the counter argument: How are we going to do all that? We have to take care of our household, we have to hold down a job so we can afford the high rent. These are all valid arguments.

GERHARD

One of Gerhard's earliest memories is of his mother pushing a baby carriage with his sister inside and piled high with their meager possessions, fleeing the oncoming Russians at the end of World War II. He recalls women screaming, though as a child he did not know they were being raped.

That is what the discussion is about, and laws are now being considered that would calculate the time spent raising children and compensate women accordingly. After all, it's hard work to raise children; it's just as much work and sometimes even harder than having a job outside the home.[6] Unfortunately, this problem was introduced with the Wende [when many of the supportive socialist institutions were abolished].

Our society often seems to be hostile to women. How many women are there in the *Bundestag* [GFR parliament]? There are a few ministers, two from the GDR: the family affairs minister and the environment minister, and Regine Hildebrandt, the welfare minister in the state of Brandenburg. She's very popular—a walking advertisement [for women in government]. So there are a few. They're not entirely disregarded.

In the *Volkskammer* [GDR parliament], we had more women. There were certain rules, as is the case with the Greens who have set the proportion at 50:50. But frankly, if you look at the executive committee of the GDR broadcasting system, there were only two women on it. And there weren't many female executives in the press. So it wasn't all that fair. We had our problems with that, too.

FRIEDA

Frieda, who is married to a scientist and has two daughters, worked as a teacher for many years.

Even at the beginning, a man's salary in the GDR was not enough to support a family, and so the wife had to work too—especially when the economy got a boost and there were refrigerators and washing machines and television sets that were terribly expensive. A man could never have bought these things on his own salary. People wanted a piece of the pie, so the women had to work too. And then women found that they liked working and having their own money. So during the forty years of partition, it became a matter of course that both should work. And the result was that retired couples from the former GDR received two pensions. And although usually retired couples in the West also received two pensions, the woman's was very small, mostly between 500 and 800 Marks, because, unlike our women, they hadn't worked their whole lives.

Here, however, compared to West Germany and West Berlin, pensions are being paid out at 85 percent. Our pensions are not fully equal yet, but the husband's and the wife's pensions together often yield more for ordinary people than what people get in the West. And that causes some envy within families. [They say:] You now have so much more than we do. They forget that mothers would get up early at five in the morning, wake their children, dress them, take them to kindergarten, come home exhausted in the evening, and pick up the children.

GILDA

Gilda also was a working mother in her younger years. However, she takes her career in radio journalism very seriously, speaking about that, as well as her adult children's vocations, without mentioning her experiences as a mother of young children.

Eighty percent of our women worked and developed themselves; they went to college, became skilled workers. And now suddenly they are faced with having to leave the workforce because there is no more demand for them. And that's what the women in the old Federal States don't understand.

And they'll never understand why our women today, those who are older now, are getting higher pensions than the women who never worked. That's even being misused, politically. In West Germany, they're saying: Well, your women are getting such high pensions. We reply: Our women worked longer than you did. You worked for six or seven years, and then you stayed home with the children.

MAX

Max is a retired Ossie factory worker, father, and grandfather.

The primary political trend is actually moving in a reverse direction, because in [the unified] system, the woman is tied to her pots and pans, and she has to raise the children. And it isn't any easier for her if she doesn't want to bear more children. Paragraph 218 [laws dealing with abortion] played an important role in the CDU [conservative Christian political party]—though, at least in some respects, [the party] had no choice but to take a positive position on that in the *Bundestag*.

Erich

After 1970, it was possible to get abortions in the GDR much as one would buy tomatoes in the supermarket.[7] I think this was good, because today it can be a problem for a young woman who gets pregnant unintentionally. It's not fair that abortion, this interruption of a pregnancy—abortion is such a gruesome word—is made difficult for women.[8]

Minister of Family Affairs Nolte supports the viewpoint that women should have children and that there should be no termination of pregnancies. She's an arch Catholic and follows the line prescribed by the Catholic church. There were vehement discussions in the *Bundestag* between her and those for the pro-choice position. This kind of law has no place in the twentieth century shortly before the millennium. Rather, it's an example of how we've taken a step backwards into the days of back-alley abortionists. In those days, many East German women went to Poland to have abortions, and, if they could, West German women went to Holland.

I know several women who had abortions here in Germany. Well, now a series of consultations has been mandated, but I don't think that there's anything wrong with that, even though each woman ought to be able to make decisions about her own body. She alone can decide whether she's in a position to have a child.

This counseling system is not really bad as long as it doesn't pressure people, as it does in Bavaria. Yes, you can refuse the counseling certificate, but it varies from state to state. After all, this is a federal system. But I think it's important that counseling is available [and that] it's a function of the state, that it's paid for by taxes—and that it's required before having an abortion. There are some situations where you can't think of any other solution until you talk it over with a third person.

Furthermore, Germany won't die out if we lift the abortion restrictions. No woman likes having an abortion, I think. An abortion is a really terrible experience for any woman. And if it's possible to avoid it, then one should at least give her the chance, even if at the moment she doesn't want the child. After all, these are therapists and psychologists counseling the women in these circumstances. I can't imagine that they would exert pressure on these women.

I'm basically opposed to pressuring women, telling them: If you have an abortion you are evil, you're bad, you are killing a life—in other words, the Catholic moral theology. I am a Protestant and I'm also homosexual. So I'm quite detached from the subject. But I have women friends with whom I've discussed this.

It's important that these consultations are true counseling sessions which delve into the woman's individual circumstances, including her psychological and intellectual situation. The moment a woman has to justify herself in front of a committee for an action that has no criminal intent and answer questions that deal with her intimate, personal life, she is turned into a virtual murderess. That's what would happen if the abortion were described as a criminal act, the killing of an incipient life.[9]

No court should be able to turn thumbs up or down, to decide. First, there should be the counseling, then it should be solely up to the woman. When all is said and done, the woman must be the one to decide, not the advisor. That is of prime importance.

Gerhard

Well, I'm not for the GDR abortion regulations, but I'm not in favor of the very strict laws that are being implemented in some of the German states. Perhaps it's a good thing that the laws are different from state to state here.

Of course, there are questions we haven't paid much attention to, for instance, the fact that there are always two parties involved, that the man also has a right to say something. This ought to be discussed. But the worst thing is that laws are usually made by men, and that men are making decisions about the rights of women.

Josephine

In the GDR there was the pill, free contraception. You didn't pay a penny for the pill; the doctor prescribed it for you; you got it. Today, you have to pay for it. After the *Wende*, actually in 1991, when the pill was no longer free, the first thing I did was to have myself sterilized. I was fully aware of what I was doing. And no doctor could dissuade me. Of course, they told me all sorts of stories: For God's sake, you're still a young woman! And I said, I'm not going to pay for contraceptive pills. I don't see why I should. I pay for health insurance, and as I see it, contraception is part of it. So for me, sterilization was the only way to go, because at that time, the operation didn't cost anything. Now it would be different; now I'd probably have to pay something for it.

KÄTHE

Käthe actually tried to get permission have an abortion in the GDR.

In 1969, when we realized that I was pregnant with a third child, I was totally shattered. I already had two small children, my husband was still attending the university, I was earning barely 300 Marks as a saleslady, and our apartment was too small, to boot. So I was unhappy, not about the child, but about our situation. And at that time, there was already a legal document that said: Women can put in a written application under special circumstances to have the pregnancy terminated within the first twelve weeks. But that was only a sort of "discretionary provision." They "can" help women, but it was always for health reasons.

So, I filled out the application and took it in. Five doctors were sitting there, a gynecologist, a pediatrician, a welfare doctor, a psychologist [only four specialists were mentioned]. They listened to me: limited living space, money, family, two small children. Everyone was for [the abortion], except the gynecologist. He was the sort of man who thinks: I'm the man and I decide, like the Pope. He said: No, this woman is healthy and she is going to have the baby. Since I was healthy and actually had only economic problems, they denied my request. And with that, my application was dismissed. I was to go home and resign myself to my fate. I was profoundly unhappy that no one had helped me, that no one wanted to help me. Well, so, we had our son, and today we're quite happy that we did. Looking back on it, it would have been a big mistake if we had gone through with it; we wouldn't have our son now.

KURT

Kurt is Käthe's husband.

Today, once again, you have to have a consultation. And I should add that the legalization did not result in a lowering of the birthrate, as occurred in the GDR when the birthrate showed a so-called pill-drop [*Pillenknick*—a crinkle, kink, or dip in the graphic representation of the statistics of the effect of the birth-control pill]. The moment women found out about the pill, the birthrate actually dropped.

FRIEDA

Frieda and her family are Catholic. One of her daughters had an affair with an Iranian exchange student.

On the whole, I'm for contraception—before it happens. We would permit that in any case, although it's not in the Catholic doctrine—in that respect we're revolutionaries. But we're against abortion. Our youngest granddaughter was born out of wedlock. When our daughter went to the doctor for a checkup, he asked her whether she wanted to keep it. We're proud that she decided to have the child. True, we weren't enthusiastic, you understand; that's obvious. But a child is a child; a child is a gift from Heaven. And this child is a gift from Heaven, too.

ERIKA

In the GDR, Erika went to work and it was possible for her to continue her education. In addition, she raised her five children.

I received my certificate of competency during GDR times. I was able to continue my education, and after my last certification, I became shift leader in the department store; I had a base pay of 640 Mark. That was the top salary. The department store manager got 750 a month. We were also on commission, and I worked the night shift for 7 Marks per night, and then 2.50 Marks on top of that for meals. So the additional pay came to 9.50 Marks a night, not including commissions. It worked like this: The commission was calculated on the basis of the total store sales and according to your salary, that is, according to a coefficient [of the base salary]. In those days, I calculated the commission myself. The higher your base salary, the higher the coefficient. I had 300 Marks in commissions. So altogether, I earned 940 Marks. That was a lot of money in the GDR.

Actually, we GDR women had to work, especially with our big family. We would have starved [*Wir hätten schwarze Zähne bekommen* (We would have gotten black [rotten] teeth)] if we had had to live on one salary. I couldn't have raised our five children even with government child allotments.[10]

PETRA

Petra is a university graduate with a doctorate in library research. After the unification, she was responsible for feminist research.

Some women from the West who were working on research projects came here looking for literature on their subjects and for people to interview. These were short-term projects that ran for only six months or one year. We got to know many of these women. Most had no children and hadn't completed their university studies, yet they were about the same age we were. And they were very surprised by us. Most professionally established women in the West had written their dissertations and decided not to have children. They kept asking: How did you manage it? It was a shock for them. They didn't have the same government support, and couldn't imagine studying at the university without having to support oneself—being able to dedicate oneself exclusively to four years of study and completing a research project. They thought this was paradise.

But after the *Wende*, many women at Humboldt University lost their jobs. All the professorships and chairs were to be reassigned, and anyone—regardless of where they came from—could apply for the positions and the new faculty could bring their entire non-professorial teaching staff with them. Whereas there had been many women on the non-professorial [research and] teaching staff in the GDR, many of the new staff people were men; so the total number of women was greatly reduced. That was a bad experience.

It was interesting to see how the visiting Western women accepted us East German women. Our university status relationship played a role in this. One always has to take all that into account at a university. Before, we never felt that so much.

JOSEPHINE

Josephine followed her husband-to-be from Sachsen to Berlin when he was assigned to a post nearby during his military training. She found employment and living quarters. The couple married and soon had a daughter.

We were married in 1978. It was love. For me, nothing else existed. My husband was stationed in Berlin, at the barracks in Adlershof, and I followed him and built a life for myself here. I looked for a job. The agricultural college in Berlin Wartenberg hired me and at first we lived in the dormitory because there were no apartments to rent in GDR times. But our single room soon became too small for us.

So I put an ad in the paper and found work and a real two-room apartment. At that time, we weren't married yet, but we could have this apartment only if we were married.

At the end of the '70s, when new housing developments were supposed to be built in Berlin, workers were drawn from all over. I [left
my job at the agricultural college and] was hired by a cooperative to
whom new apartments were made available in Marzahn. And the boss
said: Okay, we'll make a "Berlin initiative" out of it and you can have
a two-room apartment immediately, but you have to get married, otherwise we can't do it. I said: Okay, filled out the paper and got the
apartment.

We wanted to get married anyway. So it didn't matter whether it
was required or not; I was still madly in love then. It was nice. It was
a very small wedding, nothing much—not a real wedding. We just said
our "I do's" and went to eat a little something, and that was it. My
parents could never have arranged more for us, and we didn't have
much money either. My in-laws offered us money, but then we would
have had to do what they wanted. That's the only reason they offered
us the money, and I fought against that with all my might. I didn't
want all their communist friends sitting there at my wedding table,
and my "poor parents" having to sit among all those Reds. I didn't
want to do that to myself, and I didn't want to do that to my parents.

I don't know this for sure, but I think my husband somehow got
some money from his parents in spite of all that, without my knowing
about it. What he did with it, I don't know. Have no idea.

At the time, he was quite happy that, due to my resourcefulness, he
wouldn't have to go back to live with his parents after he got out of
the army. Because if I hadn't pushed for us to get away [and hadn't
found an apartment], he would have gone back there again, that's for
sure. And I found him a job in Berlin. He was happy to have a wife
who took care of everything. At that time, I didn't yet see things the
way I do now. I only became a thinking person after my divorce.

In 1980, my daughter was born. I became a housewife and felt
totally hemmed in. I felt I couldn't grow in this marriage. My life
became [too much like] the experience I had when I was young—
always having to be there as a [quasi] housewife, taking care of my
siblings whether I wanted to or not. That hadn't satisfied me in my
youth and it didn't satisfy me in my marriage. And because of that, I
quarreled with my husband. He demanded that I do this and that
because I was at home and he was working. He was young then, only
twenty-three or twenty-four, but when he came home, he expected
me to fetch his slippers. Well, I have an aversion to waiting on people
unconditionally. Always have had it. So, I pushed for a divorce.

After the divorce, he suddenly bought himself a car. As long as we
were together, we never had enough money to buy a car. I thought
this was very strange.

I had to pay a large part of the divorce costs; and because this apartment had been our marital apartment for the last four years, it was bare after that. We had bought the furniture on marital credit. In the GDR, you'd get married and then there'd be this marital credit of 5,000 Marks, I think. That was a lot of money. Today, 5,000 Marks sounds quite different than it did in those days. At that time, I earned 400 Marks net, and so 5,000 Marks was a tidy sum of money, and with that we could buy an armoire and a bed, and so we bought some things. And then we got divorced, and the question was: Who would pay back the loan? The one who kept the furniture, of course. I would have had to pay him for the furniture—except for the child's things. He wasn't allowed to empty the child's room, that was prohibited by law. But how was I to pay him? I had a child and no job because I didn't have day care for her. The alimony and the state support for the child came to, I think, a total of 250 Marks after the divorce. Of that, I had to pay 50 Marks rent and a little for electricity and gas. All of that was cheap. The relative costs were different than they are today. In spite of that, I could never have bought anything for myself. So he kept the furniture.

And still, I was very happy because I was free. I still loved my husband as a human being, but I was bogged down as long as I was with him. All chances for my development had come to a standstill; I didn't advance professionally. I had become just a housewife, actually just like my mother. I had to do whatever my husband wanted. I cooked and baked and washed and went shopping with the money he gave me, and after my six months of paid child leave were over, we had only his money to live on. There was nothing left over for me. I couldn't buy shoes for myself; I couldn't even go to the beauty parlor any more. I couldn't do anything anymore; I had to beg [for anything for myself]. And he wanted to know why I wanted to buy such and such, and then he'd look at it and say: No, that won't do. We had continuous conflict. I had to subordinate myself. To buy things, I had to ask for permission from him, my husband, whom I loved and who loved me, the father of our child. Who was he to give me permission—or not—to buy something? It just wouldn't do for him to tell me: You may not.

Even before the divorce, after the baby money stopped coming in, I found some work to do at home. But I was allowed to do that only when he wasn't there. The typewriter clatter bothered him if I worked when he was at home. As the dispute worsened, I denied myself to him sexually, because I said: No, if you dictate what I'm supposed to wear and what I can buy for myself, then I don't want to anymore. He didn't like that. So I filed the divorce papers and pushed them through.

Then, my ex-husband married an older woman who couldn't have children any more. And they really wanted my child. He said to me:

You can produce another child. And I said: You must be out of your mind. I can't produce a new child and give away my daughter—our daughter.

DOROTHEA

Dorothea divorced her husband and was left with two children to support.

After my husband started his own firm and was doing business in the millions of Marks, he became impossible to deal with. I had two children, and in 1984, I asked for a divorce. He never made any support payments. And this state, the Federal Republic, made things easy for him. They're always talking about the good social protection they have. Well, that's nonsense. When it comes to paying child support, a man can get away with anything, as long as he does it cleverly.

So, I raised the children by myself without any support payments. He often came to visit and in front of friends and acquaintances he'd put thousands of Marks on the table, to show how much he had—twenty or thirty thousand Marks—just to show he could escape the clutches of the government, give them the slip. And I must admit he succeeded in doing that. In any case, he didn't get much out of it because he died in 1995. He simply dropped dead on the way to work, surely from too much smoking and drinking over the years.

My mother would have preferred that I stay married to my husband and let him do whatever he wanted. For her, the main thing was that I not get so emancipated, that I remain a protected little girl. But that couldn't be.

Käthe

In the GDR, a mother received government support if she wanted to stay home: 90 Marks for one child, more for the second, and still more for the third. Some women had so many children by foreigners that they didn't have to work. Having children in the GDR was like a small industry. With three or more children, they were in clover. They got paid for it and didn't have to repay any marital credit.

In my family, I saw with my own eyes what happened to my sister-in-law in the West. She stayed home after the birth of her twins and the only thing she did was raise the children. The first time I was there and saw how the women simply couldn't manage with their children, I thought, something is lacking there. My sister-in-law couldn't keep a schedule and I saw only chaos in these two children. At home, we scheduled the family's activities because we had to—breakfast at 9 A.M., lunch at noon, then naptime. My sister-in-law didn't have that and to have some peace she let them have their way. As a woman, she couldn't get out of the house. She was either in her room or in the village taking the children for a walk. She wasn't able to talk with many adults, the way we did when we went to work.

I lived with four men—my husband and three sons—and I had the upper hand. Certainly I didn't beat them, but once in a while there might be a slap when I said: Time to clean up. I'll wait an hour and if the closet isn't put in order. . . . For God's sake, they'd say. Because they knew what would happen: [If they didn't put it in order, I'd] open the closet door, reach all the way into the back, pull everything out on the floor, [and create] chaos in the room. Then I'd close the door to the room. And then I knew that they'd either put things away or they'd leave them as they were—and most of the time they put them away.

Erich

I think it's very important that a parent be there for the children. It doesn't matter whether it's the father or the mother. But it's bad when both parents work ten hours a day and the children have a nanny, or their grandma or an au pair girl or, as in the GDR, the day nurseries where tiny babies grow up without their parents. In my opinion, when a couple has a child they have to decide which of them will take care of the child. Most of the time, it's the woman because the man can't nurse the baby. I think a child should have one person it's very close to, if it has loving parents. I know one case where it is the husband. The woman had her doctorate and he was still a student. Someone cared for the child while he was in class, but he would rush home afterward to raise his children because his wife was working.

But I also know a man with a pretty steady job who's now taking baby leave for a year so he can take care of his child. I assume that later on he'll be able to get his job back. His wife is a teacher and is going back to work in August. Actually, you're allowed to stay home two years. And a woman friend of mine who had a career and earned a good salary gave up her job when her child was born. Now she says it's really nice not to have to work. In the GDR, you could get six months' paid maternity leave, but even without pay, she enjoys staying home with her little child. She says she doesn't want to leave him with a stranger, to subject him to such stress.

She wants to take care of her son, and I think this is better than the state saying, with feigned solicitude: We'll take care of the children. For me, it was important to be close to my mother as well as to my father who also tried hard to take care of me. That's my personal opinion. But I don't want to force my opinion on anyone, because many people don't want to stay home at all; they find it boring.

Käthe

Typically, parents today—who come home stressed from their jobs— are content to have their children occupy themselves somehow, watching television, perhaps. It's bad that they simply have too little time for their children.

The GDR rested [its hopes] on its children, and many things were geared toward children. You could see that the institutions taking care of these children were well equipped. Maybe they didn't have all those modern toys, but the children were happy even without computers and video games.

Kurt

Well, you also have to look at leisure time and the way one arranges one's life. Today, there are completely different opportunities for people. For example, when a husband goes bowling, I can imagine the woman saying: You go, [I don't want to go bowling], I want to do such and such. Before, however, we would sit together as a family and say: Now we'll do such and such together and, on the whole, we didn't even look for an alternative.

NOTES

1. Claudia Nolte, *Das Gleichberechtigungsgesetz des Bundes: Ein Gesetz für Frauen und Männer* [The federal law for equal rights: A law for men and women] (Bonn: Bundesministerium für Familie, Senioren, Frauen und Jugend, 1995), p. 5.

2. Karl-Heinz Eberhard and Wolfram Marx (eds.), *Familiengesetzbuch sowie angrenzende Gesetze und Bestimmungen: Textausgabe* (Berlin: Staatsverlag der Deutschen Demokratischen Republik, 1989).

3. Christiane Ochs and Brigitte Stolz-Willig, Wie im Westen, so auch auf Erden? Zur Situation von Frauen in den neuen Bundesländern. In Dirk Nolte, Ralf Sitte, and Alexandra Wagner (eds.), *Wirtschaftliche und soziale Einheit Deutschlands: eine Bilanz* (Cologne: Bund Verlag, 1995), pp. 329–351. "[I]n spite of multiple measures taken to encourage women, the typical features of a job market split along gender lines existed in the GDR too: Much as in the old Federal Republic there were 'male' and 'female' professions and an excessive proportion of women were overqualified for the work they were doing, their professional chances of advancement were lower than those of men, and their average earnings were less than those of men" (p.

331); *Fünf-und-siebzig Jahre Frauen Wahlrecht* [75 years of women's voting rights] (Bonn: Bundesministerium für Familie, Senioren, Frauen und Jugend, 1995). "Among 333 delegates there were 53 women in the '*Provisorische Volkskammer*' (Provisional Parliament) elected under such [manipulated] circumstances in 1949. That is 16.1 percent. The first German *Bundestag* (the Lower House of Parliament) elected in 1949 by free and secret ballot had 410 delegates, 29 of them were women; that is 7.1 percent. The proportion of women . . . increased continually [up to] 20.5 percent . . . in the first joint German Bundestag" (pp. 5, 7).

4. Gesine Spiess, Vater Staat und seine ungleichen Töchter [Father State and his unequal daughters]. *Aus Politik und Zeitgeschichte* 41–42, 2 (October 2, 1998): 44–46. "The equal rights policies of the GDR made it possible for women to link career and family work. . . . Women felt they had equal rights . . . they had social support. . . . [In spite of that] the inequality of the sexes was systematic, but there was no awareness of it in the GDR" (p. 44).

5. Ibid. "What the West German women's movement achieved among other things was a new political awareness on the part of women." As a result, power in the public domain, sexist use of language, safe houses for abused women, and self-help groups emerged as the themes and practical achievements of the West German Women's Movement.

6. Ibid. "The gender question has its own dimension: a patriarchy . . . counts on women who, through their unpaid family and relationship work, make possible the paid work of men" (p. 46).

7. Rolf Altenhof and Eckhard Jesse (eds.), *Das wiedervereinigte Deutschland: Zwischenbilanz und Perspectiven* [Reunited Germany: Interim balance and perspectives] (Munich: [no publisher given], 1995). "Ever since 1972 GDR citizens were accustomed to a law permitting the termination of pregnancy in the first three months. This was one of the few niches in which the otherwise ever-present GDR state allowed its citizens a little 'freedom' " (p. 156).

8. Herbert Tröndle, *Strafgesetzbuch und Nebengesetze* [Book of criminal statutes and additional laws] (Munich: n.p., 1997). "Whoever terminates a pregnancy will be punished with imprisonment of up to three years or with a fine. Acts whose effect occurs before the fertilized egg is lodged in the uterus are not considered terminations of pregnancy. . . . The offense described in #218 is not committed if the [pregnant woman] . . . has submitted a certificate to the doctor according to #219 showing she has had counseling at least three days before the operation" (pp. 1110, 1116).

9. Renate Sadrozinski, *Die Ungleiche Praxis des #218* [The dissimilar application of #218] (Cologne: Heinrich Böll Stiftung, 1990). "Doctors make a decision about the termination of the pregnancy after a 'medical finding.' . . . The actual situation is characterized by sharp political confron-

tations that are being pushed forward on the one side by the Catholic church with the support of Protestant groups and various reactionary parties. On the other side . . . PRO FAMILIA . . . has pleaded that the senseless compulsory consultation and the humiliating grounds for the termination of pregnancy (*Indikationenstellung*) be given up and that the freedom to decide be guaranteed to women" (pp. 12–13).

10. 2.-2.-Rechtsvorschriften auf dem Gebiet der Förderung und Unterstützung von Ehe und Familie [Laws to promote and support marriage and family], 2.7. Verordnung über staatliches Kindergeld [Decree regarding state-funded child support], #1 and 2, in *Familiengesetzbuch* [Book of Family Law] (Berlin: Staatsverlag der DDR, 1989). Citizens and permanent residents working in the GDR receive monthly child support for their children under sixteen or until the completion of the tenth grade; 50 Marks for the first, 100 Marks after the second, and 150 Marks for three or more children. This support continues even when a child is earning money as an apprentice or other remunerative work, provided he or she attends school (pp. 74–75). Special rent subsidies and larger apartments are provided for large families (*kinderreich*, rich with children). Additional benefits accrue to single parents.

7

Youth on Their Way

Emphatically, youths are of the opinion that the "city fathers" should without delay make such decisions as will improve the life of youths.[1]

Kind man, he gives me my food
  I'll always be grateful!
Pity, I cannot embrace him!
  Because I am this man.[2]

It's just about over with the Scouts—the *Pfadfinder* and the *Wandervögel*—though today's youths do go camping. It's all over with the political youth groups, despite the youth's participation in the opposition movement that led to the Wende.[3]

The German youth movement has a two-hundred-year history, beginning with the *Sturm und Drang* (Storm and Stress) reaction to rationalism and its emphasis on nature, feeling, and emotion. Youth was seen as embodying the power of nature. This era was followed by the *Romantische Jugend* (romantic youth) characterized by passionate religiosity or unrestrained sexuality. The *Wandervögel* movement was at its height at the beginning of the twentieth century. Its members took pleasure in a closeness to nature and their connection with each other and the group. They hiked, were sporty, and strove to be hardy, to toughen themselves, much as might be required of soldiers.

In the 1920s the religious counterpart to the *Wandervögel*, the *Bündische Jugend* sprang up in the Catholic Church. To the *Bündische Jugend*, life was the celebration of creation. However, in the 1930s, this movement became vulnerable when, just a few months after Hitler came to power, democratic, socialist, and communist youth organizations were banned, and Jewish youth organizations were strictly monitored by the central agency, the *Reichsausschuβ*. All youth hostels and the entire German youth were placed under the supervision of a Nazi Youth Leader, *Reichsjugendführer* (Baldur von Schirach), whose goal it was to imbue the young with Nazi ideology and to prepare them for battle, because "with pacifist . . . phrases we shall not reconquer our positions in the world."[4] Membership in the *Hitlerjugend* became mandatory. Girls and boys were separated and organized according to age groups. The youngest boys were called *Pimpfe;* the next oldest, 10–14, were the *Deutsches Jungvolk (DJ);* and the 14–18 year olds were the *Hitlerjugend (HJ)*. Ten to 14 year old girls were the *Jungmädelbund (JM)* and the 14–18 year olds were the *Bund Deutscher Mädel (BDM)*. As a group, the Hitler Youth was enthusiastic, easily seduced, fanatic, and willing to sacrifice for Hitler and their country (*Führer and Vaterland*).

After World War II, Western youth gravitated toward the existentialism of Camus and Sartre and became the skeptical nihilistic intellectuals. Generally, youth had lost their direction in the 1950s, but the 1960s brought a response of the Marxist protest movements and the splitting into the forces of evil and good—captialist and socialist. There were groups of disciplined, paramilitary, nature-oriented heroes who gathered in tents to sing proletarian battle songs. In contrast, the anarchistic, antiauthoritarian groups were culture oriented and strove toward sexual liberation without guilt. In the East, the *Freie Deutsche Jugend (FDJ)* supplanted the *Hitlerjugend* and took over the Nazi methods of organizing and indoctrinating the country's youth, albeit the ideology was now Marxist-Leninist instead of National Socialist (Nazi). Instead of white shirts and black pants or skirts, the FDJ wore their blue shirts.[5]

The long preparation for technically demanding jobs in the second half of the twentieth century necessitated a prolongation of youth until close to age thirty years. This generation aimed—and were delegated to—do things better than their parents, to win the battles of life that their (Nazi and Communist) parents had lost. They became softer. Once again, they valued friendship, home, and nature. With the decline of the birthrate in recent years, youth has become spoiled.[6]

How it once was, the parents and grandparents are happy to tell.

WILMA

Wilma, whose son is an adult now, says:

I have the impression that children today are left to themselves more. I see too many youths hanging out in the street, too many hooligans. More was available to them in the GDR, places where young people could meet, and the schools are not so organized now. If one wants one's child to have an activity, one has to take care of it oneself and pay.

JOHANNA

Johanna explains:

Still, a lot of independent enterprises have sprung up that engage children in particular activities. These are not organizations one belongs to all one's life. They're simply programs ranging from educational museum programs to vacation programs. They're open groups in the sense that one doesn't pay dues and isn't obligated to attend. But all those groups like *Wandervögel* or the nature clubs or Greenpeace always have children's divisions, and many, many children join them. Most kids go to sports. Nowadays, there are private soccer teams and exercise programs, but none of that is equivalent to what was available before.

Wilma

Above all, there should be more public agencies where young people could turn to an adult when they have problems they don't want to discuss with their parents. It's a fact that, beginning at a certain age, teenagers model themselves after their peer group more than their family: hairstyles, speech, how to behave with girls or boys. The group decides that. Kids look for similarities, and that's often underestimated.

So much was shut down, *kaputt*, because of lack of funds. Before, the state funded youth clubs and partially funded recreational activities such as table tennis, movies, discotheques. Get-togethers [*Jugendtreffs*] were scheduled in the evening for 14–16 year olds and at night for 16–18-year-olds until midnight. Now, when a private enterprise sponsors something like this, a chaperone has to be hired. How many places will do that? It's an investment. I believe, though, that the youth club in Berlin-Marzahn was renovated.

The youths do make use of certain social work services. They're not so bad, the youths. They have their needs and they want to have something offered to them. Many want to learn a trade, but that's a problem, because these small and middle-sized concerns don't take apprentices. How can these businesses be induced to train more youths, so that we get them off the streets?[7]

If I had anything to say about it, I would first see to it that all the unemployed who don't have an apprenticeship would be trained somewhere, such as in a vocational center like the one for the skilled trades in Berlin. Then they could apply to go to the developing countries.

HORST

Horst, a grandfather, has retired from the GDR armed services. He was a member of the Hitler Youth as well as the Free German Youth, its GDR successor. His impression is:

The Nazis really understood how youths behave in groups, girls as well as boys. They managed to make the program entertaining for all the age groups. [There were *Pimpfe*, "squirts," that is, the 10–14-year-old boys in the *Jungvolk*, the young people's Hitler organization, and the *BDM (Bund Deutscher Mädel)*, Association of German Girls.] The boys were prepared for war through play, so to speak—through sports and training, and teaching about weaponry The girls, in turn, took courses in cooking, embroidery, crocheting, and child care.

Later, I found that all the humanistic principles I had developed by that time were implemented in the FDJ (Free German Youth). Nothing was strange to me: the social evenings, the education, the consultants who came in with useful information. We had first-rate people. The HJ (Hitler Youth) methods and form—the same style but not the HJ content—were continued. By the way, we used the *Hitlerjugend* premises for our meetings. It was still standing, was furnished, and we were familiar with it. We didn't experience it as an inconsistency. The sense of inconsistency and contradiction came later, when it became such a one-sided [socialist-propaganda] thing. But I say that with hindsight.

WILLIE

Willie, also a grandfather and a retired GDR policeman, is about the same age as Horst. He remembers his youth in Nazi Germany, the end of the war, and the years following.

Many of the older generation bad-mouthed us youths—said it's our fault, the whole war, the persecution of the Jews, it's our fault that the people were murdered. I said: Why? In 1933 I was two years old. I didn't vote for Hitler; you voted for Hitler and you went to war. I was still a child; I wasn't in the war; I didn't do anything.

I joined the FDJ voluntarily—many in our generation did. Under the Nazis, it had been compulsory. Every Wednesday and every Saturday at three o'clock, I had had to appear for HJ duty, always two hours, three P.M. to five P.M. Every Wednesday and every Saturday we had to march. They made us join, but we gladly participated. My father didn't force me; actually, he wasn't for it. But I was. I liked being in the *Jungvolk*. Liked to sing, to march, because that was the German Education, turning children into soldiers. We played scouting games, one team of boys against another. Lie down, seek cover, jump up, run. It was fun. I wanted to become a soldier.

And then, in 1945, we had to build a new Germany. The young were enthusiastic. The war was over; we were glad: no more murder, no more American flyers coming over to bomb us. Everyone helped. In the FDJ, the accordion player stood up front; the rest of us built. We searched for bricks among the ruins, cleaned and shaped them, all the while singing and making music. It was different from the *Hitlerjugend*—much more voluntary, much more pleasant. We had dance evenings in the FDJ.

MONIKA

Monika, Willie's daughter, was skeptical:

Dance evenings? That was different, that was a different era. When we were that age, discos started. They were organized by the school and held in different houses, all over, but they were never organized by the FDJ. If the FDJ had organized such activities, we might have gone. But we were forced to go and all they ever talked to us about was politics—always so single-minded. They always ran down capitalism. That's why the FDJ was such a drag.

The youth organizations had to march, to demonstrate, and now they're fed up with it. They don't want to be organized any more. They never wanted to be in the first place. It was really forced on them.[8]

Personally, as a child, I didn't like those group things at all. I always tried to get out of them. It was just a burden to me. Not that it was so terrible, or that it hurt me. It was just a nuisance. But imagine the consequences if I had not joined in! It never occurred to us to say no. I thought wearing a uniform was impossible; running around with those FDJ shirts was no fun. We stuffed them in our book bags, put them on at roll-call, took them off again, and threw them in some corner. Then we went on with our lives. *Na*, my son doesn't join groups either, and my daughter makes music. She's learning to play the guitar, though that's in a group.

JOSEPHINE

Josephine also grew up in the GDR. She says:

Well, I don't really have bad memories, not of the Pioneers [*Pioniere*, the younger FDJ members], anyway. In fact, I still have my identity cards with a photo, [which I keep as a souvenir of] the way I looked then. That's part of my history. Pioneers, *ja*, that was simply fun; it was a diversion. We just played a lot, because it hadn't yet become so political. There was big difference between the villages and the cities. In the village we had more freedom, at least that's how I experienced it. We had the woods, the meadows, water—we could do a whole lot more than the children in town.

The FDJ didn't start 'til eighth grade, with preparation for the initiation rites [The *Jugendweihe*, the secular, political initiation into adulthood, taking the place of a religious confirmation]. I remember that it became very political then. We had to visit the concentration camps, we had to view an incredible number of war films; and in school, in history class, we had to study all about the war en masse. It was a huge subject. And I always refused to visit the concentration camps. I never went along.

Personally, I find it repulsive that depictions of the cruelties that man inflicts upon man are shown again and again and that young people have to view them over and over again. This horrible war had been glorified in so many films, and I didn't want to see the terrible things that were done to people. I didn't want to watch how Germans—from whom I descend—annihilated other peoples.

It pained me as a child and it pains me today. It doesn't matter whether one is a Pole, or a Czech, or a Russian, or anyone else. One is a human being. And no matter what the atrocities one human being perpetrated on another, it should not be packaged in a film. And the reconstruction of the concentration camps? That's just too much! Too much!

Yes, it gives the youth every opportunity to get their hands on this "brown" [a reference to the brown uniforms of the Nazi SA, *Sturm Abteilung*, the storm troopers] material and to bring it back to life, to use it for their own "brown" goals. We wouldn't have this hate of foreigners and these frightfully high rates of hate crimes, and skinheads and boots, this attire. Where does it come from? It's Nazi-like. They are so fascistic and have this fascistic material and the "brown" frame of mind—that's all because they can view the original through this mandatory history lesson, through keeping alive the images of the concentration camps.[9]

The story is never laid to rest. It shouldn't be forgotten, of course, but it isn't right to show it over and over again.

So I refused to go and then there were these political discussions in the FDJ group: Why didn't you come along? Why did you do that? *Na ja*, I reported sick after that—one develops tricks like that. Finally, I realized, what could they do to me? Lock me up? They could come to get me, perhaps with the police. But they never did.

Instead of viewing atrocities, I did other things in the FDJ. We had to do some kind of community service, some reconstruction, taking care of the elderly, or collecting used materials; the GDR recycled old stuff, and it's not so bad to benefit the environment a bit, relieve it of some garbage. I thought this was great, swell. And it was all right with me to clean the public spaces, something for the commonweal, where I could see that others were pleased, or it looked nice. But not that other nonsense.

The school systems in the German Federal Republic (GFR) and the German Democratic Republic (GDR) resembled each other in their organization but differed markedly in their policies of admittance to higher educational programs, curricula, the names of the schools at all levels, and the availability of pre-school programs.

The emphasis in the GDR on early marriage and more than two children per family coupled with women's vocational activities made day-care facilities for babies, the *Krippe*,[10] an absolute necessity. Both the GFR and the GDR had kindergarten facilities, although they were not as numerous and not free of charge in the West. Both East and West had primary schools *(Grundschule)* from grades one to four, with additional supervised after-school activities, the *Hort* (shelter), in the GDR. In the East, this was followed by the polytechnical high school *(Politechnische Oberschule)*, that extended through the middle-school years through the first two years of high school (*mittlere Reife* [middle (level of) maturity). Education through age sixteen was compulsory and could be followed either by additional years of academic studies at an expanded high school (*erweiterte Oberschule*) or an apprenticeship with work-related part-time studies. The corresponding middle and high schools in the West were called *Realschule* and *Gymnasium* (sometimes specialized into humanistic or scientific studies [*humanistisches* or *naturwissenschaftliches Gymnasium*]). In both the GDR and GFR, the final high school examination, *Abitur*, was, and is, a prerequisite for admittance to the university and represents approximately junior college status in the United States. In the GDR, school performance was not the determining criterion for continuation at the expanded high school, sitting for the *Abitur*, and enrolling at the university. Children of working-class or farming families were given preference and later, the determinant was political loyalty.

PHILIP

Twenty-year-old Philip studied these historical themes only after the unification.

I took an advanced-standing world politics course. We studied the Nazi period for one semester. It was interesting. It's one of my favorite topics in history, and I'm still reading about it, especially Hitler and the SS-State [*Schutzstaffel*]. That was in secondary school. I think they didn't introduce it before because it's too hard for a thirteen-year-old to grasp. At that time, we studied the Romans. That's how it was set up.

I had a young teacher from the East. She leaned toward the Christian Democrats, very middle of the road. Jews were primarily spoken of, then the Social Democrats. We spoke about the Communists very infrequently; they were presented mostly as losers who did everything wrong. A lot depends on who the teacher is.

Later on, we had a lesson about the election, because it was right around the time when Berlin and Brandenburg were voting on whether to join and form a *Land*. And the next year, we spoke about the *Bundestag* election and that's when it came out that she votes CDU, that she's very conservative. If a different teacher had given the course, we might have delved more deeply into the Communists.

Otto

Otto did not have to read about the war or view films to inform himself. He experienced the war in person as a child.

Before I was old enough to join the FDJ—yes, even before the FDJ existed—my family was directly affected by the Nazi atrocities. I was here in Berlin with the exception of two years. When the bombings began, pupils, especially the elementary classes, were evacuated to protect them from the air raids. And I was put up on a large farm in the protectorate of Böhmen-Mähren. It was the best time of my childhood, but it was soon over. I was called back to Berlin—I know now that my father didn't want to leave me there because the farmer was also the district leader of the NSDAP [*Nationalsozialistische Deutsche Arbeiterpartei*, National Socialist German Workers Party, the official Nazi party], and my father was not a friend of the Nazis. Then the Russians came. For my mother and me, it was a great relief, a liberation.

It was 1945, I was eleven years old and was immediately hospitalized with scarlet fever. My mother had shingles. The city was flattened. I came out of the hospital, it must have been August, because the Western Allies had already moved in. My mother weighed less than 65 pounds, had lost her hair. I didn't recognize her, didn't want to believe she was my mother, just as I didn't want to believe that my father was dead, that the Nazis' verdict of capital punishment had really been carried out. I always believed that my father would come back sometime; anyway, I believed it for a long time as a child.

Some men did come back, among them three communists who used to meet at my parents' apartment during the Nazi-time. One died shortly afterward as result of his imprisonment. Another was very sickly until the '80s, never completely recovered. One was indomitable. These were my father's friends. They had one thing in common: they hadn't lost their spirit and they openly declared they were communists. So I also became a communist.

Horst

As a schoolboy, Horst believed that Fascism did offer some solutions.

We were taught that we were a people lacking space, while other *Völker* had a lot of space, but lacked people—like the Soviet Union, for example. It was simply amazing, this theory. And in school they showed us these maps, where Russia was pink and Germany was just a little bit of green with many black dots indicating how many people lived in one square kilometer. And over there, on the pink, there were hundreds of square kilometers with only one person living there. So I said to myself: A few people could settle there; they could work and farm. They told us: One could have a manor there because the land is available, just waiting for us Germans to settle it. Children have pretty naïve ideas—just like wanting to become locomotive conductors, or nowadays, astronauts.

But as a young adult, I was a founding member of the FDJ, because I came out of the war with the firm conviction that this must never happen again. I chose to take that path, thinking it represented the best humanistic traditions of Germany, the country in which I grew up. I decided to devote my energy to that. In the beginning, the FDJ was a liberal youth association that immediately met with great acclaim in this country. Later it adopted the official socialist position.

WERNER

Instead of turning to socialism, some young people, like Werner, chose religion.

My experiences vary. In the village, I willingly went to the Pioneers. They sang beautiful songs there, and I always liked folk music. That was for me! But afterwards, I had to bicycle every day to the district school where the FDJ met. That was rubbish! There, it was all politics, political pressure, which I tried to evade. I always learned quickly how to avoid things. I had an advantage over the others, because I didn't have to think about it first. I knew it was bad. It was easy to get out of it, because I was a commuter and couldn't go to just any evening meeting, as it would have been hard to return at night. Educationally, living in another town had disadvantages, but politically it was favorable. Of course, I attended a religious youth group, but secretly.

HILDE

Hilde's was a strict Catholic family. However, after her deportation from Czechoslovakia at the end of the war, she ceased going to church.

Church? No, no. That hardly would have been possible. I applied at the secondary school in Bautzen and the principal asked, Do you have any proof of having attended secondary school before? We had no papers, had taken along nothing, not even a birth certificate. Well, he admitted me provisionally and soon noticed that I could master the material.

From then on until 1950 I led a double life. In the mornings, I was a student and afternoons a farmworker. I was twelve years old and was put to work. I unloaded the turnips and helped harvest and thrash the grain. That was plenty hard for me, a rather small twelve-year-old.

In school, I was thoroughly indoctrinated with socialism and communism. One day, I returned from school and told my mother, You know, the Czechs were right to exile us, because we behaved terribly badly and it served us right. My mother nearly fainted. But youth know best—and it took a very long time for me to arrive at the correct point of view.

My mother refused to let me join the FDJ, but one year before my secondary school graduation, I joined anyhow. The worst of it was, I paid tuition before joining the FDJ. At that time, secondary schools still charged tuition, and we had to pay, even though my mother was a widow and single parent. However, as soon as I joined the FDJ, the tuition was waived and I even received a small monthly stipend.

I believed a lot of the ideology and we sang wonderful, beautiful songs—I respond to music. I was enthusiastic and would have liked to travel to Berlin to the *Weltfestspiele* [a sport event with political overtones, like a local Olympic festival] with the other young people, but my mother didn't let me. She kept me on a tight leash.

KURT

Kurt was born in Berlin in 1940. He, too, experienced the war in his childhood:

Our family was bombed out in Berlin, evacuated to Eastern Prussia, and returned to the Leipzig area in 1945. My father died in battle, and my mother was left with four little children. In 1955, she decided to leave East Germany, to go to the *Bundesrepublik*. I was fifteen years old and went with her, that is, she took me to Hamburg into a reception camp. I began to work in a wholesale concern and at nineteen completed my business apprenticeship. The whole thing left me completely dissatisfied, although I had every career opportunity there.

So, in November 1962, I decided to return to the GDR. That the

Berlin Wall had already gone up contributed a little to my decision, because I was already a political person.

Growing up, I had been in the young Pioneers as well as two to three years in the FDJ. The ideology was in my head, but as I had been brought up very religiously, I tried to remain in the Protestant Church—up to the point where I said: No, you have to decide; you cannot go on like this. So, I withdrew from the church and continued my studies. First, I completed my basic education, since I had interrupted my schooling after the eighth grade; then I took correspondence courses at the technical school in Dresden and graduated with the title of "economist for domestic trade."

WERNER

Werner was born during the Nazi time and attended school in the GDR.

In 1950, at age fourteen, I entered the *Oberschule* (secondary school), formerly called *Gymnasium*. First thing, during the first class, the teacher asked, Who among you is not a member of the FDJ? Besides me, there was one other student. Both of us had to stand up, and the teacher said, I expect that you will think about it carefully and join the FDJ, too. When I came home and told my mother, she immediately sent my brother to get an application form, which I filled out. Since we belonged to a discriminated-against group, it was difficult to be admitted to secondary school, then to university, and to take up certain professions. The mere fact that one was not an FDJ member aroused suspicion.

The discrimination had to do with church. It was generally known; we could be seen going to church every Sunday. During Nazi times, religious instruction was conducted in my parents' living room. The other thing was that my father was an independent artisan, another group that didn't quite belong. In the socialist state, independent enterprises were supposed to be abolished. In the GDR, the children of laborers and farmers were to be given educational advantages [a GDR version of affirmative action], and as we were neither a family of laborers nor of farmers, my chances were poor. So, I had to excel. I went to the FDJ. Only a formality such as that provided any protection.

ERNST

Ernst is a sensitive man. He tells of his difficulties and his unusual life experiences.

My mother was a housewife, my father a farmer. I was born in October 1938 and six months later, my mother married my stepfather. I appreciate that greatly, very, very greatly. He was a very kind man and still means a lot to me.

I found out late in my childhood that he wasn't my real father. That was a terrible, terrible childhood trauma. While playing with other children, I found out by chance that my real father was someone else and that everything I had believed was all wrong. The whole village knew. Everyone knew, except for me.

My stepfather, whose name I carry, wrote letters to me from the front, letters that touch my heart: "My dear, sweet, little man." No one else said that to me. He wrote it and he meant it. He fell at the Russian front. Naturally, I saved the letters. I can't read them very often because I immediately become sentimental and Verdi's *Requiem* starts running through my mind. I can't do that too often; it hurts my soul. I'd like, more than anything else, to go to Yeltsin and say, let me go to Bilek Kowo, in the vicinity of Kubanbrückenkopf. There, in that cemetery, in this row. . . . Of course, there is no cemetery there anymore; grain is probably growing there, if anything is growing there at all. I'd like to go there and dig up his bones and inter them here. Yes, that's what I would like to do.

After that, my childhood went bad. My mother remarried and it was an awful time. This man, who then wanted to be my father, was an alcoholic who beat and humiliated my mother, and I suffered watching this as a child. I don't like to think back on those times. And in the GDR, it became worse and worse.

I attended secondary school, the *Gymnasium*, up to the tenth grade and then left. Emotionally I couldn't take what was happening at home. I became an apprentice in a cooperative, stayed there three years and then went to the LPG (agricultural service) [*Landwirtschaftliche Produktionsgenossenschaft, sowjetisch Kolchose*]. I didn't like it there either. After that, I went to the district church administration, because I was very religious, and I worked there as a bookkeeper. I was brought up very religiously. That is, I basically brought myself up, because my mother was totally preoccupied with other things. Jesus was everything to me. Nothing existed for me but the church.

My FDJ membership was only pro forma, because we also had instruction in the Association for Sport and Technology, where I discovered, to my horror, that I was the best shot with the small-bore rifles. I knew that good shots were inducted into the execution firing squad, to finish off soldiers who disobeyed orders. And that contributed to my refusal to serve in the military. I followed the Fifth Commandment, "You shall not kill," and reported as a conscientious objector.

That was even worse. They threatened me with imprisonment. But it didn't matter. I would rather have gone to prison. But then I had to go away to be treated for a skin ailment on my face and torso. When I returned, I lived with a clergyman's family, had a little room there. And they said to me: You have been saved; a special army group has been formed for religious people who do not want to swear the oath. They can take a vow instead, and do not have to bear arms. That was in 1964. I went there and found myself among like-minded people. That was a very, very wonderful time. For the first time, I came out of myself. In 1966 the army service was over.

After all that, I now have to cope with the fact that the baker where my son apprenticed went bankrupt, and it didn't work out for him at the police force either. So now, *my* son—the son of a conscientious objector!—is with the Bundeswehr, the federal armed forces.

Although given preference, not all children of laborers and farmers managed to attend the last three years of secondary school (roughly equivalent to American junior college) and institutions of higher learning, such as technical or business schools or universities.

Josephine

My parents worked full time throughout my youth. My father always worked two shifts, my mother alternated through three, so they seldom saw each other except on weekends. As the oldest child, I was responsible for managing the household, preparing meals, cleaning, and—not educating—but caring for the boys.

A great responsibility. I functioned; couldn't think about it. I didn't know that one could consider other possibilities. I simply functioned, because we did what my father said. He was brought up strictly and transferred that to us. Also, we didn't have a lot of money and the children simply had to help in the house and on our plot of land. We did a little farming—fruits and vegetables, chicken and rabbits—to augment our daily subsistence. Everybody had a job. I was the oldest and had to manage the whole thing.

There was a five-year age difference between the three children. When I left home at sixteen, my youngest brother was starting school.

Petra

My mother periodically had to travel on business, so we had to take care of ourselves, even when we were very young. It was good training for independence. We were held to high standards of performance and achievement.

PHILIP

Philip, Petra's son, also had to take care of himself and two younger brothers while his parents worked.

One brother is six years younger than I, another thirteen years younger. I took care of the little one a lot after the *Wende* because my parents were so busy. I had to pick him up at the kindergarten and then play with him. The other one, well, that's a typical brother-brother relationship. When we were younger, we fought, and now we avoid each other. Maybe in five years or so it'll be different. We'll see.

JOSEPHINE

Josephine became a mother. Her divorce left her a single parent, working for her living.

In the West, it was not customary to leave children to themselves. More often, the women stayed home or worked part time during school hours. Here mothers had to work an entire shift. I thought it was better here. If I had to do it all over again, I would still put my child in day care and work, not only for the money, but to develop myself further as a human being.

It's better for both the mother and the child, because a child develops better in a group than as an only child at home. Sure, some have siblings. I worked full time as a secretary, from seven in the morning to five in the evenings, so my poor child had to go to child care, but it didn't hurt her, not at all.

My daughter was lucky; she had a very loving kindergarten-auntie, a woman over fifty, who was sweet to the children and didn't dish out that political crap. They sang songs. She was a really terrific woman. Like a grandma.

At six o'clock I'd drop off my daughter. She got up at five and I picked her up at six in the evening. Then I gave her a sandwich [Hot meals were served midday]. At seven, she went to bed. So the child was in day care twelve hours—the first to arrive and the last to leave, so that even the staff asked whether I could pick her up earlier once in a while. Yes, but when? I had to work, had an hour's trip into the town center, to Friedrichstrasse.

Despite Josephine's commitment to child care and working mothers, not all went well.

Well, she regressed a lot. She started to wet her bed again. As a
baby, as a little child, she was toilet trained quite quickly and then she
wet herself again . . . and she cried steadily. So, she was finished, done
in; I couldn't do a thing with her. I took her to a therapist. To get a
shorter workday, one had to have a doctor's order, and that had to
be renewed every six months. From then on, I picked up my daughter
at three o'clock.

Now she's eighteen, an apprentice in her second year. She's learning
to be an interior decorator. She has friends, girls and also boys, from
her business high-school [*Realschule*] class. She's always on the go,
discos and movies.

PETRA

Since the unification, the school system has changed. Petra ascer-
tained that in the GDR at most 30 percent of all students were admitted
to the college preparatory high-school program (*Erweiterte Oberschule*
[*EOS*]). As of today, it has risen to 50 percent. Petra explains:

I was admitted because I had met all the conditions: exemplary performance, single mother, and my father had been in the army. Being
from the working class played a role. I had no difficulties.

FRIEDA

Frieda's husband is an academician; they are dissenters and church
affiliated. Their daughters were refused admittance to the academic
high school.

At the beginning of the republic [GDR], it was still terrible, but in
time the former working-class and farmer's children became academicians and their children, raised in a communist family, were no
longer working class. Discrimination against communist children was
impossible, so it evolved that the secondary school places were allo-
cated according to political involvement rather than class. That is how
it was.

WERNER

Werner, who had academic aspirations, experienced great difficulties because of his religion and his opposition to authority.

Since childhood, I have been in opposition to the GDR. People used
to say the school system was so very good. I never thought so. As has

become evident, the system did not educate people, did not form them; it *de*formed them.

I have realized that accumulating information is not of primary importance; usually, common sense is all that's required to understand something. I can remember my brother laughing at me when I brought home a report card on which the homeroom teacher wrote: Werner already can think logically. That was it. That's all one needed to get by in the GDR, though the bad thing about the GDR schooling was that they deliberately tried to squelch the logical thinking.

In 1954, after four years of secondary school the following occurred: One day, the classroom door opened and the principal walked in to announce that two students would not be admitted to the final exams. The first was the worst student in the class. Worst of all, he had failed Russian. I was the other one, the best in Russian. The other one did amount to something in the end; he became a veterinarian. A few years ago, at a reunion, we openly talked about the fact that I was the only one in the class who was politically discriminated against.

PHILIP

Philip, ten years old at the time of the unification, was by and large not aware of curriculum or teaching-method differences between the GDR and the GFR.

For me, it was a smooth transition, especially since I never knew how an EOS [*Erweiterte Oberschule*, a GDR "expanded" secondary school, which includes three years academic preparation for university studies] was organized or what happened there. I can't say how it would have been different in the GDR. There weren't any big problems.

Only a few students came to our school from the West when I was in the tenth and eleventh grades. At the time, the schools here were thought to be easier, that one could get a higher grade-point average. On the other hand, many young people from East Berlin went to schools in West Berlin because they thought it would help them get better jobs afterwards. But it didn't work out that way, unless it was a school with a special reputation, like the *Lessing-Gymnasium*.

It was difficult when a new student entered the class, but not because of east-west differences. It didn't matter where the new student came from, East Berlin, or another city, or another school—from Brandenburg, from Hessen, it's all the same. At the beginning, there was some arrogance, especially on the part of the west-students, but that didn't last long. I can't really put it into words. For example, a friend of mine called Wanja—he's Serbian—grew up in Wedding, moved to West Berlin when he was twelve, and entered the class just below mine in my last year of school. His adjustment was tops.

I was an exchange student in Sweden for a year. If I had lived in the GDR [If the GDR still existed . . .], I never would have been able to go to Sweden. Now, having passed my *Abitur* (final secondary-school examination), I want to study to become a social worker. I already work in a home for the mentally retarded and it gives me great satisfaction.

Josephine

We started with the applications in the tenth grade. We all got cards to fill out, had to record which trade or occupation we wanted to learn, and had to send out the card to a firm by a certain date. Then the firms selected which of us they wanted.

I wanted awfully much to become an architect and would have had to begin with drafting, a basic occupation, because I hadn't taken the *Abitur*. I couldn't take the *Abitur*, because my grades weren't quite good enough and because my parents didn't want me to. They couldn't afford it. They wanted me to earn money.

Schools were free, but if I had taken the *Abitur*, I would have had to continue school through the twelfth grade and would have been eighteen or nineteen and not had a penny. This way, as an apprentice, I at least would have pocket money, at that time sixty-five Marks for the first six months. My parents felt secure knowing that when the others finished their *Abitur* at nineteen, I would have finished my apprenticeship and would be earning my pay.

But I didn't get the architectural drafting apprenticeship; then I wanted at least to learn technical drafting as a basis for the manufacture of machines. I didn't get a place for that, either. Finally, the application phase was over and I was still without an apprenticeship. Then my father stepped in and asked his firm whether they could do something. So I ended up there.

Between sixteen and twenty-one, I had an apprenticeship. The public transportation from the village wouldn't have gotten me to work on time, so I lived with my *Oma*, my grandmother, in the next town. I apprenticed as a secretary. At the time, I didn't like it. Today, I do. In the meanwhile I've worked myself up. I'm now a salaried business employee [*kaufmännische Angestellte*].

HORST

Horst also attended the first level of secondary school; subsequently, instead of taking an ordinary apprenticeship, he went to the *Volkspolizei* (GDR "people's" police).

I attended secondary school until the *mittlere Reife* (the first level). Then, through the FDJ, I was offered the chance to join the armed forces of this country. I went to the *Volkspolizei*, later became a career officer, and retired as a colonel.

I assume that my generation had totally different life experiences. I now live in the third German state. Everyone has to be able to cope with his country in one way or another, or he has to leave. So, as their father, I believe my children are experienced and farseeing enough to know how to make their way. It was important to me not to handicap my children in any way. For example, it was customary for an officer's son to become an officer as well. Even before their *Abitur* time, the children would be recruited and asked to take courses in line with the state's wishes. The state gave them a stipend. It gave material benefits to students who had obligated themselves to enter officers' training school or a state-approved technical program, such as television electronics, radar, or aviation electronics. It was then possible to be employed as a ranking officer right after graduation. I did not do that with my son, although I had several such offers, and he did, too. I thought it was important that he study and work at what he thinks is right for him and what interests him.

SEVEN SECONDARY SCHOOL SENIORS

Secondary school seniors met as a group to discuss the Wende and the unification:[11]

HERBERT: In 1991, I was ten years old, in the fifth grade. I did hear about the GDR escapees in Hungary and about those who left via the Czech Republic. I mean, we heard it on the Western newscasts. Here in Berlin we were able to tune in to the *bundesdeutsche* television, four channels.

RALF: We didn't think it meant the end of the GDR.

MARGARETE: No, I hadn't expected it, either.

EDIT: No one did. No one worried about the possibility that the GDR wouldn't last. That probably wasn't clear to anyone. In retrospect I think there were some indications—after all, we did know about all the people who went to Hungary so that they could then go to Austria and then across into the GFR; or that the GFR Minister of Defense, Genscher, transported the people by train from the consulate in Czechoslovakia [*sic*] to Bavaria. We did see all that.

ALBERT: Yes, that registered with us. It registered and then there were huge fights, at least in some families, about who wanted to emigrate and who didn't. The families were often very divided. An exodus in that sense was out of the question for us, simply because I was too small and my brother was just about ending school. And who could have convinced him to take such a step, to forget the East?

In school, it was noticeable that many had left, that the classes were suddenly decimated a bit. But at that age, it was not such an interesting topic. They tried to indoctrinate us. I distinctly remember one conversation about the topic of leaving the country; they listed the families who could have fled, but who stayed because they "knew very well what was best for them."

ELLEN: Whether one says one is a GDR citizen depends on the parents, their attitude to the GDR.

HERBERT: My parents didn't take such a firm position. If I wanted to join the Pioneers, I could. In any case, one didn't go there with the idea that it was something political. Hey, one went to meet one's friends, to have a little fun.

ELLEN: I learned cooking and needlework in school.

HERBERT: We had woodwork. That was mandatory.

KRISTOF: True, but I'm not absolutely in favor of FDJ afternoons. My parents were opposed to my joining, but at the time, the education was different, and they explained to me that if I didn't run with the crowd, it would be difficult for me, that I would stand there like an outsider.

My older brother was in the FDJ. He had a lot of difficulties gaining admittance to the *Abitur* because we are religious. In the GDR, religion was not looked upon kindly, and when it became known, they put a lot of obstacles in my brother's way. I was not aware of all that at the time, because I was still so young. But from the beginning, my parents told me that I should not talk about certain things in school, that it wasn't anyone else's business and might get me into trouble. I didn't understand it, and I wanted to explain to my friends what I did every afternoon. And I did not understand that I should not talk about something that makes me different from others.

HERBERT: Yes, and now the FDJ afternoons and youth clubs are no more.

ELLEN: When the Wall came down, we were at an age when we were crazy about toys, because before, we could not have them. Unwittingly, our relatives made us envious. They had the toys, we didn't.

RALF: Without wanting to glorify, I believe the quality of the instruction in the primary school was better in the GDR than in the GFR. At the end of first grade, everyone knew how to read and write.

In that sense, the GDR system was more focused on scholastic achievement. Today, it's no longer like that, although this society is actually
more achievement oriented. [According to a teacher, West German
methods in the lower grades are more child-oriented and focused on
creativity and thinking; East German methods more rote- and fact-
oriented. By seventh grade, the children exposed to the more pro-
gressive methods have caught up and mastered the subject matter.]

The teachers in school are so careful in the way they go about things
. . . as if the pupils could hit them or something like that. One gets to
be like that—one gets run over. You're lucky if you get out of the
room in one piece. No respect!

HERBERT: In the GDR, we had to be quiet in school, to listen.

RALF: That's not conveyed in the primary school anymore.

MARGARETE: But now we have more opportunities after the primary
school. I have a cousin who studied in America for a year. Now she's
back and will take her *Abitur* next year.

IRENE

Irene wanted to study. She was courageous: she left her mother in
the west to attend the university in East Berlin.

I was born in West Berlin in 1928 and lived there before it was
divided into east and west. After 1945, I lived first in the far west of
Germany because that is where my mother had been evacuated. But I
returned to Berlin.

There was only one university then, the *Humboldt Universität*. They
offered preparatory courses for children who, for various reasons—
racial, political, financial—could not complete the *Abitur*. Working-
class and farmers' children, especially, took the preparatory courses, in
order to meet the standard and to begin higher education. I, too,
wanted very much to study to become a teacher, but didn't have the
Abitur. In West Berlin, I heard about the courses and applied. I was
admitted and caught up in one-and-a-half years, passed the *Abitur*,
and was able to begin my studies.

I was very happy about that. How often I thought about my friend's
grandfather! He learned gardening at a very young age, had to leave
school, not for lack of intelligence, but for lack of money. He was one
of thirteen children in a weaver's family and had to learn gardening
because that was the only work he could get. A baron, who had a
castle in the vicinity, needed a gardener and gave the boy a tiny room
in the servants' quarter. He had to be among the first to sweep the

park in the morning, but he did not have a watch, of course, so he never could have awakened in time. So they tied a string around his big toe, hung the string out of the window, and the night watchman pulled the string at four o'clock in the morning. That became part of the night watchman's job. So, get out of bed! That's how he was trained—with a string around his toe.

Those were different times, but we had our difficulties, too. In 1948, six months before my *Abitur*, there was the *Währungsreform*, the currency reform. The Westmark, the new Deutschmark, was introduced into the English, American, and French zones. And the Russian sector didn't participate. They were quarreling. Already the split was in the making.

So West Berlin had the Westmark but I received my stipend in Ostmark, because the university was situated in the eastern part of Berlin. At first it was all right; both currencies were in use. They pasted a "B" on it, and I could pay my rent, electricity, and such things. We bought our groceries in the east, where they had opened stores for West Berliners. There were about 60,000 people who worked in the east and lived in the west, which is actually quite normal in a big city.

That was the first time I took part in a demonstration, as one who was disadvantaged by the currency reform, because in the spring of '49, the Westmark became the sole, valid currency for all three west sectors. So I had no money. When the rent came due, I would go to my landlady and give her my money and she would give it back to me, saying: I don't want this money. I want money that is valid here. Then the gas was shut off, because I couldn't pay with the proper money.

I could have said: I'll do without my studies. But why? There were 300,000 unemployed in West Berlin at the time, so I would not have found work, either. I lived with my brother and he said: You know what? We'll move to the east sector. However, that required an exchange with two people who were willing to move west [*Kopftausch*]. It had to do with the availability of food. In December 1949, we really did move to East Berlin, without an inkling of what was to come. That's how I became an Ossie.

OTTO

Otto was also educated in the GDR, and he wishes that there had been greater opportunities for personal development.

The foundation of all the education in the GDR was Marxism-Leninism. And after the students had completed their higher education and left the university, they were wearing blinders. All creativity was compromised by the ideology. Some found it disturbing, despite having gone through the entire course of education. With some of them, this Marxist-Leninist indoctrination didn't quite take—it happens, that a student doesn't take in what the teacher tries to instill. Students like that felt that the ideology cramped them intellectually, as it did in their teaching or business activities. They wanted to go away. They thought: This country is not worth staying in. There's no chance to develop here. People aren't allowed to think, even though the state constantly demands that teachers educate children to think creatively. How can a teacher do that when the boundaries are always set by the ideology?

IRENE

Irene has not been brainwashed and is not wearing blinders.

I have an advantage. I was in the BDM, the FDJ, and then went to the university. Also, I was exposed to different ideologies in my family. My father was a communist, a great-aunt was completely committed to the Nazis, and my grandmother looked as if somewhere, long ago, one of her ancestors had been Jewish. I believe that gave me a fairly broad perspective. Afterwards, with my husband and children, a certain openness prevailed as well, because one cannot live by prejudice. And the grandchildren have also experienced two different states. They adapted. They're making their way.

NOTES

1. Jutta Chalupsky et al., *Jugend in Leipzig* [Youth in Leipzig] (Leipzig: Universität Leipzig, Laboratorium für Studentenforschung, 1991). "Die große Mehrheit der Jugendlichen vertritt nachdrücklich die Meinung, die 'Stadtväter' sollten unverzüglich Entscheidungen treffen, um die Lebenssituation der Jugendlichen zu verbessern" (p. 64).

2. Heinrich Heine, *Buch der Lieder* [Book of Songs] (München: Wilhelm Goldman Verlag, 1957).

Braver Mann, er schafft mir zu essen
Will es ihm nie und nimmer vergessen!
Schade, daß ich ihn nicht küssen kann!
Denn ich bin selbst dieser brave Mann. (p. 119)

3. Klaus von Beyme, *Das politische System der Bundesrepublik Deutschland nach der Vereinigung* [The political system of the German Federal

Republic after the unification] (München: Piper, 1991). Eleven percent of 15–30-year-olds—the highest-ranking affiliation of 22 possibilities—are actively involved in the peace movement, and 64 percent who do not belong think it is a good endeavor; 10 percent are active in environmental protection and ecology, and 74 percent of non-members believe it is a good endeavor; 9 percent are active in church-related youth groups and 35 percent of non-members believe they are good. Tabelle 5.2 Organisatorische Bindungen bei den 15–30 jährigen [Table 5.2. Organizational Ties of 15- to 30-year-olds] (p. 187).

4. Karl Heinz Jahnke and Michael Buddrus, *Deutsche Jugend 1933–1945* (Hamburg: VSA Verlag, 1989), p. 14.

5. David Schoenbaum and Elizabeth Pond, *The German Question and Other German Questions* (New York: St. Martin's Press, 1996). In the west, Protestantism was carried to its logial political conclusion of Western liberal democracy. In the east, the population "internalized again the lesson of passivity and obedience" (p. 18).

6. Günther Henning, *Die Verwöhnte Generation? Lebenstile und Weltbilder 14–19 Jähriger* [The spoiled generation? Lifestyles and world views of 14–19-year-olds] (No city given: Hanns Martin Schleyer-Stiftung, 1982).

7. Herbert Merkens, Irmgard Steiner, and Gerhard Wnzke, *Lebensstile Berliner Jugendlicher 1997* [Lifestyles of Berlin Youths 1997] (Berlin: Zentrum für Europäische Bildungsforschung e. V., Freie Universität Berlin, 1998). "Das Thema Gewalt und Jugend gehört in der öffentlichen Diskussion von heute eng zusammen. . . . Rechtsextreme bekennen sich offen zu ihrem stärkeren Gewaltverhalten. Jugendliche des Typs Linksextrem dagegen sind . . . die friedfertigsten. . . . die Familien [haben] insgesamt besser ihre Aufgaben erfüll[t], als das bei vielen öffentlichen Darstellungen zu vermuten ware. . . . [Und] die Jugendliche [sind] . . . als Akteure an ihrer eigenen Entwicklung beteiligt [In today's public discussions, the topics violence and youth belong together. . . . Right-wing extremists openly admit to their pronounced violent behavior. In contrast, left-wing extremist types are . . . the most peacable. . . . All in all, the families have done a better job than one is led to believe by many public depictions. . . . [And] the youths actively share . . . in their own development] (pp. 147, 149, 163).

8. Chapulsky, *Jugend in Leipzig*. Die DDR-Jugend hat einen "Überdruß an Organisiertheit . . . nur 3% bzw. 2% der jungen Leipziger [sind] bereit, Mitglied in einer überparteilichen oder parteigebundenen Jugendorganisation zu werden." Aber mehr als 50% der Leipziger Jugend nehmen an Demonstrationen teil [The GDR youth is "weary of being organized. . . . only 3 percent, respectively 2 percent of young people in Leipzig [are] willing to become members of a non-party or party-affiliated youth organization." Yet, more than 50 percent of the youths in Leipzig participate in demonstrations] (pp. 51, 53).

9. Josephine's explanations seem too simplistic, because it is a big leap from seeing something to believing it and then acting on it. Surely deeper motivations are at play. See, for example, Magistratsverwaltung für Jugend, Familie und Sport, *Jugend und Rechtsextremismus in Berlin-Ost* [Youth and right wing extremism] (Berlin: Verlag Junge Welt, n.d.) and Kenneth Keniston, *Young Radicals* (New York: Harcourt Brace and World, 1968).

10. Barbara Hille, *Nicht nur Blauhemden. Die Situation der Jugendlichen in der DDR* [Not only blue-shirts: The situation of youths in the GDR] (Melle, Germany: Verlag Ernst Knoth, 1991), p. 18.

11. Herbert-Joachim Veen, *Eine Jugend in Deutschland* [A youth in Germany] (Opladen: Leske und Budrich, 1994). Freedom to travel is most important to 38 percent of youths; freedom of expression is in second place with 15 percent.

8

The Voters Decide

As long as millions of losers deny their shortcomings, they will remain losers . . . obedient, mousy, and programmed to be failures. . . . "Germany" was the mantra I recited to assuage my fear of . . . the consequences of what I brought about: the end of the regulated rights and duties. I was not clearly aware that, after the liberation, freedom would come.[1]

A teenage girl: "I'm for the PDS [*Partei des Demokratischen Sozialismus* (Party of Democratic Socialists Unified) far-left successor to the SED]. Grandma is for the PDS, and I'm for my grandmother!"

An older Ossie couple: "Absolutely! Not voting is worse than voting, but certainly not right-wing, not DVU [*Deutsche Volksunion* (German People's Union), far right], not CDU [*Christliche Deutsche Union* (Christian German Union), right of center], nor PDS, either."

JOHANNA

Johanna is a Wessie:

I voted for the Gray Panthers the last time, a party for seniors. They are engaged, they support a cause. That's important. Something like that is great. All without much money. And they're not sitting in their armchairs collecting thousands of Marks a month while twiddling their thumbs.

Josephine is an Ossie.

Most people vote just anything. They grumble afterwards, but they don't do anything, aren't active, don't go anywhere, or even inform themselves in an all around way. They watch television, mainly porno-channels and films. Political channels don't interest them, nor do business magazines. They're interested only in *Sybille* or some other women's magazines.

MAX

In childhood, Max's family was very poor, especially while his father was incarcerated by the Nazis.

The extremism has become much worse. The extremists are predominantly youths, the unemployed. I am interested in history, and when I see the documentaries of the Hitler era, I get the feeling that this period, these economic conditions, are almost the same as '33. Not that people want National Socialism again, but one shouldn't be surprised if, in the upcoming election, many in the East would vote PDS or DVU.

PAUL

Paul, the socialist turned businessman:

There has always been right-wing extremism in Germany, similar to the big southern landowners in the USA. Just as they always had a conservative bent, the German *Junker* [Prussian squires] nobility has always had a thing for the military. They provided the young blood for the imperial army. And the Prussian army was like [that of] Napoleon. It didn't exactly bring peace and happiness to Europe. But the Germans are feeling their oats again. It's palpable. You can tell. Those are the same forces that wanted to reverse the land reform [GDR laws nationalizing privately owned land] and buy up the land in Kaliningrad, in Königsberg, Silesia, or in the Czech Republic. They're active there.

And the government of the GFR goes right along with it: land purchases with tax funds. That's clear. However, in the eastern districts, particularly at the Oder-Neisse [rivers marking the post–World War II border between Poland and Germany] border, the Poles are very sensitive. Understandably. They don't want that conflict yet another time. And the Association of the Exiled in Germany adopted a resolution in the *Bundestag* that frightens the Poles. They object to unlimited settling of Germans there. Naturally, if Poland wants to be in the European Economic Union, and the borders are open, there is a real possibility of Germans settling there again.

Where does one find the right-extremists? We notice that youths are attracted to skinheads and violence. Among the older people it's loose talk like: Throw the foreigners out. Something like that was unimaginable here five years ago.

In business circles, when someone speaks such nonsense, I can only express my disdain with punishing looks. Fact is, the roughly 350,000 Turks were not a problem here in the past, when all the West Berliners were well off. As an island, West Berlin fared very well. It was subsidized. Everyone had work; they often flew off [on vacation]. It was wonderful. And now, though the Turks produced a lot for Germany economically, they are disliked because they don't fit into the Western picture of the world. If at least here and there a few Turks were seated in the House of Representatives [*Abgeordneten Haus*] and given positions in the civil service [*öffentlichen Dienst*], that would be an avenue toward integration.

Dorothea

Dorothea is a Wessie, a descendant of an old German-Jewish family.

Subconsciously, there's a lot of radical thinking in the west, too. Much more than one would believe. I notice it in every ordinary conversation, when young women say, for example: Foreigners have no place on German soccer teams. Why not foreigners? If someone lives here, is a player, and the team takes him on, then he has the right. Or the restitution matter: We heard over the radio that groups of gypsies should also get restitution, and actually soon, in their lifetime; not when they're deceased. And one woman got terribly excited about that: It was wrong to pay restitution, she said, even to the Jews. And then one suddenly hears the Minister of Defense, Rühe, say about the right-wing radicals: Such asocial elements have to be eliminated. It's all too much like '33.

So you can find a lot of right-wing radicalism. You only have to keep your ears open, but it's more comfortable not to. It's easier to live when you don't see so clearly. I experience it in my apartment building. We are very polite and nice with one another. When the superintendent has troubles, she comes to me. But from her remarks about others, I gather that if it were 1933–1945, she would evict me, and if we were to meet on the street, she wouldn't greet me.

A young west-woman lives in our apartment building. She has two darling little black children. It's her right and not anyone else's business. One day, the superintendent said to me: Yes, this silly goose with her briquettes, she. . . . I did not understand at all and asked, What briquettes? No sooner had I spoken than it dawned on me that she meant these two cute black children.

Paul

That people don't speak up, don't oppose, that's the fertile ground for everything. It's worrisome, and those in their thirties are quicker to take it on than I am, in my mid-forties. Surely one can contradict, but one doesn't call everyone to task.

Gerhard

Gerhard, the retired GDR journalist:

The problems of integration become noticeable in the larger political sphere. One can clearly recognize on the political landscape, in the election campaigns, that certain parties rely on the west to get the votes they need; they get nothing in the east. And in 1994, it was even clearer. For example, the FDP, a small liberal party in Germany, said: Oh, well, we are a party of the higher-income population and rely on the voters in the west. With that attitude they have voter potential only in the west, and in the East they've totally done themselves in. They are not represented in any *Landtag* [equivalent to U.S. state House of Representatives] of the former GDR. Other parties rely on the East Germans to vote for them. I find that a party in the GFR, that feels responsible for the entire region from Bayern to Ostfriesland, should not stop at the border to the east. On the other hand, a party like the PDS can't say: We are satisfied with the votes from Mecklenburg-Vorpommern to Sachsen and don't need more. They do need more, but don't bother.

Max

Max, the dissident laborer:

The worst is that the speaker for the Federal Republic said, in effect (and he created a storm in the television and in the press, both East and West): If the citizens of the new *Bundesländer* vote for the right-wing or the left (he meant especially the PDS), then one has to think twice about pumping so much money into the new *Bundesländer*.

That's not a direct quote, but it's the sense of it. What kind of a democracy is this if once again, like in the GDR, one is told which party to vote for? Democracy means I can vote for whomever I want, or no one at all. Naturally, something like that angers me mightily. On top of that, the election campaign of the Christian Democrats makes me particularly angry.

In 1945 there were several parties in the Soviet Zone: the Socialist Party, the East Christian Democrats, and the Communist Party. In April 1946, on orders of the Soviet occupation forces, the Socialists and Communists were forced to merge to become the Unified Socialist Party. It was not voluntary. Their party insignia became intertwined hands. I think this election poster makes a mockery of the SPD victims who refused to go along with it.

There were a whole lot of Socialist Party members who didn't go along with it. West Berlin didn't participate. But in the east, those who said: No, we won't do that (because the Socialist Party still existed, but not the Communist Party), those people who refused to be linked up died in Sachsenhausen. They were arrested by the Russians, sent to Sachsenhausen, and arrived when I was already there. [After the war, at age fifteen, Max was falsely accused of trumped-up charges (possibly denounced by his stepfather, who wanted him out of the house), arrested, and convicted by the Soviet occupation forces, and then interned in Sachsenhausen, a former Nazi concentration camp.] These SPD people weren't murdered. No one was shot or hanged in Sachsenhausen, but they died of starvation or sickness.

Now again, there's an ominous poster, red with two intertwined hands, and PDS-SPD written above them, meaning the red danger. It implies, if you vote SPD, then PDS and SPD will join together. And the poster refers to 1946.[2] That is why these posters enrage me. In my opinion, they are a falsification of history. The Christian Democrats do that.

JOHANNA

Johanna, from West Berlin, declares:

It is altogether impossible for someone who grows up in a democracy to understand what happened to the people who stood up against the regime. For us, particularly for me as a child, it was incomprehensible why they treated people like that. And it remained incomprehensible, because there was no concrete information available about it.

We only knew from GDR relatives that people disappeared, that in their personal lives they had to endure great pressures. We knew that some were denied a higher education if they comported themselves in certain ways. But we also knew that if they conducted themselves well vis-à-vis the system, they had chances for advancement. In our family, we had someone who had clearance to have access to secrets in the defense industry and others who were employed in the state educational institutions. And we were aware that if we westerners attracted attention there while visiting, it would affect them [negatively].

Josephine

German politics are not good. The normal, average citizen does not have the feeling that he's involved in any manner or form. Rather, we have no influence over the powers that be; and more and more [of what they do] is to our personal disadvantage. Taxes are raised, jobs are abolished, and then one finds out that the individual politicians have a lot of money. An average politician earns at least 20,000 DM a month, while an average worker gets 2,000 DM a month. America is way ahead of us. In America, the citizen has the feeling that he's included in politics. Whether it's true, doesn't matter. But there isn't the political moroseness. There, one doesn't have the feeling that some people sit around doing things I don't understand. Instead, one feels that this concerns me and that President Clinton would like to know how I'm doing. That doesn't exist here, at all. Apparently, Germany is a land of hierarchy.

When Germans take the initiative to collect money to do something, it is usually to do something bad. They do it against the hierarchy, against the politicians who admit foreigners into the country. Everything political that emanates from the *Volk* is always *against* something, like the demonstrations and protests. People get together and say: We won't stand for this anymore. That is exactly where the German citizen always engages—against the official politics. And that is our politicians' big mistake, not to take the people seriously. Here, the legal right to voter participation is not available, that is, to have a citizen referendum about certain things. Our politicians are so arrogant, they don't even want to hear from us.

I think it's a sign of magnanimity and commitment to say: Now I'll let someone else stimulate me with his ideas and vision and potential. How can I expect flexibility from an unemployed person who, by hook or by crook, keeps his head above water and whose family lives in a run-down apartment? How can I ask him to travel from here to Bremen in search of a job? How can I expect someone in such a difficult situation to be flexible when our politicians aren't mobile and don't set an example, but sit out their time in their armchairs? It doesn't matter whether Kohl is good or bad as a chancellor. Anyone, anyone, a nurse, a gas station attendant, or a chancellor—anyone who holds the same position for so long and performs the same repetitive duty becomes jaded and numb to everything else that happens all around. Anyone.

By the way, I believe Kohl will be voted out next autumn. He lost his votes in the east. He did not keep his promises. He's been in office long enough. Nothing new will come from him, and everyone who has ever visited him is familiar with his pork tripe. So something new has to happen. Unfortunately, however the new regime may line up, nothing will change for the man in the street, for the normal consumer, because the capitalists rule, not the party in power. It's as true as ever: Money rules the world. And the common people can't pull themselves up out of the mud by their bootstraps.

I don't think that our politicians, whether in Berlin or in the Republic, are up to the task of bringing east and west together. Someone who has performed the same task for a very long time is incapable of managing a sudden, profound change because, then as now, he stays in his groove. And when suddenly he is supposed to do something quite different, where should he have learned how?

After the *Wende*, the entire Berlin government remained in their posts. How could someone who used to manage a little island now be able to rule a major metropolis with totally different infrastructures and conditions? Where would he have gotten this capability?

Ernst

Ernst, who relocated from East to West:

The SED was a criminal party. They had forty years to make something out of the GDR, out of this part of Germany, but they only talked big, prophetic words. And what hot air it was! The country had only debts, nothing was left of it. Everything, all was *kaput* and run down.

Of course, an express train from Berlin to Magdeburg and all the district cities remained. The theater was well subsidized. But the operas were completely revised according to government guidelines, so that sometimes one had to ask: What is this? And the entire literature was influenced by the SED politics. So, wherever you looked, everywhere politics!

I was often appalled when I was in East Berlin. During the parades on October Seventh, the Day of the Republic, Berlin was a sea of red flags, and the idiots all ran along behind them. I never could understand how it was possible that the youth, though open [to new ideas], were so very influenced by the party.

Now, some voters have decided in favor of the opposite political direction, 13 percent for the German People's Union, the DVU, in Sachsen-Anhalt. The politicians mounted a huge campaign with posters and personal letters to the voters. No one knew quite what the DVU was, but Sachsen-Anhalt had the most unemployed. And then came the slogans: German Money for Germans, or Jobs for Germans First—although they didn't tack on: Jobs for Foreigners Only After That.

Politically, Magdeburg is extreme right; all of Sachsen-Anhalt is very right-wing. Quite horrible, very bad. I'm glad I don't have anything to do with that. I can hardly explain it, because while I lived in the GDR, I really didn't know that sort of thing existed under the surface. I did know that there were very many rowdies and young people who liked their alcohol and who sometimes became raucous, but they didn't sing genuine Nazi songs.

Now I'm horrified that this is possible. It's frightening because many are just children who don't know what they're doing, what's at stake. They didn't live through it. But it's also the government's fault. One has to confront it, not just say: These 13 percent of the voters in Sachsen-Anhalt are idiots. That is why I have to look at this critically, to tackle it politically, so that I can oppose them appropriately.

The functionaries who are suddenly sitting in the House of Representatives leave much to be desired, mentally. They don't know politics, and it's dangerous not to know. But the overwhelming opinion of the voters was: We want to show those [officials] in Bonn, that things can be different. And it's still my conviction that, above all, it was a protest [vote] here in the east, especially in Brandenburg and Mecklenburg-Vorpommern. But I surmise that next time there will be fewer DVU votes because it doesn't have a program, doesn't have an organization, doesn't actually do anything, and their delegates in the *Landtagen* don't know anything, either. They haven't learned anything, haven't the vaguest idea about parliamentary procedures, will spout any old silly thing. And they will not be reelected, because people will say: That was not the right candidate after all, he's totally inferior, can't speak, knows nothing. There is nothing we can do with him. We have to elect someone else.

ERICH

Erich, the Wessie living in the east, does not believe in protest votes.

There is an incredible amount of talk about the elections in Sachsen-Anhalt, about the so-called protest vote, and for me that's the nonword of the year, because there is no such thing as a protest vote. I think it's been disproved in the meantime. It was not the jobless who voted DVU, it's the 18- to 25-year-olds who were apprenticed or otherwise employed. I read in the *Spiegel* that the proportion of DVU voters is actually quite normal, statistically.[3]

Unemployment is a problem in the [ex-]GDR. In 1989, the western politicians, with their typical propaganda, promised flourishing landscapes, and everybody jumped for joy. They saw only the consumer side of things, and it's true, they did get consumer goods. But this capitalist system is a wicked system. It doesn't only give, it takes a lot, too. Of course, you can say: It's your own fault if you are so ignorant as not to know the fundamental rules of physics, the rule of the communicating pipes. When something goes up there, it must come down here. But that's cynical, because the people were deliberately whipped into a euphoria. People say: Mr. Kohl gave us empty promises. So they're frustrated. But one cannot always blame others, one has to do something oneself.

This hostility in the [ex-]GDR also stems from the fact that the West Germans presented themselves like victors, with the attitude: Everything you did was wrong, it was all crap, and now we're here to tell you so. And they were the very ones who could least afford to say something like that, because the first ones to come over were the unsavory business dealers.

And when the democratic government was established, not the very best of the lot came over, either. The shittiest people from the West were enticed to go east and were sent to Eisenhüttenstadt or Karl-Marx-Stadt, later Chemnitz. Very few 24-carat people came east. Most were second or third or fourth rank, frequently unpopular westerners who were pushed into community or political posts in the east. This most certainly contributed to the fact that the situation did not improve as fast as one had wished.

There are some exceptions, such as Biedenkopf, the prime minister of Sachsen. Now there is a first-rate CDU politician. He was very unpopular in the west, because he was always fighting with Kohl. Biedenkopf doesn't represent my political position, but he is a personality. And for the former mayor of Hannover, Hinrich Lehmann-Grube, coming to Leipzig was certainly no career move, but a challenge. That sort of thing didn't happen often enough.

Josephine

I vote for the party which I believe will represent my best interests and stand up for the East German population.

Yes, I care and am interested; I try to disseminate my opinion a little, can converse about it a little, but I haven't joined a party. Haven't found the right one, the one I really would like to join.

At one time, I believed firmly in the old GDR. It was always a topic, especially during my apprenticeship. Eighteen-year-olds would be seduced; my God, they organized parties and trips to pull new "material" into the party. I describe it like that, "material." People are always material, still today. And I had a phase once, when I was very interested. And maybe I would even have taken the step if someone in my firm, during my apprenticeship, hadn't said: Think about it, think about all that it involves. That person must have liked me.

Within myself, I hadn't come to a firm conclusion. I had my doubts. I learned from my father to think about what good something will bring me. In any case, one thing the party would not have given me is more money, because they wanted dues, and I knew my tiny salary would be further reduced. The finances surely played a role, but it was not only that. This pressure to run with the herd [*Herdenzwang*] probably weighed more heavily, although I didn't recognize the party's true political character so fully. That awakened in me only later.

In the GDR, while I worked for the publishers, a similar topic suddenly came up again, with the German-Soviet Friendship organization, DSF [*deutsch-sowjetische Freundschaft*]. One joined the [labor] union [FDGB] because it sometimes gave one a chance to travel. One had to pay dues there, too, but within limits; one also had to attend union meetings, but that wasn't so bad. In return, we got Christmas celebrations and some trips. That was all right. This German-Soviet Friendship, DSF, wasn't bad either. I have nothing against the Russians—that is, the Soviets (officially at that time, one wasn't allowed to say "Russians"). But why should I pay for friendship? It was a friendship between me and someone else. I was in contact with Russians. I had penpals. But pay?!

There was the "collective of socialist work," a brigade in which one had to perform especially well. And other peculiar programs were part of it. One got money for that. All the members of the brigade were supposed to be in the German-Soviet Friendship, and they always tried to blackmail me, saying. You are the only one in our group who is not in the DSF, and if you don't join, none of us will be able to be part of the collective for socialist work. And I said: You can become a collective, get your title; it doesn't bother me; I have nothing against it. But I don't want to. Anyhow, if I have to have a friendship, I'll have a German-Polish friendship. For that, one didn't have to pay.

That DSF was like my initiation [*Jugendweihe*, the secular counterpart to the religious confirmation; in the GDR, an initiation into adulthood at age 14]: You *have to* visit the concentration camp now; you *have to* view historical films. And to this "have to" I said, No! I tended my Russian friendships nevertheless.

When I married in '73, I landed in a completely political family. In this family, I was consistently in opposition.

At first I thought the family was fantastic. I came from a labor-class family; this was intelligentsia. The GDR differentiated between intelligentsia and labor. And that impressed me. I didn't have to do a thing there. I was waited on. My mother-in-law was happy finally to have a daughter. And I had heaven on earth. I had never had known anything like that. At my parents' house I worked all the time—oh, well, "all the time" sounds exaggerated, because I also have very nice memories. My parents prepared me to survive today. But I thought my husband's family was fantastic.

My husband's father was a teacher in the party system and his wife was manager of a bookstore; she was the head of it. In the GDR, book shops always performed a political function through the literature that was published.[4] I can remember the time when Wolf Biermann was expelled[5] and it became a topic in the SED school for adult education. The Biermann affair was a watershed in my life. Who is Biermann? Not a single person knew him. Only my father-in-law, and only because it became an issue in party politics.

My views were always controversial in that family. I always had held the working-class view, based on my parents' lives. But there I had contact with the perspective of the party leaders: always exhorting to more struggles and victories, more work and increased productivity. I argued about that with my father-in-law, as I did about the Biermann topic. From then on, I ceased being interested politically, and finally I distanced myself from them internally.

I also knew I could not stay in Sachsen, because it was chickenshit. Small-town stuff. There, people were kept dumb. They couldn't see past their noses. Nothing existed beyond demonstrating on the First of May and marching through the small town on the Seventh of October, Founding Day of the GDR. Why they did that, no one really knew. I never went along.

My husband served in the *Staatssicherheit (Stasi)*, but at the time I didn't know what it was. I only really learned what was up after the *Wende*. Before, I was somewhat interested, but could never speak openly about it and didn't have contact with the so-called underground. I didn't even know that an underground existed. Also, I was a bit afraid for my life, afraid of winding up in the clink, or something like that, because my in-laws were so political—especially my father-in-law, who had committed my husband to serve in the *Staatssicher-heit*. So, from that I concluded that they were part of it, but I don't know for sure. And after the Wende I never tried to find out.

Curiously, they also live in Berlin now. At some point my father-in-law was relocated from Sachsen to Berlin by his party school. From immediately after the *Wende* until his retirement, he was a caretaker [janitor] with the German railroad. It sometimes angers me that he was allowed to work there, that nothing at all happened to him. That's very emotional [for me], and I'm sometimes a little disappointed with myself, because I haven't yet read my *Stasi* files. But I don't know what it'll do to me, if I read them. That's why I avoid it.

Much has changed in the past ten years—my education, above all, but also politics. As long as I can remember, I've been vaguely aware of politics, whether east or west. I can't explain it. Even as a youth, beginning around eighth grade, when they introduced all that political stuff in school. And I've always leaned toward social democrats, although officially social democrats didn't exist in the GDR. I believe, even during that phase [I described before], when I was seventeen, eighteen, I would never have joined the SED. If anything, rather the LDPD, the liberals. But I would have done that only to get away from this red clique.

Today, it's not an issue for me; I'm still without party affiliation, but consider myself a social democrat. From time to time, I attend a few SPD party meetings. As an auditor, I can observe. That doesn't mean that I'm 100 percent behind the SPD, because in Germany—and also in other countries—you find the cult of personality. The masses follow a leading figure, and half a year later it becomes evident that he does whatever he pleases.

Most people now have no interest in politics. The friendships I cultivate are based on mutuality, are strictly private and non-political. They have their little house and their little garden or their boat, take holidays, and that's the end of it. They would never think of going to a "demo" [demonstrations or marches in support of or in opposition to a cause].

I have done all that, tried everything, since the *Wende*. I participated in a demo just to find out what happens, without really subscribing to the cause. From time to time I also visit an election campaign event, so that I'll know for whom I am voting, who the candidate is. Most people don't do that, they only talk. And then they vote. For whom they vote, you can see from the results, like the DVU.

DVU is really a very terrible thing. I'm a bit scared that it will bring the "brown" [movement] [reference to the Nazi "brown shirts," the storm troopers] to power. But I don't know what, as an individual, I can do about it. Sure, I think about what I could do myself, or whether I absolutely would have to work through an organization, or whether there are other possibilities. I haven't finished developing myself.

I've often felt that I would like to be more engaged politically. I'd like to step out of my own shadow and open my mouth and participate in the conversation. Maybe I need someone to pull me in. I read umpteen newspapers and my entire television consumption has changed completely since the *Wende*, especially in the past three or four years. I can no longer concentrate on animal films or love and la-de-dah and all that stuff. I watch primarily political and other controversial programs.

FRIEDA

Frieda was a victim of communist discrimination in the GDR:

Although one has become significantly more critical, not much has changed, except that a different stratum is engaged [in politics]. The communists are still more engaged. They go to every election, and that is the danger. Otherwise, a political frustration is evident. Not many people are interested in politics, and I fear that the fewer people vote, the more votes accrue to the communists.

The functionaries and the people with party connections who had many advantages in the GDR, such as access to scarce consumer goods and vacation spots, became worried about keeping their partially party-determined positions and more or less crept into hiding. So we got the impression that everyone was enthusiastic, that the entire population was in favor of unification with the existing federal states [*alte Bundesländer*] and was enthusiastic about it. Some said: Slowly, slowly; it has to be a gradual process. But I am convinced a drawn-out process would have made unification even more impossible. The two camps would have grown further and further apart.

We had hoped for a new party, but the *Neues Forum* was opposed to that, didn't want to try to establish itself as a party. They feared that the membership would splinter because of its many different views. They only wanted to point to the sore spots, to point out the problems with the state so that they would be corrected. They wanted to be an impetus to improvements, but didn't want to become a party.

When the GDR started to crumble, a sizable part of the population hoped for unification. Another large part wanted only to restructure the GDR into a more humane system. Naturally, if only that had come to pass, we would have been happy to have free elections and a new constitution. The constitution contained limitations pertaining to the dissidents, and we wanted to be rid of that. We wanted to vote freely.

We know exactly which politicians were in favor of unification, who contributed toward that end and who did not. But memories are short. That we owe the unification to Kohl is now forgotten.

Throughout the forty years' division (or almost fifty years if we include the first four years of the occupation) it was always said that the existing constitution is only temporary. When unification occurs, there'll be a new constitution. But nothing happened. The GDR connected up with the *Bundesrepublik*—it did not unite with it; unification is different. That engendered so much frustration, and many people feel they were just run over, that their interests were not sufficiently taken into account. Meanwhile, the government as well as the people of the old *Bundesrepublik* said: The constitution is so good that we can't imagine how it could be improved. Creating a new one would only make it worse. But that can't be proved.

These are things that make for bad feelings. For forty years, the Bonn government said that having its capital in Bonn was only an interim situation, and that should unification occur, Berlin would of course become the capital again. But it turned out not to be a matter of course, but something to be voted on in the *Bundestag*. We couldn't understand why they had to vote on it after saying for forty years that it was an interim solution.

If I were ten years younger, I would become politically active. But at least my younger daughter is politically engaged. She joined the CDU, is very involved there, and let herself be nominated for election to the city-district ministers assembly [*Stadtbezirkverordnetenversammlung*]. Every district in Berlin has a minister. She was elected, was full of spirit and idealism, and believed the other ministers were are all good people. I have to say that she has been pretty disillusioned. After she took a good look at the way everything works, how positions get pushed around, how connection and protection operate, she realized that people are the same everywhere. And that, after all, is a learning process.

The biggest adjustment has been to learn how to assert one's rights and not wait to be told what to do. Socialism regulates everything, and any change in a law or a regulation was printed in the newspaper, or one was notified directly. One was kept virtually a child.

What was so bad about the party was that it always claimed to be right about everything and demanded that everybody always be in favor of whatever was useful to the party. So, whatever was useful to the party and its leaders was supposed to be right. One wasn't allowed to judge objectively. But opinions can differ. What one might consider useful for the country did not necessarily coincide with communist thinking. It would have been dangerous for the communists if they had allowed "whatever is useful to the country" to be right. No. Right was "whatever the party says." Yes, the party was always right, and everything was taken care of. In the end, the people became largely incapable of managing their affairs.

HELGA

Helga's GDR experiences have been mixed. As a school teacher, she was often chastised for being too romantic in her choice of literature; her friends were imprisoned for their political activities; and she chafed under the totalitarian constraints. On the other hand, she valued the support she received as an artist—subsidized rents for her apartment and her studio and the low cost of food. She had an almost guaranteed market for her work.

I think the CDU representatives in the government have brutally destroyed the economy in the east. That was such a shameful, dishonorable little war that the CDU waged here, but I'm not so sure that under similar circumstances the SPD would have acted differently. When I have conversations with my friends in Frankfurt about the dismantling of the factories, I'm no longer quiet and let them talk. I tell them that an outrageous, scandalous wrong was perpetrated here.

Scientists whom they fired are now in highly paid positions in foreign countries. They destroyed intact state-sponsored clinics, threw out the salaried physicians. They used to get paid out of the 60 Mark insurance premiums every citizen had to pay. Now, many doctors are unemployed. Others became independent practitioners and organized into groups, so it's no longer called polyclinic, it's a "physicians house." A younger friend, an ear-nose-throat specialist, had a thriving practice in a polyclinic at the *Alexanderplatz* and, fortunately, could rent some space next door. That way, her patients stayed with her. She made it. But my friend who is fifty-seven years old doesn't stand a chance to open an office. It's an impossible situation.

So it shouldn't be a surprise when people stop voting for the CDU. That people are so stupid as to vote for Nazis and Fascists, as in Sachsen-Anhalt, that's a real catastrophe, but not a surprise.

I was thrilled to think that for the first time in my life, I could go into a cell to vote freely for whomever I pleased. In the past, I wouldn't have dared. It was uplifting and I was proud to be able to experience democracy. Of course, at the time, we talked about it in our circle of acquaintances: For whom are you voting? and For whom do you vote? There were a few, newspaper editors, who voted PDS. I said: How could you?! I thought it was terrible, because the PDS is the true successor to the SED. I decided for the Greens.

But things got worse and worse. I have a friend, a sculptress who survives on 1,000 Marks a month plus some additional fees from the occasional gentleman who commissions a portrait of his lady. This friend voted PDS, too, not really to elect them to the government, but to register a protest. So, for whom will I vote the next time? I'll vote PDS, for the same reason as my friend. All that CDU arrogance has to be punished. Only, the DVU, the Nazis have to be stopped.

Kurt

Kurt has always felt very connected to the GDR, but he accepts the reality of the unification.

I've always been a political person, and in the GDR I performed a great many communal tasks outside the realm of my work. I was not paid a penny for it, but I served the state. For example, I was the acting head of our residential district. I never became head, because I never could become a [party] comrade, due to the fact that I remained in contact with my mother in the west. Still, I was welcomed as a party-less person with initiative.

The GDR no longer exists and there's no point in chasing windmills. After 1990, some people approached me and asked: Won't you join the PDS, the SED successor? And I answered, Why this nonsense? What do you want? If you wanted the GDR, you should have prevented what happened. You didn't do that. Beaming with delight, you refrained from doing that. And now, Mr. Gysi (PDS) sits in Bonn in the *Bundestag* and takes his money just like all the others. He's a delegate in the *Bundestag* and makes people crazy, over and over again. This party does nothing but drive people crazy and lets them believe that everything could be different one day.

I have great respect for the general accomplishments of the CDU. I don't make a secret of it. The way I see it, no other party could have brought about [unification] as it did, nor would any other party have wanted to. Today, there are many who want to blame all kinds of things on Helmut Kohl, only because he once said there would be flourishing landscapes.

As an ex–GDR citizen, I have to say in all fairness that even though there aren't landscapes with blossoming sunflowers fully grown, I see a lot of fields where sunflowers are growing. We hadn't had that in the GDR for twenty years. That seems to me to be a historical accomplishment, attributable to the intervention of Mr. Kohl and the CDU as a whole.

HILDE

Hilde is content living in her senior residence in the west.

In the GDR, we didn't dare reveal that we had been exiled from Czechoslovakia after the war. We pretended to have "relocated" [*Umsiedler*] and were given a relocation credit of 300 Mark, which, however, had to be repaid. So, it was not like in the west, which gave compensation for the loss of one's house, garden, or farm one might have owned in erstwhile German territories in Poland or in Czechoslovakia. Compensation was paid out soon after the deportation. We had owned our own home and garden, but in the east, compensation was paid not in money, but in land—large manors carved up into pieces. The mayor told my mother that we could have a piece on which to settle, but she didn't want to take land that had belonged to someone else.

My mother joined the east-CDU and had a lot of problems as a result. Also, until the Wall was built, she used to visit her relatives in the west. And whenever she returned, she was asked how she liked it. If she said, "very well," she lost her job soon after that.

Once or twice, I was allowed to travel with her, and once my mother said to me: *Ach*, look, let's stay in the west. We would have had to stay in a camp for a while and my mother was afraid of doing that. Plus, I already had many good friends in the high school, and I didn't want to leave them. Also, I was already pretty committed to communism, so that when I saw books displayed about Nazi pilots and Nazi big shots I said to my Mommy: No, this is terrible; I don't want this. I want to go back to the GDR.

I chose the GDR, but later, as an adult in the SED, I was on the very lowest rung and sometimes felt like a lightning rod. I was a very, very lowly member of the party. When anyone had to blow off steam, I would be the one they used as a punching bag.

I was a teacher and responsible for my class. The pupils here in East Berlin had some bags with advertisements of Karstadt and Penny (department stores), which someone had sent them. And we were supposed to make sure that no pupil brought in such bags. But I couldn't get involved in such pettiness. So I would be scolded, and they probably noticed that I was no longer so committed. But I didn't dare withdraw from the SED because I probably would have been demoted and lost my job. One feared that.

OTTO

Otto is the son of an anti-fascist who was convicted and executed by the Nazis when Otto was still in grammar school.

At age fourteen, I joined the SED. Everyone was concerned and took care of me. And most likely, I would have had a great career had I not taken socialism so seriously and taken every pronouncement literally, had I not stumbled over each discrepancy between word and deed.

My run-in occurred in 1951. As the chief of a sports organization, I was accused of "democratism"—and then I was no longer chief. I became the doormat, was given a punitive transfer, and then looked for another job. Soon, my father's friends rediscovered me and said: This is impossible that a descendant of an executed antifascist and resistance fighter is left to vegetate. So, I was sent to a party school for ideological reeducation.

Then came June the 17th.[6] Even before it started, I had predicted that the higher productivity standards would drive the workers to the barricades. When June 17th came, I did not follow orders, traveled to Berlin, and then was simply axed. I appealed, was allowed to take the special examination and then was admitted to [higher education] studies. Then came the party purges. The SED leadership threw out everyone who hadn't followed the party line on June 17th. That included me. The result was that, after six months of studies, I was expelled— first thrown out of the party and then exmatriculated.

I was unemployed for two years, dragged myself around from here to there, and considered moving to the west. I refrained from that because my mother was here and she wanted absolutely no truck with the west. She said: They're no better here than the Nazis. But she didn't want to move to the west, where, she believed, the genuine Nazis were. That was her conviction. And I didn't want to leave my mother alone, or my sister, either. So I stayed here.

In 1956, the SED called me for a conversation. Khrushchev had just delivered his speech against the cult of personality, and here the Central Committee of the SED finally decided to introduce democratization. The comrades "discovered" that I was exactly the right man for that, since I had once been accused of "democratism"—whatever that meant. Now they didn't want to do without me. They assured me that all was forgotten; it had all been in error, a result of the cult of personality. If I wished to take part in the democratization process and be a party member without interruption, the party punishment would be stricken from my record. And I believed it. Believed that now it would begin, all that I imagined—socialism and democracy. *Ja! Ja!*

After three-quarters of a year, it was all over. I simply did not go through official channels. Going through official channels was not my idea of democracy. So once again I was given a punitive transfer, left the concern, stayed in the party as a sort of fellow traveler but not to fashion a career. Altogether, I didn't want to be politically active anymore.

Otto metamorphosed:

I recognized socialism as a beautiful but horribly dangerous illusion. With that, I went on my crusade. Whether or not they wanted to hear it, I told the quintessence of my story to everyone. However, capitalism as we experience it nowadays has no answers to the questions either, no solutions to the problems we confront.

So we are faced with crime and unemployment, and stand there totally helpless. Some say the administration finally has to see to it that people find their way back into the working world. That concept is like the Nazis' idea with the *Autobahn* and the communists with nationalizing everything. The Social Democrats tell me about it, the Leftists, the Christian Democrats, and so does the PDS; the Green party doesn't have any ideas either; and the FDP stands there saying: Everyone has to take care of himself. Fantastic!—but how? Please tell me. I have no answers either. I'm just as helpless. I know socialism is not it, cannot be it. This society has no answers, either. Everyone who slides over to the right looks to national socialism; those that slide over to the left look to the socialists or communists. But where are the conservatives? Do they know whether one can make something useful out of this world, so that the social and environmental problems can be solved? So that we don't face the giant companies helplessly—those with a gross income exceeding the budget of many a state, who pay no taxes but receive subsidies?

We confront these situations helplessly and have no answers. Nor do I.

I'm active in the Association of the Victims of Stalinism [*Verbände für Opfer des Stalinismus*]. I am active where the GDR history is researched and publicized. Immediately after '89—when it was clear to me that socialism could lead only to madness, that it was not an escape route—I was asked to participate in the dissolution of the secret police, and I have devoted myself to this assignment ever since February 1990.

I joined the Central Round Table Team for Security [*Arbeitsgruppe Sicherheit beim Zentralen Runden Tisch*], was sent there by the United Leftists [*Vereinigten Linken*] and later worked in the committee for the liquidation of the *MfS* [Ministry for State Security *(Ministerium für Staatssicherheit)*]. Finally, together with some friends, I occupied the *Stasi* archives.

The purpose of the occupation was to assure that the principles of the laws regulating the *Stasi* files would be included in the Unification Agreement. There were a number of laws that the East German Parliament [*Volkskammer*] had agreed would be part of the Unification Agreement and would remain in effect. However, the law requiring the *Stasi* files to be opened and made available to the public fell by the wayside. You see, they had been forgotten, or perhaps not even mentioned in the negotiations; in any case, they had not been included among the documents of the Unification Agreement.

In August 1990 we occupied the archives and sat there 'til the end of September. From there, we distributed our pamphlets and at least got a declaration of intent to pass a law in the *Bundestag* incorporating the principles of open files and public access, and to include that law in the Unification Agreement.

Time passed—the unification had taken place, a half a year had gone by, and now it was spring '91. There was still no talk of a *Stasi* file law. So we got together, those of us who absolutely couldn't let it go, three members of the erstwhile citizens committee [*Bürgerkomitee*]— one each from Dresden, Leipzig, and Berlin. This is impossible, we said. On the day of unification, the committee members had dispersed to all corners of the earth; we have to call them back together, to reactivate them and simply kick off an "initiative." So we got together a few legal experts and drew up a draft of a *Stasi*-file law. And although it was not our place, we presented the draft to the president of the *Bundestag* with the request that this bill be introduced into the *Bundestag*.

Clearly, it could not be worked out that way, The end result was that the *Bundestag* president invited us to a meeting. Sitting there were the old types who would have liked to stash everything away for thirty years. They sat at the table with us, and we argued with them. From that point on, the bill moved along and was passed into law. It is one of the few *Bundesrepublik* laws, I believe, that were initiated and introduced outside of the parliamentary procedure.

IRENE

Irene struggles with ideology and conscience. She spent her childhood in Nazi Germany, where her father was a communist and fled to save his life. Now Irene lives in the east.

Those old men in the GDR government blocked all the paths. They never lost their fear that something would happen to them, because under the Nazis they were the [persecuted] enemies. They are like an acquaintance of mine, a German who was incarcerated and condemned to death, but who escaped and emigrated to Sweden. Now he's an old man, but to this day he's still afraid. He makes appointments conspiratorily, never at the same place. It's a quirk he can't get rid of and it seems silly, but it made me realize how long the fear for one's life and one's physical safety clings to a person.

And it was the same with the old GDR geezers, the functionaries. Yes, they even banned certain books, some that were written abroad and some that were written here. I don't believe they banned them out of malice or evil, but because they were so ideologically committed that they were—yes, nuts, one could say.

In the past, problems of this ideology moved me, and naturally, still do: one has one's convictions, a religion, a *Weltanschauung*. It can be this or that, can be contrary, can include tolerance, can be intolerant—but it is one's own. One is truly convinced of something. But then it [may not be] considered moral [by others], or [might] include things that are contrary to one's conscience. In the past, in the GDR, I often said: I will not do this, it is against my conscience and I cannot do it.

For a while, I was a schoolteacher and was convinced that there were certain things I could not say to my students. And I didn't. But I discussed with them. Sometimes, I said things that were part of the curriculum of which I was not so convinced. One did that, even if in conflict. I remember the events in Hungary in 1956, and the huge discussions after Stalin's death. I had a class of older students, so sometimes I said: So far and no further! There comes a point where I had to say no. But people said: What about the party? And I answered, Luther said: Even the ecclesiastical councils can err; and I stand here and say, even the *Politbüro* of the SED can err. Nothing happened to me. But who can say whether something is really, truly, right?

It's all right with me when people are totally convinced of something right now. I have nothing against that, but sometimes I think: Who knows whether in a hundred years people will say: You destroyed the world with your technology, your industry. I won't be alive then, but still, what gives me the right to say: I am right and all the others are wrong? I always have to include myself—I can be wrong, too. But it is difficult to admit that.

Whatever their principles may have been, they gave people the strength to remain steadfast under the Nazis and in the concentration camps. But did a stronger faith, in their religions or political beliefs give them [correspondingly] more strength to withstand? To face death?

I speak of the convictions of the resistance fighters, the sufferers, the victims, not those of the of the Nazis. I mean a conviction that is seen as correct from the perspective of human values. And I want to go so far as to say that the Nazi ideology is in contempt of humanity, despicable, and wrong. We know that, and it was revealed as criminal. That a young person can be enthusiastic, led astray, and act out of conviction, that is another matter.

So I ask, to what extent may a generally accepted, good principle be unshakeable? Or should one *always* include: I, too, can err? Yes, one must, always. But how can I know whether ultimately I am right or wrong? There are no guarantees.

Even democracy is a danger, because where does freedom stop? If people have the right to think and speak freely, what may they say? What may they not say? What and whom do I restrict? And who are the guardians, the authorities, who take it upon themselves to restrict [others]?

Here, what happens is that whenever there's a march, right-wing, left-wing, the DVU, and the NPD, or whatever they are called, there's an immediate counter-demonstration protesting against it or demanding that the march be prohibited. Democracy requires one to let them march, or includes the right to march. But that's a risk. Today, ten little boys stand at the roadside and think it's fun; tomorrow, they march along. What is the mighty state to do?

In Berlin, you can observe that, with great regularity, the demonstrators are protected and the protesters are clubbed away. And that's confusing. They say that every extreme has to be gagged. We are against every extreme, right or left. But isn't it actually good that when a demonstration is mounted there are people who are against it? The police should attempt to maintain order and protect both.

After the last election put the DVU party into the *Landtag* in Sachsen-Anhalt, debates erupted about whether they should be allowed to fill the chairman's post [*Altersvorsitzender*] to which they are constitutionally entitled, or whether the election system could be altered to keep them out. The thought passed through my head: I am against them and want them out. But I said no to myself. Why, after all? By what right do I demand that they yield to me? But the question should really be: What do we do now?

Legally, this state [*Rechtsstaat*, "state under the rule of law"] can do nothing against the right and left extremists. It is caught in its own web and could fall prey to exactly the same turn of events and the same fate as the Weimar Republic, a democracy that, one can read in the history books, was defeated with its own weapons. This state also can be vanquished with its own weapons.

I see it every time the ex-GDR officials stand before the court to be tried for their misdeeds and crimes. They defeat the *Bundesrepublik Rechtsstaat* every time they manage to elude their punishment. This state, the *Bundesrepublik Deutschland*, this democracy should be strong. But it is not, and that's what I am worried about.

I have argued about this with a lot of people, who assure me again and again that over the years the state has become so firmly structured and so unassailable that no one can shatter it. They might be proved wrong if we don't think of something soon. It's difficult.

I have not thought this through completely, so I cannot say this unequivocably. But there is a big difference between the context of democracy in the USA and in the *Bundesrepublik Deutschland*. The USA has a different historical background. If you listen to the sounds emanating from Bavaria, and once in a while from the East German House of Representatives here, one fears hearing those tones that tend to bring back the "others" [Nazis]. And once they're here, that drama could start all over again.

So I hear the hope but lack the faith in my German people. So watch out!

NOTES

1. Thomas Brussig, *Helden wie wier* [Heroes like us] (Frankfurt a/M: Fischer Taschenbuch Verlag, 1998), pp. 312, 322.

2. KPD, *Kommunistische Partei Deutschlands*, and SPD, *Sozialistische Partei Deutschlands*, were united under pressure, and so on April 22–23, 1946, the *Sozialistische Einheitspartei Deutschlands*, SED, came into being. "A ban on speaking was imposed on the opponents to the fusion, [they were] incarcerated or even deported to the Soviet Union. . . . Supporters of the fusion were bribed." Wolfgang Malanowski (ed.), Die Partei war unser Leben [The Party was our life] *Spiegel Spezial*, No. 2 (1990): 120–129 [124].

3. Richard Schröder, Schluβ mit dem Elend [End the misery], *Der Spiegel*, 19 (1998): 4, 5.

4. Robert Darnton, The Good Old Days, *The New York Review of Books*,

May 16, 1991, pp. 44–48. By mixing socialist doctrine with the Prussian bureaucracy, the East Germans had created a perfect system for stifling literature while at the same time persuading themselves that they were stimulating it (p. 48). Formally, they never repressed anything at all. They simply refused to issue an official authorization slip for an objectionable text (p. 44).

5. Timothy Garton Ash, *Ein Jahrhundert wird abgewählt* [A century is voted out] (München: Deutscher Taschenbuch Verlag, 1989). "On November 16, 1976, the songwriter Wolf Biermann was stripped of his GDR citizenship during a concert in the West. Twelve leading authors wrote an open letter of protest. . . . The Honecker regime reacted viciously. Each of the undersigned was punished" (pp. 23ff).

6. Eckhard Jesse and Armin Mitter (Hrsg.), *Die Gestaltung der deutschen Einheit* [The formation of the German unity] (Bonn: Bundeszentrale für politische Bildung, 1992). The Seventeenth of June 1953 was "[t]he . . . beginning of a citizens' revolt in East Berlin and in the GDR, which was quelled by the Soviet military forces within a few hours. In response, the *Deutsche Bundestag* passed a law on August 4, 1953, designating June 17th as the 'Day of German Unity' " (p. 423).

9
Last Words

[T]he separated parts [show] . . . the picture of both those cripples who, cleaving to each other, shout their illnesses into each
other's ear and derive their self-assurance from the affliction of
the other.[1]

"An entire people, pardon me—only the people of the GDR are in
search of their new identity. An entire population seeks its new place
in a new society, while the new powers make sure that as little as
possible remains of the GDR. . . . It is called 'liquidation' when it
pertains to business enterprises; in scientific and academic establish-
ments it is called 'winding up.' . . . There are many aspects to this,
including everything in the category of 're-valuing of values.' You can
forget about all that was right before the *Wende*: ideals, models, historical traditions." These are the words of an acquaintance, who
wrote to me in 1991. And yet, he added, "I believe it is right, that
the old system collapsed, even though taking leave of many a thing
hurts."

My acquaintance was keenly aware that when the East Germans
stepped into democracy and the market economy, their experience
resembled that of adolescents who move into adulthood insofar as
"all sameness and continuities relied on earlier are questioned again
. . . [and they] are concerned with attempts at consolidating their social roles."[2]

The Germans' sense of themselves and of each other in their suddenly changed social and political environment, the urgent need for developing a personal and national coherence after decades of identifying themselves as good and each other as enemies, will be considered in the following pages.

A person's and a people's identity is complex. It is an amalgam of one's self-representations, that is, a person's inner experience of who he or she is. This includes not only inborn temperament and talents and learned skills, but also the internalization of societal values. These values typically are modeled by the family and educators and taken in, that is adopted as one's own, out of love, respect for, and fear of the elders.

The internal experience of oneself changes as one passes through the various developmental phases because one's identity is the synthesis of an ongoing interplay between the individual and the community. As the community's requirements and restrictions come to bear on an individual's temperament, inclinations, and impulses, a compromise is forged between individuality and conformity. This compromise may modify an individual's character and the sense of what and who he or she is, but it does not obliterate the sense of personal identity over time. Identity implies a continuity and stability manifested by a sense of selfsameness over the life span.

With each personal role change during the life-cycle: leaving home and school, entering the work world, marriage, parenthood, widowhood, our social identity changes, even as our sense of selfsameness remains stable. This sense of selfsameness is equally important as individuals course through the divergent roles of everyday life: subordinate or supervisor at work, parent to one's offspring and child to one's parents, host and guest. Role changes also can occur as a result of moving into a different social class, migrating to a strange culture, experiencing a natural catastrophe, or enduring an economic or political upheaval.

Even as individuals in a group are molded by their community, the synergy of individuals in a group ultimately forge the group's identity. Thus, the group gains its stability and continuity through a communal identity and sense of selfsameness. Just as a sense of one's identity strengthens individual personality organization, group identity potentiates stable social organization with mutually beneficial effects.[3]

The GDR identity had been weakened by its inability to prosper and to satisfy many of the citizens long before it was challenged by the unification with the larger, quite different political and economic organization of the GFR. After the unification, GDR citizens' group identity was assaulted by the necessity to forge a compromise between their socialist inclinations and market economy requirements. This was a difficult adjustment of fit between eastern and western German values.

Such individual and group adjustments are painful. It is the pain of finding established values discredited that my acquaintance is suffering. Who is he in the new society? Where does he fit? How can he maintain self-esteem, when "you can forget" all he believed in and represented?

Gilda, the former journalist who made a very good adjustment after a painful transition period, seems to have grasped and resolved for herself the paradox of maintaining one's sense of self even while adjusting to changed social values. She said: "I lived in this state for forty years and was in favor of it. For me it is moral to stand by my history. I cannot just push it away, because then I would push away forty years of my life."

One basic value in the socialist GDR was the principle of equality. Though the principle was accepted both officially and privately, in practice it was not realized. Another woman volunteered that: "The superiors preached water and drank the wine [*Die da oben haben Wasser gepredigt und den Wein getrunken*]."[4]

Within the context of the GDR equality principle, individuality in thought and action, that is, creativity and innovation became ever more restricted in favor of solidarity and cooperation—which in turn facilitated the palpable relatedness and warmheartedness of the East Germans. These values collided with the West German ethos of self-determination and self-actualization. However, more recently, the pendulum in the west has begun to swing again in the direction of the acceptance of duty and of the traditional German values of diligence, order, discipline, and punctuality, which had never been abandoned in the east.[5]

At the time of the *Wende* and even more so after the unification, East Germans perceived the Wessies as the arrogant victors, who are knowledgeable and successful in the market economy. (An ex-GDR interviewee experienced the unification as such an arrogant subjugation that thinking of it made him feel like throwing up [*Da kommt mir der Kaffee hoch*].) And they saw themselves as the modest Ossies, whose relatively impoverished lifestyle ultimately bore testimony to the abject failure of their socialist experiment. During the years since then, actual contacts with each other have resulted in some modifications in their views of themselves and their counterparts. East Germans reaffirmed their social values and West Germans had to acknowledge at least the competence of East German women and the social institutions that supported them (see chapters 2 and 6).

By 1998 the preconceived notions could no longer be confirmed.[6] East Germans seem to have regained their self-confidence and appreciation of the closeness that was fostered by the GDR society. East Germans to a higher degree than West Germans perceived themselves to be accepted and liked and felt confident that they could obtain help with practical problems. (Indeed, one ex-GDR interviewee listed the readiness to help another as a German attribute.) They feel less criticized and rejected and less taxed than West Germans. More so than West Germans, they experience themselves as independent, interested, and warmhearted.[7] Their relationships to parents were perceived to be markedly more positive by East Germans.

The good child-parent relationships are attributed by some to the mothers' sense of independence and self-assurance, engendered in them by their work experience, and to the "hermetic," private counterculture developed within the families as a protection against the regimentation imposed by the GDR state and the party.[8] In contrast to this "*Nischenfunktion*" (providing a nest), West German society intrudes into the family with its demands for performance at an early age.

West Germans tend to suffer more from intestinal problems, headaches, and muscle spasms. And yet, East Germans suffer ill health more frequently, particularly heart and circulatory illnesses, diabetes, and various problems with internal organs. They consume three times as much medication as West Germans.

When viewed from a psychodynamic perspective, these differences are not surprising. Other factors—such as environment and nutrition, for example—being equal, one might hypothesize that, since control of the excretory functions is among the earliest demands for performance made on the child, and since the West German family emphasizes performance, the bowels might well become the locus and carrier of stress. In the East German society, where good social relations, cooperation, mutual support, and warmheartedness are prized, aggression or expressions of hostility might be looked upon askance and possibly even dangerous to relationships. Therefore, the dependent child in the family—or the citizen dependent on the goodwill of the authorities in a totalitarian society—must control anger, perhaps repress it to protect his relationships. Under those circumstances, one might hypothesize the internal pressures would affect blood pressure, heart functions, and blood clotting.[9]

It seems then, that there exist significant differences between East and West as well as between the conscious and unconscious perceptions within each person.

To the extent that feelings are deemed unacceptable and therefore kept out of awareness, they present a danger. What cannot be acknowledged as being part of oneself is often imputed to others. The modest Ossies are uncomfortable thinking of themselves as arrogant, though they may be, when they pride themselves on their superior social morality. And the Wessie insecurities remain hidden—even from themselves—behind their competence and stiff collar with fashionable tie. Thus, the East Germans become afraid of West German arrogance and West Germans become contemptuous of East Germans' modesty and insecurity. In short, they become each other's mirrors. In the mirror each sees, in the other, the hated quality of the self. And as the internal enemy becomes an external enemy, differences between individuals and groups become exaggerated. The "other" is thereby dehumanized and victimized.

Fortunately, there are signs that the internal splits are not unbridgeable and that the views of each other are modifiable. As one interviewee put it: Talking *about* one another leads to denunciations. Talking *with* one another leads to an exchange of ideas; getting to know one another leads to understanding, compromise, and tolerance. The personal maturity of many citizens and the solidity of the democratic process promise to facilitate sufficient integration of good and bad images of self and other, so that East Germans and West Germans may develop into a coherently functioning whole with which they will one day comfortably identify themselves.

What that entity is or might be is of some concern to Germans. It is important to distinguish between the constituent political entities, the geographic boundaries, and the population living within them.

When asked, for example, what they consider to be their *Heimat*, (*Heimat* denotatively translated means "home"; the connotative meaning with its emotional and sensual overtones has no English equivalent), in 1990 many East Germans said the GDR is their *Hei-*

mat. In 1998 interviewees still did not say Germany. One died-in-the-wool socialist claims: the proletariat has no home. (Nevertheless, he takes pride in the two highest-ranking German soccer goalies, because they come from the ex-GDR.) Instead of GFR or Germany, people referred to their birthplace, or the place where they have friends and family, or anywhere they may "find good books" that can produce the comforting feelings of home. Some were more geographically oriented: "A Saxon will always remain a Saxon." Or: "I'm proud to be a Berliner, the rest doesn't matter to me." One forward-looking woman describes herself as "a European, a German-European."

Insofar as they identify themselves as "caring" Saxons or "Berliners with a tough hide" and recognize themselves also as citizens of Germany, Germans acknowledge that they are a "multilayered" people (*ein vielschichtiges Volk*). (However, many Germans shy away from the word *Volk*, because it carries the burden of the Nazi misuse of the concept for purposes of genocide.) The romantics notwithstanding, the German population in fact has been ethnically heterogeneous and has been forged into a nation as a result of social and economic developments.[10] These social and economic conditions help to explain why, though they are *ethnically* heterogeneous and reluctant to give up their emotional attachments to their regional *Heimat*, Germans are nevertheless willing to identify themselves as a nation, that is, as a population constituting a *political* entity within geographic boundaries.

The regional allegiances are supported politically by geographic remnants of feudal divisions in the form of the *Länder* (roughly equivalent to the states in the United States). In that regard, ex-GDR citizens express the opinion that a looser confederation of the GFR and the GDR would have been more acceptable to them than the merger of the old (GFR) and the new (GDR) *Länder* into the greater whole.

However, Germans do have the benefit of a common language, superordinate to the regional dialects, a reestablished standardized school curriculum, and a cultural history of which they have reason to be proud (provided "Love Parade," the summer 1998 Berlin festival resembling the Woodstock musical festival in the United States, doesn't completely obliterate the more serious literary and musical achievements). As it is possible to forge one's identity out of diverse identifications, Germans—east and west, north and south, Protestant,

Catholic, and atheist—have an opportunity to integrate their many layered identities and function as a unified nation and as a nation-state within the European Union. There are indications that even Jews are finding a home again in Germany, and Moslems might be included, should the *Ausländer* be granted a way to become German citizens.

Realizing this opportunity will require care and work. Ossies' contempt of Wessie materialism and Wessies' supercilious attitude toward the Ossies, finding them peculiar and provincial, is rather under-spread.[11] Attempts to engender guilt in others for striving toward affluence ignores the greed in oneself. Letting others feel one's contempt is shaming. Without the insults, Ossies already felt disadvantaged and deprived. And their enthusiasm about becoming "*ein Volk*" was considerably dampened by the feeling that they had been vanquished by the GFR victors, while Wessies' enthusiasm was diminished in direct proportion to the financial burden they took on as part of the unification. There is no doubt that shame (and sometimes guilt) lead to rage—not only rage against the self that has failed to live up to ideals but also, and especially, rage against the shaming other. One needs only look back on the defeated Germans' reaction to the Versailles treaty after World War I. That German shame was matched by German arrogance, which metamorphosed into un-bounded aggression. To calm themselves, to obliterate their shame with aggrandizement, their aggression was externalized, unleashed against others, who, in turn, were demeaned, shamed, and killed.

At almost any cost, this dynamic must be avoided. Both East Germans and West Germans must become conscious of their shame and their pride, if they are to be whole. It is important to avoid splitting one from the other in order to protect the self-image. Splitting acknowledges the good and imputes the bad to others, who then come to represent the rejected parts of the self. For this the others are needed and for this they need to be destroyed. They become the enemies to be conquered. No! The "bad" within must be conquered within. And the "good" can then be accepted proudly without arrogance.

East Germans have reason to take pride in their peaceful revolution of 1989. The people liberated themselves from a regime gone awry. What enabled a population trained to duck and dodge the party power, to organize themselves into an effective opposition, has remained largely a mystery. It required courage to attend the prayers for peace in the Berlin Gethsemanekirche and, when exiting the church, to risk being apprehended. People were loaded onto trucks and transported to the police station, where they had to undress and line up against the wall naked. They were kept under arrest for at least twenty-four hours, often longer. These harsh measures further inflamed the people, resulting in the mass movement that led to the events of October-November 1989.

The 1980s political demonstrations in the GDR have been likened to those in the 1960s in the democratic West. Both movements were expressions of dissatisfaction with establishment policies and practices and with the consequent social injustices. However, unlike the protests in the United States, France, and West Germany, the 1960s protests in the Soviet Union's sphere of influence were quickly aborted with the help of tanks, rendering activism meaningless and protest almost certainly damaging to the participants.[12]

In the 1980s the Soviet Union moderated its internal political atmosphere and its international stance, thereby reducing the chances of overwhelming damage to members of an opposition movement. And Hungary's opening of its borders to the West was the "world-historical event," the requisite mobilizing catalyst for a rebellion.[13]

If these were the contextual circumstances, what were the protester's motivations? And what personal characteristics distinguish protesters?

Indeed, the East Germans' motivation for actively opposing the establishment and leadership of the *real existierender Sozialismus* (actually existing [in contrast to ideal] socialism) resembled the motivation of 1960s young American radicals. Both groups were disillusioned. They were confronted with the inadequacies of their respective systems and the failure of the very institutions established to relieve inequities and to assist the victims—communist victims of Nazism; proletarian victims of capitalism; female victims of male dominance. Taught to identify with the plight of the underdog, East German activists saw the need for the revision of their institutions and took personal responsibility for opposing their country's totalitarian leadership.

Although partially imbued with a victim mentality, activist members of the opposition to the establishment had the countervailing benefit of having been presented with strong socialist ideals and a picture of an outside enemy—especially the "capitalist" GFR—as a target for their aggression. For this reason, the GDR activists did not totally fall prey to self-pity, nor did they become helpless and inhibited to the point of inaction.

It is also plausible that, like the 1960s "Young Radicals" in the United States, the 1980s activists in the GDR coming from families with high ethical standards subscribe to their parents' expressed ideals and are committed to implementing those values.[14] Typically, for lack of opportunity or courage, the 1960s parents did not implement or fight for their ideals. For the parents of members of the 1980s GDR movement, it was impossible to prevail against the political circumstances of the 1960s and 1970s. Indeed, many were not inclined to oppose. They were ideologically so committed that they became "informal" associates of the *Stasi*, spying and informing on neighbors, friends, and family. However, the younger GDR activists were sufficiently concerned about their grandparents' perpetrator or not-so-innocent bystander roles during the Nazi era, that they decided to participate in the opposition. They wanted to be able to answer their children affirmatively, instead of evasively, should the question "And what did you do?" ever be posed.[15]

Activists tend to grow up in a warm family atmosphere, and the sons' ties to their mother are very strong during the early years. The father is respected for his principles, honesty, idealism, and political interest. However, this is often offset by the father's acquiescence, weakness, and unsuccessful implementation of his principles. Thus the gift for empathy and nurturance, learned at mother's knee, combined with an identification with father's principles and ideals prepares the activist for a concern for political justice and social welfare. However, activists protect themselves against the danger of identification with father's weak, ineffectual side by means of a negative identification with this parental attribute: Activists express their convictions, stand firm, protest when necessary. Otto did so to his detriment. He identified with father's communist principles, stood up for them, but failed to protect himself against the identification with father's ineffectual side. Otto's father was ineffectual in protecting himself against the Nazis, and Otto all but provoked the SED into victimizing him. Only when Otto chose to function in an oppositional group, at the time of the *Wende* and the unification was his activism successful.

The emphasis on deferring to the group in the GDR socialist culture and the necessity for establishing robust social relations in an atmosphere of austerity may well have prepared activists for the opposition movement. Once a member, an activist could find in the movement's social structure support for a synthesis of conscious and unconscious motivations, harmony of self and communal principles, and decisive action.

Now, the totalitarian regime of the GDR is of the past. And so is the savior, Chancellor "Helmut" of the West. The idealized image of the GFR, which momentarily replaced the East Germans' picture of the capitalist enemy, has been tarnished. For their part, the West Germans resent having become victims of the "insatiable" victims in their decrepit territory. The images they have of each other, based on a split of their own acceptable and unacceptable attributes, is difficult for Ossies and Wessies to relinquish in the face of an imperfect reality. The "cripples" cleave to each other and are ambivalent about being "*ein Volk*."

Healing themselves and each other will require quite as much activism as the *Wende* and the unification. It is to be hoped that the east-west symbiosis, based on chronic complementary disabilities, will be addressed before a crisis occurs. True, for almost a decade the state and the people's resources have been dedicated to reestablishing an economic and social balance in the politically unified Germany. Meanwhile, Wessies and Ossies have met, learned more about one another, and sometimes informally explored each other's perspectives. However, the unification on a grassroots level would benefit from a more formal procedure. Of utmost importance for East Germans' and West Germans' identification with their unified country is a joint definition of and acceptance of a superordinate goal.[16] It is not enough to point a finger at the radical youth on the right and on the left. They are but the mouthpiece and the delegates of disgruntled and conflicted middle-aged and middle-class citizens who are too refined to express their hateful feelings. Educators, clergy, psychologists, executives of large concerns, and local politicians are in a position to intervene, "to explore possibilities for resolving difficult issues in mutually satisfactory ways [in] problem-solving workshops,"[17] or at least to create a safe milieu where citizens can express and listen to their respective feelings and thoughts. The methods to implement such programs have been tried and found useful. Group process is no longer a radical idea. Where are the "committed" to begin a "proactive" movement toward a person-to-person, people-to-people unification?

NOTES

1. Leonhard Froese, *Was soll aus Deutschland werden?* (München: Wilhelm Goldmann Verlag, 1968). "Die geschiedenen Teile [zeigen] . . . das Bild jener beiden Krüppel, die sich aneinandergeklammert gegenseitig ihre Krankheiten ins Ohr schreien und von denen der eine sein Selbstbewβtsein aus dem Gebrechen des anderen bezieht" (p. 5).

2. Erik H. Erikson, Identity and the Life Cycle, in *Psychological Issues* (New York: International Universities Press, 1959), pp. 18–171 [89].

3. Ibid. "[T]he mutual complementation of ethos and ego, of group identity and ego identity, puts greater common potential at the disposal of both ego synthesis and social organization" (p. 23).

4. Heike Solga, Klassenlagen und soziale Ungleichheit in der GDR [Social class positions and social inequality in the GDR], *Aus Politik und Zeitgeschichte: Beilage zur Wochenzeitung Das Parlament*, Vol. 46 (November 8, 1996), pp. 18–27. "How is inequality established? . . . In the 1980s, children of parents in the bureaucracy (*Dienstklasse*) had more than six times the chances [for educational and vocational advancement] than children from other social classes [working class, e.g.]. . . . [And] only in the eighties were men and women equally able to attain entry into the bureaucracy based on their own career achievements. The process of establishing the new bureaucracy in the fifties and sixties took place without women. This process was concluded well-nigh exclusively around the careers of men. The educational laws (*Bildungsgesetz*) of 1965, as well as the 1970's special measures of the feminist politics, furthering women, were of significance [in this regard]" (p. 24).

5. Barbara Haenschke, *Identitätsentwicklung in Zeiten des Umbruchs in Deutschland* [Identity development in times of radical change] (Berichte aus dem Zentrum für Gerechtigkeitsforschung an der Universität Potsdam: Veränderungserfahrungen in den neuen Bundesländern nachder Wiedervereinigung, 1998), (pp. 47–69).

6. Elmar Brähler, Michael Beyer, Aike Hessel, and Yvonne Richter, *Soziale Befindlichkeiten in Ost und West* [Social conditions in east and west] (Berichte aus dem Zentrum für Gerechtigkeitsforschung an der Universität Potsdam: Veränderungserfahrungen in den neuen Bundesländern nachder Wiedervereinigung, 1998), (pp. 34–46).

7. Aike Hessel, Michael Geyer, Julia Würz, and Elmar Brähler, Psychische Befindlichkeiten in Ost- und Westdeutschland, *Aus Politik und Zeitgeschichte: Beilage zur Wochenzeitung Das Parlament*, Vol. 13 (March 21, 1997), pp. 15–24. This study confirms that the East Germans tend to experience themselves as social, somewhat more labile in their feelings, interested, diligent, and less aggressive. The authors view these attributes as

internalized middle-class values to be differentiated from the "late-capitalist-experience society" in which diffuse anxiety, feelings of being overwhelmed, and unhappiness can be observed. When the research data was broken down according to age groups, significant east-west differences became apparent: East Germans under twenty-five years old tend to be more apathetic and more aggressive than their western counterparts, the reverse being true for those over twenty-five.

8. Ibid.

9. Ibid. The authors indicate a possible association between stress and somatic illness, but do not account for the differences between East and West; J.W. Pennebaker, Traumatic experience and psychosomatic disease: Exploring the roles of behavioral inhibition, obsession, and confiding. *Canadian Psychology*, 26: 82–95. Pennebaker's research results clearly show the relationship between stress, somatic symptoms, and the salutary effect of "confiding." The relief of confiding in the family or societal representatives, the very people whose values are the cause of the stress, is obviously not possible.

10. Michael Wintle, *Culture and Identity in Europe: Perceptions of Divergence and Unity in Past and Present* (Brookfield: Avebury, 1996).

11. Detlef Pollack, Das Bedürfnis nach sozialer Anerkennung: Der Wandel der Akzeptanz von Demokratie und Marktwirtschaft in Ostdeutschland [The need for social recognition: The change in the acceptance in East Germany of democracy and market economy], *Aus Politik und Zeitgeschichte: Beilage zur Wochenzeitung Das Parlament*, Vol. 13 (March 21, 1997), pp. 3–14.

12. Kenneth Keniston, *Young Radicals: Notes on Committed Youth* (New York: Harcourt Brace and World, 1968), p. 314. Most of what follows will be based on Keniston's results of his in-depth investigations of alienated and committed youth.

13. Ibid.

14. Ibid. In contrast, the "alienated" do not take action, tend to be more "disturbed psychologically," and do not necessarily subscribe to their parents' ideals (p. 302).

15. Daniel Goleman, Scientist at Work: Ervin Staub: Studying the Pivotal Role of Bystanders, *New York Times*, Tuesday, June 22, 1993, pp. C1, C6. "The failure . . . to do or say anything about excessive violence is taken as a tacit acceptance, which encourages it. . . . If bystanders—people who are neither perpetrators nor victims—object firmly . . . it can slow or even stop the whole process."

16. Nadim N. Rouhana and Daniel Bar-Tal, Psychological Dynamics of Intractable Ethnonational Conflicts, *American Psychologist* 53: 7 (1998): 761–770. See also E. Azar, *The Management of Protracted Social Conflict: Theory and Cases* (Hampshire, England: Gower 1990), and W. G. Stephan

and C. W. Stephan, *Intergroup Relations* (Dubuque, IA: Brown and Benchmark, 1996), and H. Tajfel (ed.), *Social Identity and Intergroup Relations* (Cambridge, England: Cambridge University Press, 1996).

17. Herbert C. Kelman, Social-psychological Contributions to Peacemaking and Peacebuilding in the Middle East, *Applied Psychology: An International Review* 47: 1 (1998): 5–28.

The Speakers

All names are fictitious.

DOROTHEA, 51: Dorothea has attractive facial features, had important things to say, and survived her tears during the interview, although at first she was a reluctant project participant, concerned about not being qualified, worried about being too obese to fit through the door, afraid of breaking down in tears.

In September 1947, Dorothea was born out of wedlock in Palestine. Her parents—a Jewish mother and an Arab father—were unable to marry and had to terminate their great love relationship after the creation of the State of Israel, because Dorothea's paternal grandfather, a powerful figure in the Arab world, swore to have her mother killed. Subsequently, her father left the Middle East to live on another continent.

Dorothea's maternal grandparents had left Nazi Germany and reached Palestine via a circuitous route. Her grandfather, an attorney, was recalled to Germany to participate in the post–World War II legal proceedings. In 1959 her mother followed with Dorothea and her older sister in order to give her daughters "a European education." Dorothea married twice and has three children. She is proficient in three languages, competent in bookkeeping, in the use of computers, and as a secretary. Currently, she is an assistant (*Wissenschaftliche Mitarbeiterin*) at a research institute.

ERICH, 34: Erich, an only child, was born in Düsseldorf, West Germany, in August 1964. His mother, Hungarian-born, is a piano teacher. His father, a German citizen, is descended from French Huguenots who were driven out of Alsace long ago. His father, born in 1929, was too young to be drafted and avoided the *Volkssturm* (German territorial army) by taking to his bed for six weeks with a feigned heart problem, to which a physician friend attested.

Erich attended primary school and *Gymnasium* in Düsseldorf, was deferred from military service, then studied management and languages at Humboldt University in East Berlin. He apprenticed in an advertising firm in the west and now is partner in an advertising firm in East Berlin, where his knowledge of Russian, English, and Hungarian is of great advantage. Erich lives alone in a former warehouse district of Berlin. He has renovated his small apartment in very modern style. He volunteered the information that he is homosexual.

ERIKA (FAMILY WANGLER), 65: Erika, one of eight children, is a *Volksdeutsche*. She was born April 1933 in a tiny village, near Lublin in Poland. Her parents owned several acres of land, a cow, and a one-room wattle-and-daub house. Her mother tongue is German, and she learned to speak Polish, Russian, and some Yiddish, because "several kinds of people lived in our area." In 1940, Hitler brought the *Volksdeutsche* from Poland into Posen, from whence the family was deported in cattle cars when the Russians reconquered the territory in January 1945. In Brück, Germany, the family slept on straw in a church hall. In August 1945, her father returned from the war crippled and died after several years of illness. The children took turns taking care of their father, who had to have help with every bodily function, and they worked on neighboring farms to help support the family.

Erika met Willie in 1949, became pregnant, and married in 1950. The couple has four sons and one daughter. One married son died of cancer at age thirty-eight, a great sorrow, especially since their daughter-in-law does not encourage her children to have close relations with their grandparents.

Erika is religious. She baptized her first two children, but by the time the other three were born, Willie had forced Erika to resign from the church, because he had become a policeman in the GDR, where religion was frowned upon. When the family moved to Berlin, Erika was homesick and cried bitterly. In time, she adjusted, but never felt truly at home.

Erika left school after the sixth grade, apprenticed as a salesperson, and continued her vocational education throughout her working years, attaining supervisory status and earning quite a high salary. She was able to buy herself a Trabi, the East German equivalent of a Volkswagen. Unbeknownst to her husband and against his wishes, she maintained contact with family members in West Germany and friends in the United States. She has visited the United States since the travel restrictions were lifted.

ERNST, 60: Diminutive Ernst had neatly set out coffee and cookies in preparation for the interview in the small West Berlin house his wife inherited after the unification. Ernst was born out of wedlock in a Sachsen village in October 1938. He believed that his stepfather, whose name he carries, was his real father, until he was shocked by finding out the truth from playmates. The stepfather was a dear man who wrote very loving letters to him until he was killed in battle. Ernst's mother's second husband was an alcoholic who beat the mother. Ernst left home, became a devout Christian, a conscientious objector, and a lover of music. A visit to a concentration camp in his young adulthood motivated him to do humanitarian service. He became a nurse, married, and has two children.

In 1983, Ernst searched for and found his biological father, a half brother, and stepmother living in West Germany. He had learned the father's whereabouts from a ninety-year-old woman who also told him that his father had visited the village and kept himself informed about Ernst's progress. Obtaining permission to leave the GDR to visit his father's family was fraught with such difficulties and chicanery that on one occasion Ernst broke down and cried at the police station. He sent a letter to Erich Honecker, stating that he has not committed any crime, feels deprived of his rights like a Jew in Nazi Germany, and that he believes he has a right to get to know his father. Ernst's pleas for "wisdom from the representative of one part of the German people" brought the desired result.

Subsequently, an emotional meeting took place, his stepmother accepted him as a second son, and she and his father were happy to accept Ernst's son and daughter as grandchildren.

FRIEDA, 70: Frieda, unpretentious but extremely articulate, was born in Dresden in June 1928. Her father was an independent businessman, her mother a telephone operator. Frieda studied to be a teacher and practiced her profession for several years, but resigned from her position for political reasons and devoted herself to her husband, a scientist, and her two daughters. They live in a traditionally furnished one-family house in a residential—with its unpaved streets, almost rural—section of Berlin. All members of the family are devoutly—but not fanatically—Catholic. Frieda thinks for herself, and has done so her entire life. Already as a girl in her parents' home, she incurred her father's displeasure when she brought home political posters representing a point of view her parents did not share. In the GDR, she defined herself as a dissident and was treated as such by the authorities, who denied one daughter a university preparatory education because she practiced their religion. Despite this, she became a meteorologist. The other daughter managed to complete the *Abitur* at a church-sponsored high school, but had to "eat crow" and join the FDJ before matriculating at the university to study library science. Frieda refers to this as her daughter's "darkest hour."

GILDA, 67, and GERHARD, 63: Gilda and Gerhard, retired broadcast journalists, live on the outskirts of Berlin in the upstairs apartment of what was once a large one-family house. Gerhard tends the garden, where on summer afternoons the couple enjoys chatting and reading. For both members of this couple, this is a second marriage; both have children by their first spouses.

Gilda feels deprived of a proper childhood and twice betrayed: first in 1945 and again by the propaganda, lies, restrictions, and failure of the GDR socialist regime, whose leaders had promised to build a better world but sought their own advantage instead. In 1991, after forty years' membership in the SED, the couple decided to resign and not to join any other political party. Gilda's feelings ranged from disappointment to hate and impotence; she feared choking on her rage. Finally, she suffered from angina pectoris. By 1998, she had recovered, and the couple had adapted.

Gilda was born in Zwickau, Sachsen, 1931; Gerhard was born in Berlin, 1935. Their World War II memories are still very vivid, and they described them in great detail: frightening bombings, the sight of dead people and horses, fear of the Russians, and years of hunger after the war's end—when, it seemed to Gilda, American soldiers preferred to throw away food rather than give it to German children. For a long time, both Gilda and Gerhard, but especially Gerhard, had post–traumatic stress symptoms: nightmares, anxieties, and startle reactions.

Gerhard's father, an employed businessman, was conscripted into the *Volkssturm* (people's territorial army) late in the war; his mother was a librarian. He had one younger sister. Gerhard grew up "non-political" and näive until age ten, when he began to "register" the events around him.

Gilda's father, a factory employee, was on the Nazi "blacklist" because he was a social democrat. He engaged in intense discussions with his oldest son, a fascist. Gilda, joined the BDM, the Hitler Youth organization for girls, but became disillusioned when she began to realize "where it led." After the war, her father was employed by the municipality to deal with the black marketeers. In 1947, for unknown reasons, he was poisoned with methyl alcohol and died, leaving Gilda's mother to care for her four children. Gilda described their great poverty and her decision to forego a medical education in order not to burden the family. Gilda's next-older brother encouraged her to join the FDJ, but then left to live in the West, It was his presence there that caused the East German authorities to deny Gilda permission to travel to Western countries as a journalist.

HANS (WANGLER), 40: Hans is Erika and Willie's third son, born in 1958. As a late teenager, according to his parents, he caused them much grief, walking around with a "boom box," going on rampages, fighting, drinking (*"mit der Kofferheule unterm Arm, randalieren und grölen und Westen gucken. . . . Alkohol getrunken und rumgeschlagen*), and looking to the West, picking up not only "the good" but also "the bad" things and wanting to live in the Western way. On one occasion, Hans jumped the Berlin Wall at a point where there was a fence (instead of masonry), was arrested, and jailed. His mother hired lawyers, who succeeded in having his sentence reduced to several months.

Hans is a taxi driver, divorced, and father of one son. Now he opposes the West, much as he rebelled against the DDR as a young man. In the interview this translated into adolescent-type argumentativeness toward the interviewer from the United States.

HELGA, 67: Helga, born August 1931, is the only child of a coal miner and a housewife. They lived in a village in the Lausitz area. Her handsome father's interest, talent, and activity in photography (and one might speculate its possible usefulness to the war effort) raised the family's social and economic status in the community. They occupied a seven-room apartment in a three-family house. Although her father was a Nazi party member, Helga claims he was not actively engaged. Nevertheless, at war's end he shot himself and several relatives who wanted to commit suicide. Helga's refusal saved her, her mother, and her grandmother, who lived to see the Russians rape the women and set the village afire. The three women left for another town, where Helga's mother became a seamstress and supported Helga through her university training. Out of loyalty to her mother, Helga remained in the GDR, though she had an opportunity to leave prior to 1962. Despite some difficulties in the socialist society during her years as a teacher, East Germany—not Germany—is her home. Her marriage to a photojournalist enabled her to leave teaching and work side by side with him until she became a mother in 1968. Over the years, Helga developed her artistic talents to a professional level and, after the divorce from her alcoholic husband, has supported herself through the sale of her pictures and ceramics. At the time of the Wende, her fear of what she imagined the future would bring sent her into a depression. She would commit suicide, she said, if she were less cowardly. (She rejected the comparison with her father at that other turn of historical events in 1945.) Helga survived, is financially comfortable, and lives by herself in an attractive apartment. She also survived a cancer operation, continues to be in a long-term relationship, and is generally in good spirits.

HILDE, 65: Belying her talents, Hilde looks plain and dowdy. She was born in Trautenau, Böhmen, Czechoslovakia, in May 1933. Her father, a civil servant, did not return from the war. After the war, the Czechs deported her family, although they were practicing Catholics and certainly not Nazis. She and her mother, grandmother, and aunt were rounded up at four in the morning, told they would be sent to do farm work, and would be able to return home after two weeks. (This turned out to be a lie.) They were allowed to gather up a few pieces of old clothes, a bowl, and two spoons before being loaded into open cattle cars and transported to Germany. On the way, they had to make sure that the sparks from the coal-fueled locomotive would not set them afire. They had nothing to drink on that hot day. After the train crossed the border, her mother prevailed on them to sneak out of the train; she did not want to go further away from Czechoslovakia, believing they would soon return home because the deportation was surely a mistake. So, twelve-year-old Hilde began her life in East Germany by wandering along village streets and begging farmers to give them food and shelter. Before long, Hilde enrolled in school, became a teacher, and since 1950 has kept a daily journal, chronicling her life and the events in the GDR.

She was married, divorced, and has two adult children and several grandchildren.

HORST, 67: Horst was born out of wedlock in 1931 in Riesal, Sachsen. Subsequently, his mother married, but Horst grew up in his maternal grandparents' house, carrying yet another name, all of which caused him much embarrassment in the local school. Sometime between eighteen and twenty-two, Horst tried to meet his father, but he had died; he did get to know his paternal grandparents, "very simple people," who farmed a little, kept a goat. The maternal grandfather worked in the steel industry. The first inklings of international capitalism were awakened in Horst when he realized that the armament factory in which his grandfather worked was never bombed because it was partially financed by British capital. At fourteen he was drafted to assist refugees from Pommern and Silesia who streamed into Dresden and on February 13, 1945, during the great bombing of Dresden, Horst had to run for his life.

IRENE, 70: Irene is a Berliner, born in June 1928. She looks younger than her years, has an energetic, slightly masculine gait, and blond hair and used lipstick before it was general practice in the east (at the time of the first interview in 1990). During World War II, Irene's mother had been evacuated to the west of Germany, where Irene joined her upon returning from her own evacuation to Czechoslovakia, until returning to Berlin to pursue her university studies. She is married to a man whose work in the GDR took him to conferences in Western countries.

Irene's mother was a teacher who lost her job when Irene's father, a member of the Communist Party, emigrated to Sweden to escape the Nazis. The family was atheist, but after Hitler's ascension to power, the mother had Irene and her two siblings baptized. Irene thinks her grandmother has a Jewish appearance, and there seems to have been an illegitimate child, possibly Jewish, somewhere in the ancestry. Irene describes her brother as a "delicate, dark-haired, brown-eyed dreamer . . . not very aryan." After the parents divorced, the mother had a companion, who might also have been Jewish, because he disappeared suddenly. The grandmother was the only family member who helped Jews. One aunt was a fervent Nazi.

Despite her mother's efforts to educate her humanistically, Irene became an enthusiastic member of the BDM. She enjoyed marching and wearing the uniform, as did her sister, although her older brother (born 1923) had refused to join the HJ but was drafted into the *Wehrmacht*. He was stationed in the north of Norway, where he connected with Norwegian resistance fighters. Irene's world and values collapsed when their teacher, who had accompanied her class of evacuees to Czechoslovakia, deserted them to flee the conquering allies. The girls were stranded. Fearing the Russians who were in Berlin and hating the "Amis," they did not know which way to turn. Irene was without shelter and food, and without news from her mother since 1944.

After her return to Berlin, Irene joined the FDJ and the SED, hoping for a socially just, peaceful world, only to be disappointed again as totalitarianism took hold once more, albeit "with a different content."

Irene bore three children: a son who died at age eight after having been run over by a car, and twins, of whom the boy committed suicide in his twenties and the girl has struggled with depressions since her late adolescence. Irene carries on, remaining thoughtful and introspective.

JOHANNA, 36: Johanna is a tall, slender, sportily attired young woman. She was interviewed in her bright, sun-filled office, which is furnished with sleek blond cupboards, tables, and chairs.

She was born in West Berlin, Tempelhof, in March 1962. She attended primary school and high school and then trained to become an instructor in religion. She is now director of a mission program in the Catholic church. Her father was a technician and her mother a teacher of religion. Johanna decided to work in religious education because, in the absence of any strong interest in any other fields, she decided to earn her living by continuing the work she had enjoyed doing for several years as a volunteer. Hers was not a (conscious) decision to follow in her mother's footsteps. Johanna never married and has always lived on the "island" that was West Berlin.

JOSEPHINE, 42: Josephine was born on Christmas day, 1956, but, looking fit in her white pants and red shirt, appears at least ten years younger than her age. It was surprising to learn that she has an eighteen-year-old daughter. Similarly, her stylishly furnished apartment in a typical GDR project, complete with balcony, gives not a hint of her very modest beginnings. Josephine divorced her husband soon after their daughter was born and subsequently had a fifteen-year relationship, which broke up for "personal" reasons. She is intent on improving herself and continuing to grow with the times.

Josephine was born out of wedlock in Cologne, West Germany, while her mother stayed with a brother (who had remained in Cologne where he had been a prisoner of war). After returning to the east, her mother married her father, and two boys were born. The family lived in a village in the vicinity of Chemnitz, Sachsen. Both parents worked, her father as a toolmaker, her mother as a cook. She had to perform many of the household tasks and take care of the younger brothers. Neither brother has been married, though each has one child; one brother has been awarded custody of his son.

KURT, 58: In appearance and manner, Kurt is quite undistinguished, polite but lacking grace. Kurt was born in April 1940 in Berlin and evacuated to East Prussia in 1945 when the family was bombed out. Later they returned to Leipzig. His father did not come home from the war. In 1955, his mother moved to Hamburg via West Berlin with three of her four children. The oldest son, married, remained in the GDR.

Before being assigned an apartment in Recklinghausen, Nordrhein-Westfalen, the family temporarily lived in a reception camp, which suited Kurt not at all. At sixteen, Kurt separated from his mother, who had established a relationship with another man, and began a three-year apprenticeship with room and board in the Lüneburger Heide, south of Hamburg, followed by three years' work experience. The Berlin Wall, which had been built by then, contributed to Kurt's November 1962 decision to return to his brother in the GDR. Kurt was—and remained—a "political person" with an ideology he had learned in the Young Pioneers and the Free German Youth, prior to his stay in the west. For a while, Kurt attempted to be a committed socialist as well as a religious Protestant, but soon realized this was untenable. He chose socialism.

His wife, Käthe, participated in the second part of the interview. They have three adult sons.

MAX, 68: Max is a large, gray-haired man, whose second wife is of small stature and somewhat oriental features. She did not participate in the interview, except to supply one or two names Max had difficulty recalling. Max's first marriage failed as a result of his "rigid attitudes toward gender roles and child rearing."

Max was born in February 1930 in Völpke, the second son of his devoutly Catholic parents. His father was a coal miner and his mother a housewife; his grandparents were poor and illiterate. When he was ten, the father lost his job and was jailed by the Nazis for distributing

social democrat flyers. Max was ashamed that his father was imprisoned and pretended not to know when asked about him. The family
received a small monthly welfare payment, but they had to vacate the
coal miner's apartment and move to a tiny one-room plus kitchen.
Mother became a cleaning woman in the church; Max taught himself
to repair radios and earned some money to contribute to the household. Upon his release, the father told nothing of his experiences,
looked for occasional work, and then found a job loading heavy
stones onto trucks. One year later, the father died of a heart attack
while reading the newspaper at the kitchen table. Subsequently Max
spent much time alone while his brother was an apprentice and his
mother worked. Neighbors often took care of him, fed and pampered
him. In 1942, his mother remarried, this time to a committed Nazi.
He was strict with Max and beat the mother.

Max joined the *Hitlerjugend*, where he enjoyed the outdoor activities and learned to build model airplanes, but his "arm became lame"
(from the Nazi salute). After the war, Max and another youth found
a land mine, were arrested by the Russians, and released the next day.
The following year, 1946, Max's case was reopened. He suspects his
stepfather of denouncing him, so as to get him out of the house. This
time Max was sent to Sachsenhausen, where conditions resembled
those prevailing during Nazi times. At the time of his release, Max
was sixteen, six feet tall, weighing ninety pounds; to this day, he
suffers somatic and psychological post–traumatic stress symptoms. He
vowed never to join a political party and therefore has had problems
at work and has struggled for years to straighten out his pension and
his compensation for internment. To him, communist "liberation"
from Nazism was no more than "the same music, different lyrics."

MONIKA (FAMILY WANGLER): Monika is a secretary in her middle
thirties, a divorced mother of two. She recently moved into an apartment in her parents' housing complex, where she grew up. She participated enthusiastically in the family interview. (Because she was not
interviewed individually, nor did her parents speak of her in detail,
very little is known about her life.)

OTTO, 64: Otto was born in Düsseldorf, West Germany, in February 1934. His mother was Catholic; his father, a Protestant, converted to comply with the Catholic Church's prohibition against
"mixed" marriages. His father was a toolmaker, his mother a secretary. In 1936 the family moved to Berlin because, there, his father
earned four times the salary he had received in Düsseldorf. Otto is

married to a (now retired) kindergarten teacher; his sister, two years his junior, lives next door to him.

After the bombing of Berlin began, Otto was evacuated to a farm in Böhmen-Mähren, Czechoslovakia, where he spent the "most beautiful" time of his life. However, it was short-lived, because his father refused to leave him with the farmer, who was the head of the NSDAP local Nazi party. As a toolmaker in the defense industry at Daimler-Benz, the father was deferred from military service. Except for 100 Germans, the Daimler-Benz workers were war prisoners or deportees. They formed an anti-Hitler resistance group and collaborated with some leading communists in the underground movement. In July 1943, several of the communists were arrested. Six weeks later, his father was arrested, convicted, and sentenced to death. Neither his mother nor the attorneys she hired succeeded in having the sentence commuted. At the end of September, the father was shot. Hoping his father would return, young Otto refused to believe it.

Soon after his father's arrest, an upstairs neighbor, a leader in the Nazi women's organization, grabbed Otto, shook him, boxed his ears, slammed his head against the wall, and called him "Jew brat" and "Bolshevik pig." Another neighbor saved him. Otto did not forget the effects of fanaticism, which he had felt on his own body.

Though Otto and his mother were relieved when the Russians liberated them from the Nazis and though he became member of the "Anti-fa" (anti-fascist) children's group and of the FDJ, in his adulthood Otto, like his father, became resistant to the socialist dictatorial regime. As a result, he did not strike his stride until after the Wende, when he participated in the democratic political system.

PAUL (FAMILY ALBERT), 45: Paul was born in February 1953, the younger of two brothers. Their father, who had been in the GDR army, died suddenly of a cerebral stroke when Paul was thirteen. While the boys were young, their mother stayed home and later worked in a bank. Both boys completed their *Abitur*, and Paul continued his studies in economics and data processing under the auspices of the police division of the GDR armed forces. (Under the Soviet occupation, all armed services were combined as *bewaffnete Organe*, because officially no military forces were allowed.) His great grandmother was German, married to a Pole—or a Russian, the status remaining unclear because of the changing borders between the two countries. The family lived in East Prussia, Germany, where they remained "stateless," that is, without citizenship; as a result, the older

sons were spared having to serve in the army until the 1940s, when
the family was granted German citizenship so that the younger sons,
including Paul's father, could be drafted.

PETRA (FAMILY ALBERT), 45: Petra is a sleek, dark-haired, attractive, and energetic woman, married to Paul. She earned her doctorate
in philosophy at Humboldt University, submitting her dissertation
when her third son was about two years old.

Petra, born in October 1953 in the district of Neubrandenburg,
in the north of East Germany, is the oldest of three children. When
she was four, her parents divorced, necessitating the mother's return
to work as a salesperson in a trading company. One set of grandparents lived nearby, nevertheless, the children had to shift for themselves when mother's work took her out of town. Petra believes this
was good training for independence. She attempted unsuccessfully to
make contact with her father during her young adulthood.

PHILLIP (FAMILY ALBERT), 20: Phillip is an attractive young man,
a bit unsure of himself in the interview. He was born in 1978, graduated from high school with *Abitur*, and is now discharging his civil
service (instead of *Bundeswehr* service) by working with mentally retarded adults. He plans to become a social worker. His two brothers
are fourteen and seven years old. Like his mother in her childhood,
Phillip frequently had to take care of himself and the siblings while
his parents worked.

SOPHIE, 63: Born in August 1935, Sophie is a plain, serious person.
Never married, she lives to this day in her (deceased) parents' West
Berlin apartment and uses their stolid furnishings. Her father was a
mathematician and engineer, her mother a translator. She completed
high school with the *Abitur*. Mathematics, chemistry, and biology
constituted her university concentration, but she had to abandon
these studies when she developed an allergic reaction to certain chemicals. She became a teacher, is now retired, but tutors privately.

Their convictions and concern for Sophie's Jewish uncle-by-
marriage motivated her parents to become active in the anti-Nazi
resistance. Sophie "took over" by joining Amnesty International,
working for human rights and recently women's rights, in particular.

THORSTEN (WANGLER): Thorsten is an owner of a pub, married
and a father. He briefly attended the family interview, seemed a little
embarrassed about his success as an entrepreneur and denied making
a good living—insisting he gets by. Nevertheless, he seems comfortable in the unified German culture, content with his work, and

though excited about his first vacation to a foreign country—to begin the next morning—he was apprehensive about air travel. Under the circumstances, no information about his life as a youth became available.

WERNER, 62: In appearance and manner Werner is the professorial type. With his physician wife and two daughters he lives in a spacious, attractive apartment in an old Berlin building. He was born in 1936, to anti-Nazi parents. "Simple" people, who differentiated between "propaganda and truth," they followed their conscience. During the Nazi era, his parents conducted religious education in their living room. Father was a housepainter. Mother trained as a housemaid in the castle of the crown prince, worked herself up to *Beschließerin* (in charge of the keys) in a diplomat's household (where she met Einstein and von Weizsäcker), and became multilingual during ten years in the German embassy in Paris.

In the GDR, Werner encountered difficulties in school and at work as a result of the confluence of his naïveté in human relations and politics, an underestimation of the Soviet-backed GDR, and an over-estimation of himself. He was spied upon by *Stasi* associates. Despite his undisguised opposition to the regime and to socialism, he was permitted to complete his education, but he never achieved professorial rank. Following in his parents' footsteps, he secretly lectured to aspiring clergy at an independent seminary. Unemployed now and feeling very poor, he devotes his expertise and time to an organization of people persecuted by Stalin.

WILLIE (FAMILY WANGLER), 67: Willie was born to a tailor and a housewife in 1931, in Hamburg. Willie had five siblings: a set of twin brothers who died at six months, when Willie was five; a three-month-old brother who died in an air raid in 1943, when Willie was twelve; and two sisters, of whom one died in 1988. Willie's father did not return from the war.

In 1941, Willie was evacuated to Vienna, where he, a working-class child, lived uncomfortably with foster parents, their twelve-year-old son, and a maid. The foster father was an artist and a captain in the cavalry and therefore often absent from home. At school in Vienna, Willie found several other Hamburg evacuees, and together they battled the Viennese schoolmates. The foster brother persuaded Willie to become a *Pimpf* (the youngest Hitler Youth group). This displeased Willie's father, who had belonged to the Communist Party until 1933, at which time he resigned, without, however, joining the

Nazi Party—the reason he never attained the rank of master-tailor. Despite frequent letters from his mother in Hamburg and his father at the front, Willie was homesick and worried that during air raids or on the battlefield harm would come to his parents and siblings. After one year, he returned home, only to be evacuated again to Bayern after having been bombed out in Hamburg. This time, he was in the company of his mother and one sister, but the father decided they could not stay because the village was too Catholic. Therefore, after about six weeks, the family moved to relatives in Wittenberg, in the region to become the DDR.

Willie learned to be a machinist, but when the factory was closed, the machines to be shipped to the USSR as war reparation, Willie joined the transit police and later the regular DDR police force. He married Erika in 1950; together they have five children. In 1989 he was very disappointed in the DDR leadership and could not understand how Erich Honecker, the erstwhile roofer, who had been incarcerated by the Nazis, could be so self-serving and betray his people. In contrast, Willie's children say, he is an "honest communist."

WILMA, 53: Stately, elegant Wilma picked me up at the *U-Bahn* (subway) stop in her white, four-door Mercedes sedan and drove me to her large, sumptuously furnished one-family house. She was born to a detective and a secretary in Mark Brandenburg, in December 1945. After the parents' divorce, Wilma and her brother lived with their financially secure and musical father for two years. Later they returned to their mother, who lived in Cologne with her second husband. Wilma began her apprenticeship in insurance sales at age fourteen and later trained for but never practiced nursing. Subsequently, she lived in several other West German cities until she came to East Berlin. Her husband is a banker and her only son, a lawyer. She is an office administrator. She has suffered and grown through her husband's extramarital affair, his alcoholism and discharge from his position at the bank, her depression after her beloved brother's death of lung cancer, and her own operation to remove what turned out to be a non-cancerous breast tumor. She has become a more self-assured, liberated woman. Since childhood she has been deeply religious, committed to the Seventh Day Adventists.

STUDENTS AND TEACHERS: Seven students, aged nineteen to twenty, were interviewed as a group. At the time of the interview, these students had just completed their university preparatory program at the *Gymnasium* (equivalent to an American high school plus junior college.) They come from lower-middle-class and professional families. The group setting did not lend itself to an exploration of personal history.

Five *Gymnasium* teachers were interviewed in a separate group. No biographical information is available.

The remaining interview protocols were confirmatory of the Speakers' statements, but they are not included in this manuscript.

Appendix

To discover how individual lives had been affected by the German unification, forty-one people were interviewed. Twenty-eight interview partners were chosen from the respondents to identical advertisements in two Berlin newspapers. Geographic location and time constraints eliminated some respondents. An effort was made to balance women and men, young and old, east and west interview partners. In addition to the chosen newspaper respondents, twelve additional participants were referred by acquaintances and one by an interviewee. Quite obviously, this is not a random sample of Germans, east and west, not even of Berliners. However, informal observations and conversations with acquaintances and friends, their parents and children, taxi drivers, and a manicurist pointed to a general consistency in responses over and above the idiosyncratic perceptions of each interview partner.

Of the 41 interview partners, 25 were women, 16 men.

There were 17 seniors (born before 1945), 8 women and 9 men.

Fifteen were of the middle generation (born 1945–1964), 9 women and 6 men.

Eight were youths (born in 1978–79), 4 women and 4 men.

One young married woman (born 1968).

Among the interviewees were several West Germans, some of whom had recently found jobs in the east and two who had relocated to the east. Two formerly East Germans had relocated west.

Their vocations ranged from skilled worker to independently established printer to artist; there were assistant researchers, office administrators, a male nurse, recent graduates (*Abiturienten*); three are affiliated with a university (of these, two have doctorates); of two men who used to be in the police force, one has a doctorate; one army officer also holds a doctorate. Several teachers and journalists participated, and two semiprofessional educators (*Erzieherin*).

The majority of the interviews were conducted with individuals; however, in three cases men invited their wives to sit in, and two of these actively participated. In addition, one group of teachers, one group of youths, and two families with adult children were interviewed (for over three hours each).

Eight people had been interviewed twice before: early summer 1990, roughly half a year after the Berlin Wall was opened and again summer 1991 after the *Währungsunion*. All but one of these eight were affected by personal tragedies in the interim; however, these did not overshadow some significant attitudinal and lifestyle changes, which the interviewees attributed directly to the effects of the unification.

As was true in 1988, 1990–91, and 1992, the focus of the investigation is on ordinary citizens. Their status, affiliations, unusually good or bad deeds, fortune or misfortune were not criteria for selection, indeed, were unknown before the interviews.

Interviews lasted two to three hours and were semistructured: Respondents were given free reign to speak about how they had fared in their work and private life since the *Wende* and the unification. Toward the end of the conversation, the interviewer asked about specific areas of interest that the interviewee might have ignored or avoided, as for instance, their interest and participation in political matters, then and now, or their explanation of the phenomenon of totalitarianism in the same country twice in a row, though representing two utterly different ideologies.

Interviews were recorded on audiotape and transcribed. To protect the interviewees, no last names were mentioned on the tapes. All names in the manuscript are fictitious, and certain identifying data has been omitted.

The protocols were read to discern themes, such as women at work and women at home. The themes emerging from each record were categorized such that a composite of segments from several interviews constitutes the core of a chapter. The author's explanatory and interpretive comments are interspersed with the interview material and are summarized in a concluding chapter.

Glossary

Abitur	Final academic high school examination, a prerequisite for university admittance
ABM	*Arbeitbeschaffungsmaßnahmen*/Measures for obtaining work/jobs (includes retraining opportunities)
BDM	*Bund Deutscher Mädel*/League of German Girls (14- to 18-year-old female Hitler Youths)
BfA	*Büro für Arbeit*/Employment Office
BLG	*Betriebsgewerkschaftsleistungens-Vorsitzender*/Head of factory/business labor-union (members) performance
BRD/GFR	*Bundesrepublik Deutschland*/German Federal Republic
Bundesland/Bundesländer	State(s) of the BRD: "old" belonging to the original BRD; "new" belonging to the ex-DDR territory
CDU	*Christliche Demokratische Union*/Christian Democratic Union (right-of-center political party)
DDR/GDR	*Deutsche Demokratische Republik*/German Democratic Republic
Deutschmark	West German currency

Dienstleistungskombinat	Service-combine (socialist alternative to independent artisans)
DJ	*Deutsches Jungvolk*/German Young People (10- to 14-year-old male Hitler Youth)
DSF/GSF	*deutsch-sovietische Freundschaft*/German-Soviet friendship
DVU	*Deutsche Volksunion*/German People's Union (ultra right-wing political party)
EOS	*Erveiterte Oberschule*/expanded secondary school which includes three years of academic preparation for university studies
(F)DGB	*(Freier) Deutscher Gewerkschaftsbund*/(Free) German Labor Union
FDJ	*Freie Deutsche Jugend*/Free German Youth (state-sponsored youth organization)
FDP	*Freie Deutsche Partei*/Free German Party
HJ	*Hitlerjugend*/14- to 18-year-old Hitler Youth
JM	*Jungmädelbund*/Young Girls League (10- to 14-year-old female Hitler Youth)
KoKo	*Kommerzielle Koordinierungsstelle*/Commerce-Coordination Bureau
KPD	*Kommunistische Partei Deutschlands*/Communist Party
LDPD	*Liberal Demokratische Partei Deutschlands*/German Liberal Democratic Party
LPG	*Landwirtschaftliche Produktionsgesellschaft*/Agricultural Production Cooperatives in the GDR
LVO	*Landesverteidigungsordnung*/Laws for the Defense of the Country
MfS	*Mitarbeiter für Staatssicherheit*/Stasi collaborator
NSDAP	*Nationalsozialistische Deutsche Arbeiterpartei*/National Socialist German Workers Party—Nazi Party

NVA	*Nationale Volksarmee*/National People's Army (DDR)
PDS	*Partei des Demokratischen Sozialismus*/Party of Democratic Socialism (successor to the SED, the official party of the DDR)
SED	*Sozialistische Einheitspartei Deutschlands*/Unified Socialist Party (DDR-mandated unification of the KPD and SPD)
SFB	*Sender Freies Berlin*/Free-Berlin Transmitter (Radio)
SPD	*Sozialistische Partei Deutschlands*/Socialist Party of Germany
Währungsunion	Introduction of the Deutschmark as the official currency in the GDR
ZK	*Zentralkomitee*/Central Committee (SED)

Selected Bibliography

Altenhof, Rolf, and Jesse Eckhard (eds.) (1995). *Das wiedervereinigte Deutschland: Zwischenbilanz und Perspectiven* [Reunited Germany: Interim balance and perspectives]. Düsseldorf, Germany: Droste.

Ash, Timothy Garton (1989). *Ein Jahrhundert wird abgewählt* [A century is voted out]. München: Deutscher Taschenbuch Verlag.

Bahrmann, Hannes, and Christoph Links (1994). *Chronik der Wende: die DDR zwischen 7. Oktober und 18. Dezember 1989* [Chronicle of the Wende: The GDR between October 7th and December 18th, 1989]. Berlin: Ch. Links Verlag.

Beyme, Klaus von (1991). *Das politische System der Bundesrepublik Deutschland nach der Vereinigung* [The political system of the German Federal Republic after the Unification]. München: Piper.

Brussig, Thomas (1998). *Helden wie wier.* [Heroes like us]. Frankfurt a/M: Fischer Taschenbuch Verlag, 312, 322.

Chalupsky, Jutta, et al. (1991). *Jugend in Leipzig* [Youth in Leipzig]. Leipzig: Universität Leipzig, Laboratorium für Studentenforschung,

Darnton, Robert (1991). The Good Old Days, *The New York Review of Books*, May 16, 44–48.

Eberhard, Karl-Heinz, and Wolfram Marx (eds.) (1989). *Familiengesetzbuch sowie angrenzende Gesetze und Bestimmungen: Textausgabe.* Berlin: Staatsverlag der Deutschen Demokratischen Republik.

Evers, Adalbert (1995). Das politische Defizit der Wohlfahrtsgesellschaft. [The political deficit of the welfare society], *Universitas*, 50, 590, 734.

Henning, Günther (1982). *Die Verwöhnte Generation? Lebenstile und Weltbilder 14–19 Jähriger* [The spoiled generation? Lifestyles and world views of 14–19 year-olds]. Hanns Martin Schleyer-Stiftung.

Jürgs, Michael (1998). *Die Treuhändler—Wie Helden und Halunken die DDR verkauften* [The fiduciary trustees: How heroes and scoundrels sold the GDR]. Munich: Droehmersche Verlagsanstalt Th. Knaur Nachf., 9.

Keniston, Kenneth (1968). *Young Radicals*. New York: Harcourt Brace and World.

Magistratsverwaltung für Jugend, Familie und Sport (no date). *Jugend und Rechtsextremismus in Berlin-Ost* [Youth and Rightwing extremism in Berlin-East]. Verlag Junge Welt.

Malanowski, Wolfgang (ed.) (1990). *Die Partei war unser Leben* [The Party was our life]. *Spiegel Spezial*, No. 2, 120–129.

Merkens, Herbert, Irmgard Steiner, and Gerhard Wnzke (1998). *Lebensstile Berliner Jugendlicher 1997* [Lifestyles of Berlin Youths 1997]. Berlin: Zentrum für Europäische Bildungsforschung e.V., Freie Universität Berlin.

Nolte, Claudia (1995). *Das Gleichberechtigungsgesetz des Bundes: Ein Gesetz für Frauen und Männer* [The federal law for equal rights: A law for men and women]. Bonn: Bundesministerium für Familie, Senioren, Frauen und Jugend, 5.

Nolte, Dirk, Ralf Sitte, and Alexandra Wagner (eds.) (1995). *Wirtschaftliche und soziale Einheit Deutschlands: eine Bilanz* [German economic and social unity]. Cologne: Bund Verlag.

Ochs, Christiane, and Brigitte Stolz-Willig (1995). Wie im Westen, so auch auf Erden? Zur Situation der Frauen in den neuen Bundesländern. In Dirk Nolte, Ralf Sitte, and Alexandra Wagner (eds.), *Wirtschaftliche und soziale Einheit Deutschlands* [German economic and social unity]. Cologne: Bund Verlag, 329–351.

Sadrozinski, Renate (1990). *Die Ungleiche Praxis des #218* [The dissimilar application of #218]. Cologne: Heinrich Böll Stiftung.

Schoenbaum, David, and Elizabeth Pond (1996). *The German Question and Other German Questions*. New York: St. Martin's Press.

Schröder, Richard (1998). "Schluss mit dem Mitleid." *Der Spiegel*, No. 19, April 26, 4.

75 Jahre Frauen Wahlrecht [75 years of women's voting rights]. Bonn: Bundesministerium für Familie, Senioren, Frauen und Jugend.

Solga, Heike (1996). Klassenlagen und soziale Ungleichheit in der DDR [(Social) classes and social inequities]. *Aus Politik und Zeitgeschichte*, Vol. 46/96, 18–27.

Spiess, Gesine (1998). Vater Staat und seine ungleichen Töchter [Father state and his unequal daughters]. *Aus Politik und Zeitgeschichte*, Vol. 41–42, October 2, 44–46.

Tröndle, Herbert (1997). *Strafgesetzbuch und Nebengesetze* [Book of criminal statutes and additional laws]. Munich: (no publisher given).

Veen, Herbert-Joachim (1994). *Eine Jugend in Deutschland*. Opladen: Leske und Budrich.

Index

Entries in **bold** indicate interviewees.

About the Author

CHARLOTTE KAHN is a psychoanalyst and family therapist in private practice. She has served on the faculties of colleges, universities, and postgraduate psychoanalytic training institutions since 1966. Dr. Kahn has published extensively and is the coeditor of *Immigration: Personal Narrative, Psychological Analysis* and *Children Surviving Persecution* (Praeger, 1998).

ISBN 0-275-96357-8